TRAUMATIC STRESS
IN POLICE OFFICERS

TRAUMATIC STRESS IN POLICE OFFICERS

A Career-Length Assessment from Recruitment to Retirement

By

DOUGLAS PATON, Ph.D.

School of Psychology
University of Tasmania
Launceston, Tasmania, Australia

JOHN M. VIOLANTI, Ph.D.

School of Public Health and Health Professions
Department of Social and Preventive Medicine
State University of New York at Buffalo

KARENA BURKE, Ph.D.

School of Psychology
University of Tasmania
Launceston, Tasmania, Australia

ANNE GEHRKE, MS

BG Institute Occupational Health and Safety
Dresden, Germany
German Federation of Institutions for Statutory
Accident Insurance and Prevention

CHARLES C THOMAS • PUBLISHER, LTD.
Springfield • Illinois • U.S.A.

Published and Distributed Throughout the World by

CHARLES C THOMAS • PUBLISHER, LTD.
2600 South First Street
Springfield, Illinois 62794-9265

This book is protected by copyright. No part of
it may be reproduced in any manner without written
permission from the publisher. All rights reserved.

© 2009 by CHARLES C THOMAS • PUBLISHER, LTD.

ISBN 978-0-398-07893-5 (hard)
ISBN 978-0-398-07894-2 (paper)

Library of Congress Catalog Card Number: 2009016526

With THOMAS BOOKS *careful attention is given to all details of manufacturing and design. It is the Publisher's desire to present books that are satisfactory as to their physical qualities and artistic possibilities and appropriate for their particular use.* THOMAS BOOKS *will be true to those laws of quality that assure a good name and good will.*

Printed in the United States of America
MM-R-3

Library of Congress Cataloging in Publication Data

Traumatic stress in police officers: a career length assessment from recruitment to retirement / by Douglas Paton...[et al.]
 p. cm.
 Includes biographical references and index.
 ISBN 978-0-398-07893-5 (hard)–ISBN 978-0-398-07894-2 (pbk.)
 1. Police– Job stress – United States – 2. Police psychology – United States. I. Paton, Douglas. II. Title.

HV7936.J63T73 2009
158.7'208836320973–dc22   2009016526

PREFACE

If a comprehensive understanding of the nature and effectiveness of the police role in dealing with adverse trauma events is to be developed, it is necessary to empirically integrate such events into the police career path. At present, there is no comprehensive resource to address this issue. There is a growing recognition that stress risk can in some cases begin prior to police work and extend after retirement from police work. It thus becomes necessary to incorporate pre-employment and the retirement period into accounts of the psychological impact of policing. Similarly, the implications of the changing gender balance in police agencies needs to be accommodated. To date, these issues have not been explored systematically within a framework that embraces the whole career of police officers. Such an approach is essential if we are better able to understand the complex and changing interactions that affect the psychological well-being of police officers. This approach is based on the premises that:

- officers can experience both positive and negative outcomes as a result of confronting highly challenging events which may coexist
- these outcomes are influenced by different resilience and vulnerability mechanisms
- the organizational environment and practices, the family environment, and the societal environment introduce significant and independent influences on these outcomes
- changes in factors such as gender and ethnic composition contribute to issues that influence the nature of the organizational environment
- posttrauma outcomes are influenced by the interaction between individual, team and organizational levels of analysis
- positive and negative posttrauma outcomes are also influenced by factors that, over the course of officers' careers, commence prior to their employment and persist beyond the point at which they retire or disengage from police work

We propose with this book to develop a viable resource to explore interactive issues of trauma over the entire police career course. The book will draw upon empirical research to provide an evidence-based approach to traumatic stress risk management. We will start with police officer pre-employment experiences and conclude with a discussion of the implications of disengagement or retirement from the police role.

The contents of the proposed text will include:

- Incorporation of police trauma into a life-career course perspective
- Changing context and nature of police work (e.g., sources of trauma and uncertainty, community relations)
- Recruitment, selection, and socialization in the context of critical incident and terrorist work (e.g., pre-employment experiences, organizational influences on capacity to confront uncertainty, developing resilience within an organizational context)
- Changing gender balance in policing
- Training and development in uncertain times
- Managing risk, resilience, vulnerability, and adversarial growth
- Organizational context (e.g., management systems, organizational culture)
- Family dynamics and issues
- Team: inter and intraorganizational
- Health and mental health
- Consequences of long-term exposure to hazards
- Disengagement and retirement

We feel that this book is unique in two ways. First, the majority of volumes on police psychological issues do not differentiate with regard to career stage. Second, very few books reflect complex patterns of interaction between vulnerability and resilience characteristics that occur at individual, team, group, and organizational levels, as well as involving interaction between these levels. This book will be one of the first to pull these various threads together and provide a comprehensive account of the impact of trauma throughout the police career. This work will provide a framework that police agencies can use to develop their officers and their organizations in ways that enhance their capability to confront an increasingly uncertain future. It will also be useful as a teaching tool for police officers, mental health professionals, and supportive organizations.

CONTENTS

Chapter   *Page*

1. CONCEPTUALIZATION: THE POLICE CAREER COURSE AND TRAUMA STRESS 3
    Introduction 3
    The Life-Course Model 4
        Life-Course Theory 5
        Life-Course Theory and Trauma 7
        Important Life-Course Theory Concepts and Issues 8
    Posttraumatic Stress Disorder: Life-Course Impact 9
    Police Career Pathways and Trauma 11
        An Early Example: Stress "Stages" of a Police Career ... 12
        The Impact of Pre-employment Trauma 14
        Assimilation into the Police Role 16
        Individual Assimilation 17
        Social Assimilation 18
        Coping Efficacy and the Acquired Police Role 20
        The Police Role and Relationships 21
        Increased Trauma Potential 22
        External Life Events: Transitions to Depression 23
    Risk 24
    After the Battle Is Over: Retirement and Trauma 27
    Conclusion 28

2. ORGANIZATIONAL INFLUENCES ON CRITICAL INCIDENT STRESS RISK 30
    Introduction 30
    Identifying Sources of Diversity 31
    The Influence of Organizational Life 33
        Risk in Operational Contexts 35

Organizational Context 37
    Organizational Climate and Culture 39
    Organizational Factors 41
    Operational and Organizational Risk 42
Conclusion 45

3. FROM CIVILIAN TO RECRUIT: SELECTING THE
   RIGHT STUFF 48
   Introduction 48
   Selection 50
       Dimensions of the Five Factor Model 52
       Personality and Police Performance 53
       Comparing Police and the Public 57
   The Personality Profile of Police Recruits 58
       Comparing Recruits and the General Population ... 59
   Deciding to Enter Police Work: Motivations and
       Expectations 63
       Motivators 64
           Family 64
           Power 65
       Satisfiers 66
           Prior Experience 66
           People 67
   Pre-employment Traumatic Experience 69
   Prior Traumatic Experience 70

4. FROM RECRUIT TO OFFICER: TRANSITION AND
   SOCIALIZATION 73
   Introduction 73
   Prior Traumatic Experience 74
       Prior Trauma and Vulnerability 76
       Prior Trauma and Resilience 77
   Prior and Early Career Traumatic Experience 78
       The Number of Operational Critical Incidents 78
       On Versus Off-Duty Experiences 79
       Hassles and Uplifts and Posttrauma Outcomes 80
       The Influence of Pre-Employment and Operational
           Traumatic Experience on Posttraumatic Growth
           (PTG) 82

Adjusting to Work in a Police Agency 84
    Socialization 86
    Academy Training 86
        Academic Environment 88
        Atmosphere 88
    Transition 89
        Administration and Procedures 90
        Practical Skills 91
        Jobs 83
        Public Response 94
        Public Understanding and Expectations 95
    Impersonality 95
    Media Reporting 96
    Coping 98

5. MALADAPTIVE COPING DURING THE POLICE
    CAREER 101
    Introduction 101
    Police Coping Efficacy 101
        Coping Impact: "Acting Out" the Police Role ... 103
    Alcohol Abuse 103
    Suicide 105
        Trauma and Police Suicide 107
    Family Disruption 109
    Intervention Strategies 109
        Trauma Risk Management 110
        Alcohol Abuse 111
        Suicide Prevention 111
    The Intervention Role of the Police Supervisor 112
    Peer Support Programs in Law Enforcement 113

6. GENDER DIFFERENCES IN POLICING 115
    Introduction 115
    Police Culture and Women Officers 117
        Women Officers and Critical Incident Stress Risk 120
        Gender and Social Support 121

7. THE CHANGING NATURE OF EXPOSURE DURING THE
    POLICE CAREER: TERRORISM AND TRAUMA ... 125

Introduction 125
Terrorist Response as a Sequential Process 126
    Mobilization–Response to Terror Events 127
    Stress Risk During Response to Acts of Terrorism 129
    Event Characteristics 131
    Organizational Factors 135
        The Interagency Environment 136
    Managing Risk After the Event 137
Conclusion 139

8. ACCOMMODATING TERRORISM AS RISK FACTOR:
    THE ORGANIZATIONAL PERSPECTIVE 141
    Introduction 141
    Acts of Terrorism and the Environment of Contemporary
        Policing 143
    Organizational Learning, Change and Future Capability 145
        Organizational Change 147
        Organizational Influences on Officer Thinking, Well-Being
            and Performance 148
        Agency Planning and Officer Deployment 149
        Decision Making 149
        The Multiagency and Multijurisdictional Context 150
        Organizational Influence on Response Schema 151
        Organizational Influence on Managing Risk after
            the Event 154
    Conclusion 155

9. THE LIFE OF ESTABLISHED OFFICERS 157
    Introduction 157
    Satisfaction and Its Antecedents 157
        Organizational Climate and Job Satisfaction 159
        Occupational Experiences and Individual
            Characteristics 160
    Coping 161
        Emotional Social Support 161
        Denial 163
        Behavioral Disengagement 163
        Extraversion 164
    Established Officers: Perceptions of Police Life 164

External Aspects 165
    Family and Friends 165
    Public 166
Occupational Experiences 167
    Frustrations 171
    Camaraderie and Support 172
Personal Influences 175
General Coping 175
Critical Incident Response 177
Personal Change 179

10. MANAGING CRITICAL INCIDENT STRESS RISK: INTEGRATING PERSON, TEAM, AND ORGANIZATIONAL FACTORS 182
    Introduction 182
    A Life Course Critical Incident Intervention 183
        Integrating Officer, Team, and Organizational Factors 184
            Modeling Resilience 184
    Organizational Characteristics, Coping, and Resilience 185
    Empowerment 187
        Empowerment as an Enabling Process 187
        Critical Incidents, Incident Assessment, and Behavior 190
        Empowerment Schema and Resilience 193
        Access to Resources 195
        Trust 196
        Dispositional Influences 196
        Modeling Empowerment and Resilience 197
        Senior Officer Support and Empowerment 197
        Peer Cohesion and Empowerment 198
        Hardiness and Empowerment 199
    Conclusion 200

11. DISENGAGEMENT FROM POLICE SERVICE: THE IMPACT OF A CAREER END 202
    Introduction 202
    Police Retirement 203
        Police Retirement and Feelings of Loss 206
    Vestiges of Trauma After Disengagement 207
        Residuals of Police Occupational Trauma 207

       Addiction to Prior Occupational Trauma 209
       Prior Trauma and the Loss of Group Support 211
       The Police Family: Issues of Left-Over Trauma 212
       Conclusions 213

12. CONCLUSION 215
       Benefits and Limitations 218
       Lessons and Implications 219

References 225
Index 249
About the Authors 255

TRAUMATIC STRESS
IN POLICE OFFICERS

Chapter 1

CONCEPTUALIZATION: THE POLICE CAREER COURSE AND TRAUMA STRESS

INTRODUCTION

The average career length of a police officer in the United States is approximately 20–25 years. Most officers complete their career paths for that period of time and then retire to civilian life. During this time, serving officers face the prospect of repeated exposure to potentially traumatic or critical events. Understandably, this aspect of police work has attracted considerable interest. However, most of the research into traumatic stress phenomena in police officers has focused on the consequences of specific events that are located at a single point in an officer's career. While informative, such brief snapshots (from a whole of career perspective) can provide only limited insights into a reality that will extend over decades and in which the events and the context in which events are experienced is evolving. Adopting a career-length perspective provides a more comprehensive approach to understanding how the implications of repeated traumatic or critical experiences and events unfold over time in the context of changing organizational and societal circumstances.

Adopting a career-length perspective makes it easier to appreciate a need to consider how traumatic experiences interact with one another over time and it increases awareness of the need to consider how changes in the nature of police work and the societal context in which officers and agencies operate over time can influence the kinds of incidents officers will have to contend with, their implications for well-being, and the need to develop interventions accordingly. For example, increased recognition of the risk posed by terrorism has influenced how police agencies plan, how they deploy officers, and it has affected the resource and equipment needs required by officers. These changes, in turn, have influenced how officers interpret and respond to critical incidents and it has had significant implications for how officers and the police agency relate to society (see Chapters 8 and 9). The objective of this book is to demonstrate how adopting a career perspective can provide a more comprehensive conceptualization of traumatic stress processes as they apply to police officers and agencies and provide a framework that can be used to guide research and intervention agenda in ways that reflects the changes that can occur over the course of a police career that can span decades.

The purpose of this chapter is to develop a conceptual basis for understanding the impact of trauma throughout the career course of police officers. We will first develop a conceptual perspective of the police career, borrowing from the rubric of life-course theory (Elder, 1996). Second, we will discuss how pre-employment traumatic experiences influence officer's experience of the critical incidents they encounter as serving officers throughout their careers. Third, officers' assimilation into the police "role" and the impact of trauma within that role will be discussed. Fourth, this chapter considers how demographic (e.g., gender) and societal (e.g., terrorism) factors introduce significant changes into the context of policing in ways that affect the traumatic stress risk faced by officers. Fifth, the perspectives arising from the preceding discussions are integrated into a conceptual model for managing critical incident stress risk. Finally, the spillover of residual trauma into police retirement will be discussed. This chapter will also introduce some conceptual issues that can inform understanding of a life-course perspective on traumatic stress in police officers. Discussion commences with an introduction to the conceptual perspective that life-course theory brings to understanding traumatic stress processes in police officers and agencies.

THE LIFE-COURSE MODEL

The life-course perspective is an ideal conceptualization on which to base a police career model. In its simplest sense, the life course may be defined as the "duration of a person's existence" (Riley, 1986). (For an excellent review of life course theory, see *Crime and the Life Course*, Michael L. Benson, Roxbury Publishing, 2001.) Elder (1985, 1996) a leading figure in life-course research, defines the life course as the interconnected trajectories that a person has as they go through life. A trajectory is a sequence of linked states within a conceptually defined range of behavior or experience. It is a pathway over the life span. As people move through this trajectory, they graduate from one level to another. Transitions are always embedded in trajectories, and the states that make up a trajectory are always linked to one another by transitions (Elder, 1996).

Life-Course Theory

According to Elder (1985), the life-course perspective is based on four central premises, which can be summarized as the following:

- Aging and developmental change must be viewed as continuous processes that occur throughout life.
- Trajectories in different realms of life are interconnected and have reciprocal effects on one another.
- Human development is influenced by social and historical conditions.
- Efforts to optimize human development through preventive or corrective interventions will be most effective if they are sensitive to the developmental needs and capabilities of particular age periods in the life span.

The first premise is simple to understand—as persons go through life, they change from beginning to end. There is no such thing as a "static" life, and this holds true for biological, psychological, and social change.

According to the second premise of the life-course perspective, trajectories in these different life domains are intimately connected and have reciprocal effects on each other (Elder, 1985). Biological change can effect social change, and psychological disruption (such as trauma) can affect us biologically and socially. The third premise that life pathways are multidetermined and influenced by social and historical conditions and changes (Magnusson & Bergman, 1990) is interesting. Our individual lives are linked to the lives of others in the sense that changes in the lives of persons around us can have an impact on our own trajectories (Elder, 1996).

A good example of the kind of interdependency envisaged by Elder concerns the ways in which families and other significant individuals help shape the life course. This issue is examined in more detail in Chapter 3, which introduces how family history of police work can influence officer's perceptions of their role even before they enter the profession. However, families represent only one source of influence on our lives.

Broader social conditions and changes also influence the life course. Our lives carry the imprint of what happens in our particular social worlds (Elder, 1992). If our social world undergoes rapid change, it can disrupt our lives and change the timing and direction of life. Events that involve trauma for example can disrupt life dramatically, visibly, and quickly. Just such a change occurred on September 11th 2001. The events of 9/11 represented a significant transition point, and one with far-reaching implications for understanding and managing traumatic stress processes in police officers (see Chapters 7 and 8).

Other social changes occur incrementally and work their effects more slowly, less visibly, but just as profoundly. Examples of the latter include, for example, entry into police work and officers' subsequent socialization into police life. These change processes are examined in Chapters 3 and 4, and again in Chapter 9, as officers' relationships with the society (and its members) they protect and serve develop over time. These relationships, in turn, influence how officers make sense of their world and respond to events.

The fourth premise of the life-course perspective simply alerts us to the fact that people are influenced by different things at different stages of life. The timing of events and interventions is crucial to their effect. What may be an effective intervention strategy for one may not work as well for other officers. Timing is important as it relates to the effects of both unplanned events and planned interventions that occur in the life course (Laub, Nagin, & Sampson, 1998). This perspective has important implications for police officers who experience rigorous selection, training and socialization processes designed to facilitate their ability to exercise their role competently and with integrity.

The life-course perspective holds to the principle of contextualism, which argues that development cannot be separated from the context in which it occurs (Dannefer, 1984). Related to the principle of contextualism is the *life-stage principle,* which holds that the way that individual and social events affect people is influenced by where they are in their career span when events occur (Elder, 1995). For police officers, a highly significant context is the police organization that selects and trains them and represents the context in which they are socialized into an environment that promotes and sustains a level of cohesion that is rarely matched by any other profession (see Chapters 2, 3 and 4). At the same time that internal (to the police organization) socialization increases coherence amongst officers, relationships with the external environment are increasingly characterized by a sense of insularity. The implications of this for officers' sense making mechanisms that their stress risk is discussed in Chapters 2, 4, 9 and 11. These insights also allow life-course theory to offer insights into traumatic stress processes.

Life-Course Theory and Trauma

According to this theory, there exist three key dimensions in a police career as related to trauma: frequency, seriousness, and length of exposure. Frequency refers to the number of traumatic events a person is exposed to during a certain period of time. Individual trauma exposure frequency varies dramatically among persons, with some having very high rates and others very low ones (Turkewitz & Darlynne, 1993). Exposure rates also may vary over time throughout an individual's career. An important question is what events of the life course influence individual trauma exposure rates. Certainly occupations like policing can exert such an influence. Duration or career length is an important dimension of a career perspective. It is also important to understand the relationship between duration and frequency. While normally considered only within the context of operational policing, this perspective must expand to include the period prior to and after officers are operational (see Chapters 3, 4 and 11).

What the life-course perspective adds to the examination of traumatic or critical incident stress over a police career is greater recognition of the reciprocal, mutually interacting connections between trajectories in police trauma and trajectories in other domains of life. It assumes that trajectories in police trauma exposure can be better understood if they are viewed within the total context of the individual's life and, specifically, in relation to the content of the present book, their career as a police officer.

The life-course perspective is attuned to the role of history and sociological factors in shaping individual life courses. One recent factor that has emerged and that can have a profound effect on the life course of police officers is terrorism. It does so as a result of how it has created significant changes in the way in which citizens and police officers alike relate to their social environment (see Chapters 7 and 8). The advent of terrorism is used to illustrate how trajectories can be influenced in significant ways.

What this means in practice is that a comprehensive understanding of traumatic or critical incident stress processes in policing must accommodate both turning or transitional points (e.g., selection, training, becoming operational, having a family, retiring) that arise over the course of a career and the fact that these can have a cumulative effect on the person and the context in which they operate. The advent of terrorism has demonstrated how new turning or transitional points can emerge. The implications of terrorism as a transitional point are discussed specifically in Chapters 7 and 8. The example of terrorism is used to illustrate how new and significant transition points can emerge and what this can mean for the contexts (organizational and societal) in which officer's career trajectories unfold. The importance of this issue in particular derives from its implications for how agencies and officers relate to the wider society. A life-course perspective is well suited to modeling the dynamic nature of policing through its emphasis on trajectories and transitions and its adoption of the concept of cumulative continuity. These are discussed in the next section.

Important Life-Course Theory Concepts and Issues

- Trajectories and transitions—Transitions also are important because they can represent turning points or change in the life course. A trademark of life-course studies is the dual focus on continuity and change. Life course researchers attempt to understand how early experiences are linked to adult outcomes and how transitions or turning points may lead to change in life-course trajectories.
- Cumulative continuity—A particularly important issue in the life-course perspective involves cumulative continuity. Cumulative continuity refers to the way in which exposure at one point in life

influences opportunities and behavior later in life. Early trauma experiences, for example, can influence later trauma exposures; effects may be cumulative. This means that it is essential to examine traumatic experiences over the whole life, including before and after employment, and to recognize that this is central to the development of a comprehensive understanding of traumatic/critical incident stress in serving officers.

A life-course perspective applied to the police career may be a valuable tool in helping to understand both the immediate and long-term effects of career length critical incident exposure on police officers. The future value of a life-course approach will depend for its success on elucidating new mechanisms and pathways as well as its ability to explain social, psychological, and temporal patterns of trauma exposure and its consequences. A mechanism that fills this need is discussed in Chapter 10 where a model designed to accommodate the iterative interaction between critical incidents and the organizational context in which incidents are experienced is presented.

POSTTRAUMATIC STRESS DISORDER: LIFE-COURSE IMPACT

As outlined in life-course theory, social and cultural experiences can lead to transitions that change lives. Posttraumatic stress disorder (PTSD), as a result of traumatic experiences, can certainly be a life-altering event. Several researchers have suggested that PTSD can pervade through a lifetime. Elder, George, Shanahan, Kaplan and Howard (1996), for example, suggest that contextual features of stress are located temporally within the intersection of personal lives and history. Some examples that integrate life course themes with stress were war, child abuse, and caregiving.

Elder, Shananan, Clipp, and Colerick (1994) used longitudinal data to examine whether social disruptions resulting from late service entry increased the risk of adverse change in adult health. Apart from preservice factors, the authors found that the late-mobilized men were at greatest risk of negative trajectories on physical health. Work-life disadvantages account in part for this health effect. Pathways that link stress and physical decline were discussed in relation to social disruption or discontinuity.

Elder, Gimbel, and Ivie (1991) suggested that military service creates discontinuity in men's lives by removing them from age-graded careers and subjecting them to the dictates of a world in which one's past or life history has no importance. This article examined the extent to which military service represented subjective turning points in their lives. Military service specifically, rather than war generally, was recalled as the life-changing experience. Men in this study were most likely to define past events as turning points when those events had positive effects and were perceived to cause substantial change in their lives. It is possible to infer similar consequences in officers how a profession characterized by highly cohesive relationships. This discussion also highlights a need for intervention designed to facilitate the experience of salutogenic outcomes over the course of the career and not just in relation a specific incident. This issue takes on added significance in the context of the growing incidence of DSM-IV disorders in the population.

Kessler, Berglund, Demler, Jin, Merikangas et al. (2005) estimated lifetime prevalence and age-of-onset distributions of DSM-IV disorders in the recently completed National Comorbidity Survey Replication (NCS-R). Lifetime prevalence estimates were as follows: anxiety disorders, 28.8 percent; mood disorders, 20.8 percent; impulse-control disorders, 24.8 percent; substance use disorders, 14.6 percent; any disorder, 46.4 percent. The estimate for PTSD is 6.8 percent. Later onsets are mostly of comorbid conditions, with estimated lifetime risk of any disorder at age 75 years (50.8%) only slightly higher than observed lifetime prevalence (46.4%). Lifetime prevalence estimates are higher in recent cohorts than in earlier cohorts. The authors concluded that half of Americans will meet the criteria for a DSM-IV disorder sometime in their life, with first onset usually in childhood or adolescence. Interventions aimed at prevention or early treatment need to focus on youth. Recognition of the potential for such early experience highlights the importance of accommodating it within the selection and training interventions adopted by police agencies (see Chapters 3 and 4).

Wright, Carter, and Cullen (2005) suggested that military service disconnects men from past social and personal disadvantages and thus potentially alters normal life-course patterns of development. Through latent growth curve models, the authors examined the impact of military service in Vietnam on drug use and arrests across the life course.

Longitudinal data collected by the Marion County Youth study (1964–1979) were used to track a sample of men over a 15-year period. Analyses of these data revealed substantial nonrandom selection effects associated with service in Vietnam.

Cohan and Cole (2002) examined changes in marriage, birth, and divorce rates following Hurricane Hugo. Time-series analysis indicated that the year following the hurricane, marriage, birth, and divorce rates increased in the 24 counties declared disaster areas compared with the 22 other counties in the state. Taken together, the results suggested that a life-threatening event motivated people to take significant action in their close relationships that altered their life course.

Huff (1999) examined how veterans understand and give meaning to the life events that they have experienced following their service in the Vietnam conflict. All of these veterans also believed that Vietnam had significantly altered their subsequent life course and initial expectations. Many veterans diagnosed with PTSD report having experienced major life events such as employment, marriage, and parenthood "off-time": a number of these events were experienced later than the veterans had expected. Delays in employment, marriage, and parenting were perceived as providing an important period of adjustment following their combat experience. In contrast to the thesis that life events experienced off-time are typically negative in their effects on individuals' subsequent life course, the findings of this research suggest strongly that for some groups such as combat veterans, the off-timing of life events may provide important advantages.

POLICE CAREER PATHWAYS AND TRAUMA

The socialization process of a police officer from "civilian" to "police officer" and back to "civilian" is analogous to a life role. In terms of life-course perspective theory, there are many normative (e.g., socialization) as well as disruptive (e.g., 9/11) transition phases within a police career. These can, as introduced earlier, be interconnected. For example, the events of 9/11 have left an indelible mark on the environment of contemporary policing, changed the way subsequent generations of officers are socialized, and affected how officers think about their work and the society they serve. Phases typically are

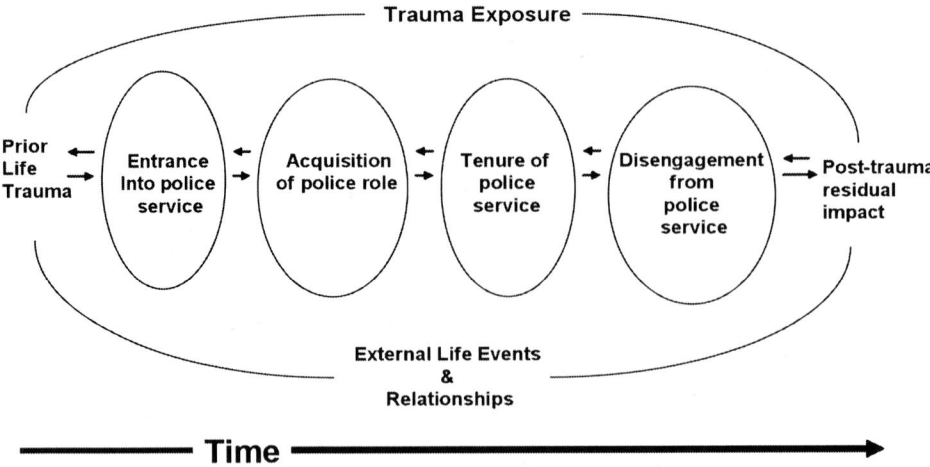

Figure 1.1. Police career course trauma model.

separated from each other by transitions and tend to be ordered in the sense that certain events are expected to precede or follow other events most of the time. This section outlines trajectories and stages of the police career and their relationship to trauma. Figure 1.1 outlines a conceptual model of the police career course and trauma.

An Early Example: Stress "Stages" of a Police Career

An early example of a police career course was suggested by Violanti (1983), who comments that police officers go through transitory "stages" during their careers and that these stages affect the officer's perception of stress:

- **Reality Stage (0–5 years)**–The *reality stage* occurs in police work during the first five years. This pattern can be equated with "reality shock," a realization by the rookie officer that real police work is quite different than what is learned in the academy.
- **Disenchantment Stage (6–13 years)**–Stress should increase sharply during this stage as the young officer is exposed to "real-life" job experience. This may be true for two reasons. First, the rookie officer has never experienced actual police work and is probably startled by such scenes as dead bodies or suffering accident victims. Second, the officer perceives the demands of "real" police work as taxing his personal response capability. The state-

ment "I don't think I can handle the job" is common among young officers. For these reasons, the first stage of an officer's career is increasingly stressful. The *disenchantment stage* generally occurs during year 6 and continues until mid-career. In some respects, the disenchantment stage is an extension of reality shock experienced in the first five years. Idealistic notions fostered in the police academy become further and further apart from reality during this stage. This is a time of bitter disappointment for many officers, a realization that pressures and demands of the police system far outweigh their ability to respond successfully. Officers become disenchanted with an unappreciative public and police administration; many of them adopt cynicism as a coping mechanism. Stress should continue to increase during this stage, above that of the alarm state. This is true because officers feel a sense of personal failure in being unable to handle the demands of policing. They may perceive themselves as "not having an effect" on crime, their own careers, and the common good.

- **Personalization Stage (14–20 years)**–At the end of mid-career and until possible retirement at 20 years, officers go through a *personalization stage*. During this time, the officer begins a renewed emphasis on personal rather than police work goals. During the personalization stage, the officer may no longer "worry" about the demands of policing. It is possible that, as officers approach mid-career, their ideas about what important change are. For example, failure at police tasks may be less important than in earlier years. This change in values can have a decreasing effect on stress. Demands of policing that are perceived as less important, and the diminished fear of failure will contribute to this decrease.
- **Introspection Stage (20 years and over)**–The period after 20 years of service is a time of reflection for officers. This period is indicative of the "old timer" who looks back on early career years as "the good old days." This is the *introspection stage,* a time when officers are somewhat more secure in their jobs. After 20 years of service, officers appear to worry even less about job demands and failure. Most departments allow retirement at 20 years, and offices know that they may leave at any time. Those who stay do so because the "job is now easy," or they lack other suitable employment.

The Impact of Pre-employment Trauma

Part of the life-course perspective involves developmental stages of early life as well as police career exposure. Person who enter police work may come in with emotional baggage: prior trauma. This may have a synergistic effect on trauma experienced as a police officer. Buchanan, Stephens, and Long (2001) suggest that within those occupations where exposure to trauma is high, previous trauma is an additional risk factor which may adversely impact on job performance and ultimately on resignation intention. These authors conducted a study of traumatic experiences of new police recruits and present in-service officers. They found that the percentage of recruits who reported traumatic events (70.6%) was at the high end of the ranges reported from other samples of younger adults. The results of this study have important implications for the health of people entering professions where they may be exposed to traumatic experiences. If they begin work with unresolved trauma, they may have poorer performance and be among the first to seek early retirement. Furthermore, current interventions for managing trauma at the workplace, such as psychological debriefing following a critical incident, do not function retrospectively.

Burke, Shakespeare-Finch, Paton, and Ryan (2006) investigated the process of adaptation in newly recruited police officers. Highlighted were incidences of difficulty in adjusting to the role of police officer, such as predictors of elevated stress and symptoms of posttraumatic stress disorder (PTSD). These authors examined personality, prior experience, and coping strategies of newly recruited police officers. Results demonstrated that the officer's personality profiles showed elevated levels of extraversion. Common coping strategies include positive reinterpretation, acceptance, and planning. Measures of PTSD and positive posttrauma changes were higher in recruits who had endured a traumatic incident prior to joining the service, compared to recruits who had endured stressful, rather than traumatic, events. On entry to the police academy, officers bring with them a plethora of previous life experiences, both positive and negative. In many states and countries, officers enter policing having been selected because their individual characteristics indicate that they are likely to be resilient to the effects of operational stress and trauma (Goldfarb & Aumiller, 2004).

The Burke et al. (2006) paper reported baseline data for a group of police recruits during training at the police academy. The aim was to provide an outline of the personality characteristics, stress levels, and coping strategies with which these individuals enter the profession, with a long-term focus of examining the predictors of officer adjustment. The level of individual traumatic exposure prior to academy entry was also explored. Officers are expected to show similar levels of neuroticism, openness, agreeableness, and conscientiousness to adult population norms. Other researchers (Thompson & Solomon, 1991) have found higher levels of extraversion amongst the police when compared to normative data and therefore, we do not expect this phenomenon to differ in the current population (see Chapter 3).

It is also expected that there will be a positive relationship between stress and maladaptive coping strategies, and a negative relationship between stress and adaptive coping strategies (see Chapter 5). The personality trait of neuroticism is expected to exhibit positive associations with maladaptive coping mechanisms and with stress, and negative associations with adaptive coping mechanisms. Extraversion is expected to have positive associations with using social support as a coping mechanism. It is predicted that there will be significant differences in levels of PTSD symptomatology and reported levels of posttraumatic growth (PTG), with the recruits having experienced a prior traumatic life event, as defined by the DSM-IV-TR (American Psychiatric Association (APA), 2000), exhibiting significantly higher levels of both PTSD symptomatology and PTG than recruits having experienced no traumatic life event.

Huddleston, Paton, and Stephens (2006) point out that while high levels of traumatic stress symptoms at point of entry may increase vulnerability, the manner in which this experience interacts with other kinds of experience within the police role may moderate any relationship with subsequent vulnerability, and may even enhance adaptive capacity and resilience. These issues are examined in more detail in Chapters 3 and 4.

Several mechanisms could thus be proposed to account for this possibility, including, for example, access to social support, or the capacity to use training and operational experiences to render prior experiences coherent and meaningful. These authors add that prior traumatic experiences may have contributed to officers' motivation to enter police work. Police officers choose to enter a profession that explicitly increases the likelihood of their exposure to traumatic and threatening events. Previous experience of traumatic events could increase the likelihood of recruits entering police work both with more realistic expectations of what they could experience and be called upon to deal with and recognition of the importance of being able to deal with these events in the course of fulfilling their professional role. Under these circumstances, they may interpret their experience as providing insights into the importance of helping people (who are faced with significant adversity) in ways that could have salutary and beneficial consequences for them and the communities they have elected to serve. This discussion introduces a need for future research to consider how motivation to enter police work influences subsequent well-being. This issue has, in a formal sense, been neglected in research into traumatic stress processes and adjustment in police officers. This oversight is rectified in Chapters 3 and 4.

Assimilation into the Police Role

Police officers exposed to traumatic events during the course of their careers have an increased vulnerability to posttraumatic stress disorder (PTSD) (Paton & Violanti, 1996). Part of this vulnerability may be attributed to a lack of efficacious coping strategies employed by officers to deal with these events (Patterson, 2001). Current coping models give emphasis to psychological and personal coping resources to deal with distressful situations. Lazarus and Folkman (1984), for example, suggest that coping involves a constantly changing behavioral and cognitive effort to mange external distress. The nature of police work calls for officers to deal with stress from two separate, but related, domains; the operational and the organizational. The influence of each domain on the coping repertoire of officers is examined in Chapters 4 and 9. It is also important to recognize the unique role that the police organization plays in coping.

Coping refers to any response that serves to prevent, avoid, or control psychological symptomatology (Pearlin & Schooler, 1978). The present model suggests that the role of police officer may be used exclusively to cope with traumatic situations. The police role is thus distinguished here as a social coping resource, represented by interpersonal networks among other officers, relationships, and groups.

A common trait of the police role is the use of distinctive behavior patterns for problem resolution. During the work experiential process, officers tend to assimilate a mode of dichotomized decision making–the situation is either "right or wrong" and there is no discretionary middle ground (Blau, 1994). This type of occupationally induced thought process may constrict consideration of alternatives for the amelioration of trauma. Dependence on the police role as a primary life role may also discourage officers from using other more flexible roles as resources to deal with trauma (Thoits, 1986).

Entry into policing involves a process of abrupt resocialization. A first step in that process is assimilation into the police role (Violanti, 1997). Assimilation refers to the rookie officer's adaptation of a new work role (see Chapters 3 and 4) and appears to occur interactively at individual and social levels (Harris, 1973). As noted below, the acquisition process is very strong in initial police training and continues to dominate officer's lives throughout their career (see Chapter 9).

Individual Assimilation

Socialization into the police role begins early in police training, which attempts to instill a sense of superhuman emotional strength in officers (Violanti, 1990). By the time recruits leave the academy, their attachment to the police role has increased far beyond what it was when they entered (Paton & Violanti, 1996).

To the new officer, police work may at first seem exciting and adventurous. Officers can become addicted to their work from what Gilmartin (1990) termed the "brotherhood of biochemistry," a physiological as well as social dependency on the police role. Gilmartin (1986) suggested in that police role created a "learned perceptual set" which led officers to alter the manner in which they interact with the environment. Officers adapted to excitement and danger, were depressed in calm periods, and became detached from any role unrelated to police work.

Solursh (1988), in his analysis of combat officers, found that the combination of mutually excitatory states of danger and recall of such danger led to depression in officers. Van der Kolk (1987) theorized that persons involved in highly stressful jobs may actually become addicted to traumatic exposures. Increased physiological arousal brought about by dangerous or exciting events decreases the officer's ability to assess the nature of current challenges and interferes with rational decision processes. Furthermore, these processes do not occur in a social vacuum. Rather, they occur in a highly cohesive context characterized by interaction under highly challenging circumstances with officers with very similar beliefs about their role and experiences of the performance of that role, with the outcomes of these collective experiences sustaining the police culture.

Social Assimilation

Social factors perpetuate reliance by officers on the police role as a coping resource (see above). The formal and informal police culture may exert considerable influence on the individual in this regard. The formal police organization is said to strongly demand individual adherence to the police role. In response to outside influence, police organizations attempt to facilitate officers' adjustment using organizational design (see Chapter 3), controlling the behavior of organizational members to maintain an image of the police role (Violanti, 1981). As a result, the police organization is unique and can be distinguished from other organizations by the intensity with which it restricts officers into their work role—intensity resulting from rather powerful combinations of militaristic and bureaucratic control methods (Violanti, 1997). The typical police organization may be said to "compound the felony" against officers in terms of control: they are coerced to think and behave in ways consistent with the police role in a continuously changing environment and punished when they do not conform (Gross, 1973).

Proscription of role by the police organization constricts officers into rigid behavior patterns, which in turn decreases their propensity to assume other roles (Kirshman, 1983). One result of such constriction is what Harris (1973) termed "false personalization," a facade of behavior that forces officers to act out roles contrary to true identities and feelings. Officers who employ false personalization may forsake true psychological self-representations and adopt role standards prescribed by the police organization (Kirshman, 1983).

The informal police structure also applies pressure on officers to conform to the police role. This close-knit subculture prescribes a theme of solidarity among officers designed to help them deal with a perceived rejection from society (Burbeck & Furnham, 1985). Quite often, however, formal and informal police cultures are at odds with each other, likely a reaction to the rigid structure and role requirements of the formal organization. As a result, the informal police culture may set up its own role requirements with strong pressure to conform. The foremost requirement is loyalty; an officer never "rats" on another officer, and the code of secrecy remains very influential (Brown, 1981).

These observations point to the important role that the culture of the police organization has for how officers think, react, and operate. It thus deserves special consideration in a model that places considerable importance on the relationship between social context and the trajectories that define officers' critical incident experiences. The preceding discussion introduces the fact that it is not the police organization per se that exercises this influence, but the organizational culture.

Organizational culture can be defined culture as a pattern of fundamental assumptions that are discovered or devised and sustained by a given group (Schein, 1990). Because these assumptions have proven effective in the past, they have been deemed sufficiently important to be taught and transmitted to new members and sustained in established members as the correct way to perceive, think, and feel in relation to the issues and problems that arise in a profession. Culture, according to Schein, comprises artifacts, espoused values, and basic underlying assumptions that emerge from shared experiences over (relatively long) periods of time in order to deal with fundamental problems of adapting to the external world and achieving internal integration and consistency. The outcome of this process is a "collective pool of knowledge that determines what is appropriate behavior, directs understanding and gives guidance on how to resolve problems" (Kampanakis, 2000, p. 2).

Culture is transmitted and sustained through the process of socialization that commences with recruitment and selection (Chapter 3) and proceeds via training and officers entry into organizational life (Chapters 4 and 9). It is subsequently sustained by officers progressive immersion into organizational life that involves their using "a body of knowledge that emerges through the shared application of practical skills to concrete problems encountered in daily routines and the normal course of activities" (Kampanakis, 2000, p. 3). Experiences shared by group members' result in knowledge how to act and how to think about work. Culture has a significant influence on officers' experiences of traumatic events and their consequences (Pieper & Maercker, 1999), including how they cope with and adapt to critical experiences.

Coping Efficacy and the Acquired Police Role

The second part of this model suggests that once officers acquire the police role, dependence on this role as a coping resource may affect trauma symptomatology. Cognitive, social, and inflexible styles associated with the police role may hinder efficacious coping and thus precipitate risk factors associated with PTSD.

Constrictive Inflexibility—Officers socialized into the police role take on an array of predispositions and behaviors which become a permanent part of their personality (Bonafacio, 1991). A prominent feature of the police personality cluster is the cynical notion of reality (Regoli & Poole, 1979). Police officers are by no means existentialists, and their view of reality as a "black and white" issue is common.

Schniedman (1986) suggested that an essence of good adjustment to stress is to be able to view frustrating life situations as existential dichotomies rather than black and white situations. Adjustment to social frustration lies in the individual's ability to make discriminations along the continuum of "black and white" solutions. Police officers' view of themselves as problem solvers precludes the luxury of searching for meaning in work events, and while such a view may be conducive to good police work, it does not lend well to dealing with stress.

Thus, dependency on the police role as a primary coping resource appears to constrict cognitive flexibility. In addition, this dependency leads officers to forsake other social roles which may be useful in coping with traumatic events. The influence of socialization and acculturation and officers' progressive immersion into the police culture on this process is discussed in Chapters 3, 4, and 9. Progressive immersion into the police culture and the growing sense of separation from family and friends that occurs in this context has the effect of constricting social roles.

Diminished Use of Other Social Roles—Attributes of the police role may affect the representational cognitive structure of officers, which defines the self as having purpose and meaning in the social environment. When meaning is lost, the officer can become isolated through role restriction increasing the potential for PTSD (Turner & Roszell, 1994). How this process may be enacted is considered in Chapter 4. Its importance as a life course issue stems from the relationship between role identity and stress.

Thoits (1983, 1986) found that psychological symtomatology varies inversely with the number of role identities possessed. Thoits (1986) argued that individuals conceptualize the cognitive self as a set of social "identities," that refer to assigned positions in the social structure accepted by the individual. Thus, the more social identities a person has, the less potential that person will have for psychological trauma. Linville (1987) concluded symptomatology may be influenced by differences in the complexity of self-representations. Identity role complexity thus appears to protect the self from being overwhelmed by psychological trauma. Consequently, socialization and acculturation processes that restrict roles have significant implications for understanding how traumatic stress processes are influenced by career experiences.

Rosenberg and Pearlin (1978) found a positive relationship between the importance assigned to roles and the impact of life challenges. Gecas and Seff (1990) found a significant positive relationship between the importance attached to roles and self-esteem at work and home. Stryker and Serpe (1982) hypothesized that individuals tend to organize role identities in relation to the social environment and place such identities in a "salience hierarchy." The more salient the role, the greater will be the impact of a traumatic event. Similar to these studies, the present model suggests that utilization of the police role as a primary self-representation may discourage utilization of other life roles to cope with trauma. As a consequence, police officers may deal with trauma almost exclusively from the standpoint of their work role (see Chapters 3, 4, and 9) and this has several implications for their operational performance and their well-being.

The Police Role and Relationships

Reliance on the police role may impair interpersonal relationships for the traumatized officer. The police role calls for depersonalization—interpersonal relationships, on the other hand, call for human emotion. Police officers learn to not let emotion affect their work. When officers are off-duty, however, they have difficulty turning their emotions back on. They remain stuck in prescribed "tough guy" roles that are seen as necessary to be an effective police officer (Madamba, 1986). As a result, the personal relationships of police officers are not personal at all; they are more like a transaction on the street (Stratton, 1978). The implications of these issues are dealt with in Chapters 4 and 9.

Increased Trauma Potential

Police work factors likely to increase the risk of exposure to trauma are danger, shift work, public apathy, a sense of uselessness, and dealing with human misery and death (Spielberger, Westberry, Grier, & Greenfield, 1981). Other traumatic events involve shootings, witnessing death and mutilation, disasters, and abused or maltreated children (Violanti & Aron, 1994). Exposure to trauma without adequate resources for coping may increase the potential for PTSD (American Psychiatric Association, 2000). As police officers encounter trauma through their career, they tax available coping resources to the maximum. Unfortunately, as the present model posits, officers strongly assimilated to the police role may lack important coping resources such as mental flexibility, other life roles, and supportive relationships (Turvey, 1996).

The police role model suggests that assimilation of officers into the police role restricts cognitive flexibility and the use of other life roles, thus impairing their ability to deal with psychological trauma. As a result, the potential for PTSD among exposed police officers may increase. This model does not imply causality, nor is it intended to explain the variance of PTSD rates among police officers. Certainly, police officers are differentially affected psychologically or by job exposure, status, rank, or length of service. Consequently, a life source perspective is a prerequisite to developing understanding of the crucial temporal aspects of how traumatic stress phenomena manifest themselves in police officers. The police role may be only a part of a complex interaction involving the individual, police organization, relationships within the police structure, and society at large. The implications of formal activities, such as training, and informal processes that reflect socialization and acculturation for the development of these competencies are discussed in Chapter 4.

There are some methodological questions about the use of multiple roles to ameliorate trauma. Gerson (1976), for example, theorized that multiple roles increase rather than decrease traumatic symptoms because individuals may encounter role conflict or overload and have difficulty managing roles. Repetti, Matthews, and Waldron (1989) theorized that demands from multiple roles can result in strain in other roles.

Others have argued that police officers do not occupy only one role but instead are faced with a multitude of roles as part of their jobs, resulting in role ambiguity, overload, and conflict (Kelling & Pate, 1975). In response, Marks (1977) hypothesized that human time and energy are flexible and therefore role strain will not always result from occupying multiple roles. The present model characterizes the role of police officer as a state of behavior rather than a work function. Thus, our model maintains that there is no multiplicity associated with the role of police officer, behavior considerations are primary, and tasks and functions are secondary.

A second question concerns the causal direction between use of roles and psychological symptomatology. The multiple role hypothesis posits that occupying multiple social roles positively affects psychological well-being, although it is possible that a pre-existing selection process is operative. Incoming officers with higher levels of psychological well-being may be resistant to cognitive constriction and more willing to become involved in other life roles (Verbugge, 1983).

External Life Events: Transitions to Depression

Although repeated exposures to acute work stressors (e.g., violent criminal acts, sad and disturbing situations, and physically demanding responses) can lead to trauma symptomatology and depression, police officers must also deal with stressors external to work. Contending with negative life events (e.g., divorce, serious family or personal illness, and financial difficulties) can affect both the psychological and physiological well-being of officers as well (Shakespeare-Finch, Paton, & Violanti, 2003).

The psychological effects of experiencing life events have been well studied. Life events often precede depressive episodes and psychiatric disorders such as anxiety states, alcoholism, bulimia, and schizophrenia (Kendler, Karkowski, & Prescott, 1998; Kendler, Kessler, Neale, Heath, & Eaves, 1993), contribute to depression, and are associated with greater risk of illness (Brown & Harris, 1989).

Police career courses can be affected by such events in terms of psychological disruption. Hartley, Violanti, Fekedulegn, Andrew, and

Burchfiel (2006) examined to what extent negative life events and traumatic police incidents are associated with depression in police officers. Officers averaged nearly three life events during the previous year. Among most reported life events were the death of a close relative or friend, decrease in income, and serious arguments with spouse, boss, or coworkers. Results revealed associations between exposure to negative life events and depression. Depression increased as the number of negative life events increased. An increasing stepwise trend in depression scores was observed between officers experiencing a low, medium, and high number of negative life events, a finding consistent with work by Patton et al. (2003). Further analyses revealed that experiencing a high number of negative life events over the past year nearly doubled depression scores in this sample of police officers. This police sample averaged over four traumatic police incidents during the previous year. A stepwise trend was observed among police officers experiencing one or more traumatic incidents; depression scores increased as the number of incidents experienced increased. This is not, however, the only outcome that can ensue.

RISK

Police officers can expect to experience challenging critical incidents (emergencies and disasters) several times over the course of a career likely to span several decades. Critical incidents have traditionally been viewed as precursors to the development of acute and chronic posttraumatic stress reactions. However, growing evidence for such experiences to be associated with positive outcomes has fueled calls for a reappraisal of this aspect of police work (Moran & Colless, 1995; Paton, 2006). Positive outcomes include exercising professional skills to achieve highly meaningful outcomes, posttraumatic growth, enhanced professional capability, a greater appreciation for family, and an enhanced sense of control over significant adverse events. Furthermore, a growing body of evidence suggests that positive (adaptation and growth) and negative (deficit/pathology) outcomes are discrete and coexist (Hart, Wearing, & Heady, 1995; Huddleston, Paton, & Stephens, 2006; Linley & Joseph, 2004; Paton & Burke, 2007; Tedeschi & Calhoun, 2003). If a comprehensive account of this aspect of police work is to be forthcoming, a new conceptualization of critical incident stress, and one capable of accommodating these diverse outcomes, is required.

The starting point for this process is recognition that traumatic stress symptoms (e.g., intrusive ideation) reflect the experience of a state of psychological disequilibrium as a result of a person's inability to organize elements of their atypical experience in meaningful ways (Janoff-Bulman, 1992; Paton, 1994). Rather than it being an automatic precursor of posttraumatic pathology, disequilibrium can be resolved by the development of new mental models (new equilibrium state) characterized by either growth (e.g., posttraumatic growth) or loss (e.g., learned avoidance of threat situations). In the context of the life course model upon which the present text is based, this confers upon critical incidents a capacity to be conceptualized as significant transition points in the career trajectories of officers.

Which outcome occurs is less a function of the experience per se and more a result of how it interacts with elements that increase officer's susceptibility to experiencing loss from exposure to a critical incident (i.e., increase vulnerability) and those that facilitate adaptation and growth (Paton, 2006; Paton & Burke, 2007). Rather than posttraumatic pathology being inevitable, the risk paradigm suggests that it is best defined as a probability. Importantly, it also advocates that it is necessary to accommodate the probability of a positive outcome.

If the factors that influence each eventuality can be identified, police organizations will be in a better position to make choices about the outcomes their officers can experience. In order to guide organizational analysis and action, a framework capable of integrating these issues is required. The risk concept is an appropriate candidate for this role.

While its contemporary usage is synonymous with loss, Dake (1992) reminds us that the term "risk" was originally coined to account for the *gains* and the *losses* that could occur under conditions of uncertainty. This confers upon the risk management paradigm a capacity to encapsulate both growth/adaptation and deficit/loss outcomes in models of traumatic stress processes (Dake, 1992; Paton, 2006). This has several implications for the way in which the content of the present text is framed. Foremost amongst these is the fact that it should not be assumed that the organizational and career factors discussed in subsequent chapters automatically increase the likelihood of officers experiencing traumatic stress pathology. Rather, they should be regarded as factors that can, depending on circumstances, increase the probability of officers experiencing either growth or loss outcomes (i.e., as influencing risk rather than presuming a specific outcome). Furthermore, since it is not possible to lay responsibility for traumatic stress or adaptive outcomes at the door of the events (e.g., body recovery from an air crash, dealing with a hostage situation, a mass shooting, etc.), it is appropriate to label these events not as traumatic incidents but as critical incidents.

Paton and Violanti (1996) adopted this approach to emphasize how an event became critical as a result of its potential to create psychological disequilibrium because it fell outside and/or exceeded normal or expected response parameters. In this sense, factors are framed as critical incident stress risk factors and this terminology is used in subsequent chapters to emphasize a need to adopt a neutral standpoint when researching the consequences and career implications of critical incident experiences. This is particularly important when dealing with a profession whose members face the prospect of repetitive exposure to incidents over a period of several decades. Adopting a neutral starting point, and accepting a need to consider the potential for events to result in gains or losses, makes it easier to accept a need for proactive intervention (Paton, Violanti, & Smith, 2003).

This should not be taken to imply that everything can be managed. It is acknowledged that this may not always be possible (e.g., response to major disasters). However, knowledge of risk factors that underpin resilience, even if they can't be changed, can inform the process of residual risk assessment (Violanti, 2006). This process identifies those issues that are significant predictors of risk, but which cannot be managed within the risk management process. Issues identified here can be used to, for example, advise officers of sources of risk that can inform future training needs analysis or counseling processes.

Conceptualizing traumatic stress within such a framework has important ramifications for police officers. While the nature of police work precludes preventing exposure to critical incidents, and therefore to events that affect officers' stress risk, choices made within the risk management process will influence individual, team, and organizational outcomes. Consequently, intervention should focus on altering the consequences of hazard exposure through better planning and preparedness; that is, by reducing the prevalence of vulnerability factors and facilitating and sustaining those personal, group, and organizational factors that enhance resilience. While risk can be managed actively during the period of an officer's career, this becomes less tenable once the officer has retired. The significance of the latter stems from the fact that termination of a police career does not mean that traumatic stress risk is eliminated overnight.

AFTER THE BATTLE IS OVER: RETIREMENT AND TRAUMA

The impact of trauma in police work does not end upon separation from police service. The issue will be dealt with on more detail in Chapter 11. Briefly, there has been some work done on trauma carried over from war and other traumatic events.

Liston (2003), for example, identified trauma symptoms experienced by World War II combat veterans as well as coping strategies that these veterans have found to be helpful for healing and adapting to civilian life and the later years. While several of the respondents began talking openly about their war experiences shortly after the war, most did not do so until their later years. Several of the men stayed in the military, and most who repatriated were healing in a different way. Anxious to move on with their lives, they channeled their energy into humanizing activities that provided feelings of control such as finding work, pursuing an education, raising a family, and engaging in hobbies. During their retirement years, many of the respondents have become more involved with their respective veterans groups and regularly attend service reunions. When triggered in this safe environment, coupled with the passage of time, combat trauma is successfully integrated. Faced with the death of loved ones and comrades, deteriorating health, and their own mortality, many of the veterans are talking and writing about their war experiences in their advanced years.

Hyer and Leon (1994) addressed acute, delayed, and chronic PTSD among the elderly, including a brief review of studies that have focused on later-life veterans with PTSD. Particular attention was paid to the interaction of relevant aging variables with trauma variables in an attempt to elucidate the phenomenology of later-life PTSD. These include variables from normative aging, geriatric psychopathology, and psychotherapeutic techniques, as all contribute to the manifestation of later-life PTSD.

Davison, Pless, Gugliucci, King, Salgado, Sprio, and Bachrach (2006) provided preliminary evidence for a phenomenon observed in aging combat veterans termed late-onset stress symptomatology (LOSS). LOSS is a hypothesized phenomenon among older veterans who (a) experienced highly stressful combat events in early adulthood; (b) functioned successfully throughout their lives, with no chronic stress-related disorders; but (c) begin to register increased combat-related thoughts, feelings, reminiscences, memories, or symptoms commensurate with the changes and challenges of aging, sometimes decades after their combat experiences. Using a qualitative focus group methodology with 47 World War II, Korean Conflict, and Vietnam War veterans, the authors obtained preliminary evidence for the presence of LOSS as defined, identified some of its features, revealed some normative late-life stressors that may precipitate LOSS, and uncovered potential intrapersonal risk and resilience factors for LOSS.

Krause, Shaw, and Cairney (2004) evaluated (1) the relationship between exposure to trauma over the life course and physical health status in old age; (2) the relationship between trauma and health varies across three cohorts of older adults: the young-old (ages 65–74), the old-old (ages 75–84), and the oldest old (age 85 and over); and (3) examined whether the age at which a trauma was encountered is related to health in late life. Data from a nationwide survey of older people (N = 1,518) reveal that trauma is associated with worse health. Moreover, the young-old appear to be at greatest risk. Finally, data suggest that trauma arising between the ages of 18 and 30 years, as well as ages 31 to 64 years, has the strongest relationship with current health. This is exactly the age at which most officers will retire. A life-course perspective makes it easier to appreciate why the research and intervention net needs to cast wider than the period of operational employment to include retirement. Several mechanisms could thus be proposed to account for this possibility.

CONCLUSION

This chapter has presented several basic conceptual components of the life course model as applied to trauma and police work. In sum, the impact of trauma, whether it be positive growth or pathogenic affect, depends on timing and circumstance through the police career path. For example, at what point in the police career the most meaningful trauma occurred, where and how it occurred, its intensity and meaning, how peers and the organization responded, and the timeliness and efficacy of intervention or treatment. As our model in Figure 1.1 suggests, there exists bidirectional causal pathways at all stages of the career, and any one of the aforementioned factors can adversely (or positively) determine the final impact of trauma exposure and symptomatology. The chapters which follow in this book examine these concepts in more detail and provide explanations for the course of traumatic stress in police work and offer some solutions on how we may deal with this perplexing problem.

The introduction to this chapter discussed the importance of understanding the context in which life events and transitions take place. For officers, this is the police organization. It is to a discussion of this important context that this book now turns.

Chapter 2

ORGANIZATIONAL INFLUENCES ON CRITICAL INCIDENT STRESS RISK

INTRODUCTION

In the previous chapter, the discussion of life-course theory introduced the need to consider the connections between the domains within which life trajectories take place, and in which the events and interventions that influence development occur. This chapter picks up on this issue and focuses on a domain that has highly significant implications for the life trajectories of police officers; the police organization. This chapter introduces the context, the police organization, in which the experiences (e.g., socialization) and interventions (e.g., training, performance appraisal) that officers encounter are enacted. It also introduces how officer's interpretations of the processes that govern organizational activity influence their critical incident stress risk.

Discussion focuses specifically on how the contextual features and organizational nuances of the police profession and police work influence officer adjustment, stress, and well-being. The examination of these issues follows Abdollahi's (2002) classification of police stress as comprising occupational and organizational contexts. Occupational stressors describe the demands that occur by virtue of the police officer being involved in their operational duties. Organizational stressors, on the other hand, are context driven events, and can include administrative issues as well as demands on officers generated by the bureaucratic, hierarchical nature of the profession. The first issue involves asking how these facets influence critical incident stress risk. Since traumatic phenomena typically manifest themselves in officers following their involvement in a challenging incident, it is easy to see how operational factors would influence risk. Not so for organizational factors that tend to be implicit or taken-for-granted facets of officers' experience. In other words, because they are a constant in the working life of officers, they are less likely to be implicated in explaining the consequences of any one event or even recognized as having the potential to influence reactions to events that take place in the community.

Given this difference, it is not surprising that the majority of studies into police stress have focused on the volatile nature of the job which police officers perform. It cannot be disputed that police officers often encounter disturbing situations which, given the very nature of police work, cannot be avoided. This work has, consequently, located the major source of stress experienced by police as a direct result of the operational tasks they perform. There is little debate that the events faced by officers in an operational capacity can be potentially harmful and life threatening. What is open to debate, however, is whether these events induce similar responses in all officers. A growing body of evidence attests to the fact that reactions to critical incidents (e.g., the prevalence of posttrauma pathology) and how officer's themselves interpret their critical incident experiences are marked by considerable diversity.

IDENTIFYING SOURCES OF DIVERSITY

The prevalence rate for the development of PTSD in police officers lies between 7 percent and 20 percent (e.g., Carlier, Lamberts, & Gersons, 2000; Carlier, Lamberts, Gersons, & Berthold, 1997; Hodgins, Creamer, & Bell, 2001). These data highlight the fact that amongst officers who experience the same/similar types of events, some (albeit a small proportion) do experience pathological outcomes. However, others (i.e., 80–93%) involved in the same events do not and, furthermore, may demonstrate a capacity to adapt and experience beneficial outcomes from the self same experience.

For example, North et al. (2002) observed that, following involvement in the response to the Oklahoma City terrorist bombing, some officers reported increased job satisfaction. This was linked to the sense of pride in their performance and with improved relationships with managers. Other officers, however, reported a decline in job satisfaction from their experience of this critical incident. Differences of this nature highlight a need to understand why officers who attended the same event can experience very different outcomes. Recognition of this diversity introduces a need to explain why some officers are more at risk of developing adverse outcomes than others and why some officers appear to be more resilient.

The validity of the assumed link between operational experience and pathological outcome can also be called into question when it is considered that the most common rewarding aspects identified by American police officers were variety and arresting fugitives (Newmann & Ricker-Reed, 2004) and excitement and helping people (Storch & Panzarella, 1996). Kop, Euwema, and Schaufeli (1999) found that Dutch police officers reported positive aspects of policing as resulting from contact with civilians and variation of work. Recent research thus recognizes that there is a positive side to policing, and argues that officers derive positive occupational outcomes from the very situations that lead the lay person to assume the job is stressful (e.g., Burke & Paton, 2006a; Hart, Wearing, & Heady, 1995). Furthermore, lay perception of the nature of police work need not correspond to officers' views of their work.

Despite their high exposure to adverse situations, police officers generally report similar or higher levels of job satisfaction compared with those employed in "less stressful" occupations (Hart, 1999). Reasons for this apparently counterintuitive observation become clearer if positive and negative outcomes are conceptualized as discrete rather than as lying at opposite ends of a continuum (Hart et al., 1993). Thus, an event attended by an officer may be distressing or traumatic initially, but provide them with a great deal of satisfaction in knowing that they have handled a situation to the best of their ability, even if, in the process, they experienced some level of distress (e.g., saved a life despite facing personal threat). The beneficial aspects of policing reported above can be traced to officers' operational experiences, with at least some of them reflecting challenging (stressful) and potentially traumatic (arresting fugitives) work experiences. Moreover, this facet of work can be identified as having beneficial effects.

Since dramatic differences in outcomes, from pathological to growth, cannot be attributed wholly to the operational itself, other factors must be influencing how officers interpret and make sense of their experiences. Several factors can be implicated to help account for this differential reactivity. Some variance will likely arise from differences (e.g., traffic control versus body recovery at the same incident) in the way officers experience a given event (Paton & Violanti, 2007). However, it is clear from the above studies that responsibility for stress in police officers cannot be laid wholly at the operational door. Some variance can be attributed to individual differences in psychological reactivity, past experiences, and levels of acculturation that influence how officers interpret experiences (see Chapters 3 and 4). Another possibility, and the area being introduced in this chapter, is that officer's experience of the police organization itself may contribute to stress risk. If this line of argument is to have any currency, it is necessary to identify how the "organization" can influence risk.

To this point, it has been argued that while attendance at, and exposure to, adverse incidents are an integral aspect of policing, those individuals employed as police officers have an expectation that they will be involved in these volatile situations. Operational exposure to stressful and traumatic situations are defining aspects of the police officer's role, and in many cases, may be the very thing that motivated people to join the profession. Therefore, if occupational experiences and consequences are consistent with officers' expectations, it is likely that they will pose little threat to levels of well-being, and consequently, have little impact on an officer's risk of stress. If the answer to the question of locating critical incident stress risk does not lie solely with officers' operational experiences, what about Abdollahi's (2002) other category, organizational factors.

THE INFLUENCE OF ORGANIZATIONAL LIFE

In the main, the influence of organizational factors on officer well-being has generally been perceived as peripheral, and not deemed as salient to officers' psychological functioning as the operational content of policing (Abdollahi, 2002; Alexander & Wells, 1991; Burke & Paton, 2006b; Paton & Burke, 2007; Paton, 1994). However, core aspects of organizational culture (e.g., its influence on training content, operational tactics, and bureaucratic reporting requirements) make a significant contribution to the context in which operational experiences are interpreted and responses take place. For example, autocratic management influences the scope for responding to emergent demands during critical incident response (Alexander & Wells, 1991). This example illustrates how an aspect of organizational culture (maintenance of autocratic management style irrespective of circumstances) can, by constraining officers' ability to respond quickly to dynamic, evolving events, increase stress risk (Paton & Flin, 1999). This example raises an interesting issue. It can be taken to imply that officer's expectations about their critical incident experiences can extend beyond the incident to embrace the organizational procedures they experience as a result of fulfilling their operational role. That is, they expect organizational procedures and processes to support the performance of their operational role. After all, serving the community is what policing is all about.

Thus the degree to which organizational characteristics are consistent with officer's beliefs about the core functions of police work can facilitate or hinder officer adjustment, performance, and well-being (Hart & Cooper, 2001; Burke & Paton, 2006a, 2006b; Leong et al., 1996; Paton et al., 2003). Thus, if organizational procedures support effective performance in one's operational role, officers are less likely to find their beliefs about policing challenged and are less likely to need to adapt their interpretive mechanisms to reconcile what they see as contradictory demands. If, however, organizational procedures impose demands on officers that are inconsistent with their operational beliefs, the consequent need to adapt their interpretive schema increases the psychological demands they face, with the pressure coming from the organizational rather than the operational context. To accommodate this possibility, research in policing has begun to focus on factors that influence officer's perception of the day-to-day organizational context of the police experience. That is, how the processes and procedures that have become implicit aspects of the daily work environment influence how officers come to develop consistent ways of thinking about and responding to events and how inconsistencies between officer's expectations of police work and their perceptions of organizational procedures (e.g., making an arrest versus completing the associated paperwork) constitute a stressor.

The last point introduces a need to accommodate the fact that the organizational climate also encompasses the bureaucratic and political aspects of work life. These facets of officers' experience influence both the daily demands on officers (i.e., operational stressors) and their subsequent critical incident stress risk (e.g., as a result of the tactical management procedures they prescribe; the degree of autonomy allowed to officers; attitudes to mental health). The realization that organizational systems and procedures sustain the bureaucratic and political imperatives of the police agency as much they do the pursuance of core policing activities may not be consistent with the schematic expectations an officer had of policing. It can be this aspect of work that shatters assumptions and contributes to the experience of adverse psychological outcomes (Violanti & Paton, 1999). Officer's experience of the organization can thus influence their vulnerability and resilience in several ways (Paton, 2006). These range from influencing how officers interpret events to differences between officer and organization with regard to the emphasis on different facets of the event (e.g., making an arrest versus the associated paperwork). In this context, it is possible to appreciate how interaction between operational and organizational factors influences critical incident stress risk.

Risk in Operational Contexts

The potential for the operational duties police officers perform to expose them to challenging critical incidents is high. Such experiences include, for example, officer involved shootings (Coman & Evans, 1991; Gersons 1989; Kroes, 1974); encountering victims of crimes and fatalities (Alexander & Wells, 1991; Kroes, 1985; Kroes et al., 1974); community relations (Brown & Campbell, 1994; Kroes, 1985; Violanti & Aron, 1993; Wilson, 1968); encountering violent/unpredictable situations (Blau, 1994; Wells, Getman & Blau, 1988); dealings with the judicial system (Kroes, 1974; Kroes et al., 1985); and public scrutiny and media coverage of high profile incidents (Davidson & Veno, 1980; Kroes, 1985). While the potential for these events to constitute significant personal, team and organizational challenges is not disputed, the belief that these events represent the only or the most significant influences on critical incident stress risk can be questioned.

The assumed link between the experience of a challenging event and a traumatic stress reaction derives from the fact that research on police officer well-being has traditionally been embedded within the pathogenic paradigm. This has fostered a belief that stress is a function, predominantly, of the operational situations officers face and that exposure to stressors will inevitably result in pathological outcomes.

While attendance at, and exposure to, challenging incidents are an integral aspect of policing, officers know this prior to becoming operational, and therefore have some expectation of being involved in volatile situations (Gist & Woodall, 2000). Furthermore, the training officers receive does increase their knowledge of what they may encounter, and is designed to facilitate their ability to respond to and cope with challenging events and their consequences. This suggests that a significant critical incident stress risk factor will be the degree to which officers' training and incident management procedures used to put training into practice affects risk (Alexander & Wells, 1991; Gist & Woodall, 2000; Paton, 1994; Paton, 2006; Pennebaker, 2000).

The fact that the nature and content of training officers receive reflects organizational choices about how they believe officers should think about and respond to (operationally and psychologically) critical incidents illustrates how decisions made as a result of implicit organizational beliefs and historical precedent can create a unique source of critical incident risk. Paton and Violanti (2007) discuss how the choices made by the organization (e.g., the focus of training needs analysis, training content, and mode of delivery, and how training is put into practice and evaluated) reflects the action of organizational decisions derived from historical operating environments. As such, by potentially reducing the applicability of these processes to the contemporary environment, these choices play a significant role in determining officers' critical incident stress risk. To put it another way, organizational awareness, or otherwise, of changing environmental characteristics (see Chapters 7 and 8) influences the degree to which officers are prepared, physically and psychologically, for the situations they are likely to be called on to respond to.

Nor is it only officers' competencies that are affected. Organizational influence can also extend to the quality of their psychological preparedness (Kampanakis, 2000; Paton, 1994). Police organizations cannot prevent officers being involved in critical incidents, but they can influence the degree to which officers are prepared for such eventualities. Whether this occurs, and the quality of preparedness that ensues, is a function of the degree to which the pool of knowledge developed to guide organizational choices is appropriate for resolving the problems the organization faces (Kampanakis, 2000). This may not be the case when dealing with atypical critical incidents (Alexander & Wells, 1991–see Chapters 7 and 8). Consequently, if a comprehensive account of critical incident stress risk in police officers is to be developed, it will be important to cast the explanatory net wider than the events officer's experience to encompass the role of the organizational context (e.g., the actions and attitudes of senior officers and colleagues, officer's interpretation of procedures) as a risk factor.

ORGANIZATIONAL CONTEXT

The organizational context represents a salient influence on officer socialization, adjustment, functioning, and well-being (Burke & Paton, 2006; Hart et al., 1993, 1995; Paton & Violanti, 2007; Paton et al., 2003). For example, the way in which selection procedures operate, the role of academy training in socialization, and decisions about training content and evaluation, all of which reflect prevailing organizational cultural beliefs (see Chapter 3). When considered from the perspective of a life course model, it becomes easier to appreciate how the processes that unfold over the officer's career can make a significant contribution to the context in which officer's experience and interpret work life.

As a result of officers' progressive immersion in the culture, the organization comes to exert greater influence on how officers interpret their experiences and attempt to make sense of or impose coherence upon them (Gist & Woodall, 2000; Paton, 2006; Pennebaker, 2000; Pollock et al., 2003). Specifically, it is by investigating how officers impose meaning on their organizational experiences that we can understand how organizational contexts influence stress risk.

Recent research that has pursued this line of inquiry has argued that officers perceptions of how organizational structures, functions, climate, and procedures impinge on them and their work (e.g., as hassles that add to the demands they encounter or as uplifts that make them feel good—see below) reduce future vulnerability or nurture future resilience (Paton, 2006; Paton & Burke, 2007). The positive experience of the organization (e.g., uplifts—see below) has been identified as playing a significant role in sustaining a sense of coherence between the occupational roles, identities, and expectations of officers (Dunning, 2003), and is thus implicated as a resilience factor.

In contrast, negative organizational experiences (e.g., hassles) are implicated in the breakdown of organizational coherence and can, consequently, exert a negative influence on officers' professional identity and future performance capability (Paton & Stephens, 1996). For example, officers enter a profession they see as providing a helping role. Implicit in their expectations is that the structure and culture of the organization would support this. However, factors such as, for example, bureaucratic procedures and organizational practices regarding the allocation of blame that call this assumption into question, reduce the degree to which officers can reconcile different aspects of their experience (operational and organizational) to create an overall sense of cohesion, and lay the foundation for adverse psychological outcomes due to a perceived fracture the psychological contract between the officer and the organization (MacLeod & Paton, 1999; Paton & Stephens, 1996). This means that the operational experiences of police officers cannot be realistically understood in isolation from the wider organizational context and the procedures and practices that it endorses or discourages (Anshel, 2002; Burke & Paton, 2006a, 2006b; Haarr, 2005; Hart et al., 1995; Burke et al., 2006; Paton & Burke, 2007). It follows that if a comprehensive understanding of critical incident stress processes and outcomes is to be developed, the culture and climate of the organization in which these experiences actually take place, and how these facets of organizational life translate into the daily experience of officers, must also be considered.

The development of organizationally-derived sense making processes has its roots in the socialization practices that officers experience as recruits and is sustained through, for example, the training and performance appraisal procedures that they encounter throughout their career. The beliefs engendered by these organizational interventions are further maintained by, for example, exposure to senior officer attitudes to emotional disclosure and how they attribute blame for operational problems, feedback from training evaluations, interaction with the criminal justice system, and the relative emphasis they place on operational versus bureaucratic performance. These processes conspire over time to influence the development of the interpretive frameworks or schemata officers use when responding to operational events.

Following Dunning.s (2003) lead, the foundation for understanding organizational influence is the degree to which officers perceive the actions taken and promoted by the police organization, particularly in the provision of operational guidelines, as making sense to them in terms of their occupational expectations and experiences. If these guidelines do not facilitate officers' ability to maintain a sense of coherence and impose meaning on all aspects of a critical incident (that encompasses not only the event but also how the organization prescribes such things as response and reporting requirements, etc.) the risk of adverse stress outcomes is increased and the likelihood that a given experience will contribute to the development of officer and organizational capability is diminished. To understand how officer-organizational transactions influence well-being, we need to understand how the organizational culture influences officer' interpretive processes and how these, in turn, influence their critical incident stress risk.

Organizational Climate and Culture

Officers' operational and organizational experiences are enacted in the context of their wider organizational membership. The process of cultural assimilation is affected through, for example, selection, socialization, and training processes whose content, delivery and assessment reflect prevailing organizational cultural beliefs about such things as duties, responsibilities and "correct" procedures (Kampanakis, 2000). Core aspects of organizational culture (e.g., its influence on training, operational tactics) make a significant contribution to the context in which operational experiences are interpreted and response occurs (Alexander & Wells, 1991), and organizational cultures can be differentiated with regard to their effect on officer's posttraumatic stress outcomes (Paton, Smith, Ramsey, & Akande, 1999). This reflects how, over time, immersion in the organizational culture (see Chapters 3, 4 and 9) result in the progressive development of consistency in how officers perceive, think, and feel in relation to the issues and problems that arise in work environments (Schein, 1990). The end product is the "collective pool of knowledge that determines what is appropriate behavior, directs understanding and gives guidance on how to resolve problems" discussed by Kampanakis (2000, p. 2). Because it plays a key role in facilitating adaptation to external events and achieving internal integration and consistency, organizational culture exercises a strong influence on how life trajectories evolve, and, in so doing, exerts a significant influence on officers' experiences of traumatic events and their consequences (Pieper & Maercker, 1999).

As officers interact with these organizationally sanctioned and sustained procedures, they develop ways of thinking, mental models, that come to implicitly influence how they conceptualize and respond to incidents (Paton & Jackson, 2002). These organizationally sanctioned and sustained procedures thus make a significant contribution to the context in which officers experience work life and critical incidents (e.g., as a result of the tactical management procedures they prescribe, the degree of autonomy allowed to officers, organizational attitudes to stress, etc.). The organizational climate also encompasses the bureaucratic and political aspects of work life, and these facets of officers' experience influence both the daily demands on officers and their vulnerability to posttraumatic stress reactions (Violanti & Paton, 1999). Consequently, operational and organizational factors should be regarded as playing complementary roles in the processes that influence occupational and critical incident stress risk (Burke & Paton, 2006; Gist & Woodall, 2000; Hart, 1999; Hart et al., 1995; Paton & Burke, 2007; Paton & Violanti, 2007). While a considerable body of research in policing has examined critical incident stress from the perspective of officer's involvement in specific incidents, few, however, have considered how officers' experience of their routine, day-to-day organizational procedures influences stress risk.

The predictive utility of daily work experiences on officer wellbeing was investigated by Burke & Paton (2006b). They found that the inclusion of daily *organizational* experiences (both positive and negative) in an hierarchical multiple regression explained significantly more of the variance in police officer job satisfaction than *operational* experiences (i.e., those factors usually held to be stressors for police officers) alone. The addition of organizational hassles contributed a further 20 percent predictive power. Burke and Paton also noted that the experience of operational hassles (e.g., arresting criminals, dealing with victims) actually increased job satisfaction. Conceptually, this makes sense as policing involves people who enter a profession they see as providing a helping role (Gist & Woodall, 2000; Haarr, 2005), with the expectation that the structure and culture of the organization would support this ideal. If the organization does not match these expectations, there is potential for the organization to contribute to increasing stress risk.

Organizational Factors

The climate of an organization can be conceptualized as a framework that guides officer's interpretation of experiences in ways that can nurture or constrain their ability to impose coherence and meaning onto atypical critical incident events (Dunning, 2003; Pollock et al., 2003). The actions taken and promoted by the police organization particularly in the provision of operational guidelines must make sense to the employees in terms of their occupational expectations and experiences. These guidelines may fail in the context of non-routine (i.e., critical incident) events unless the organization develops procedures specifically to cater for such eventualities (Alexander & Wells, 1991; Gist & Woodall, 2000; Paton, 1994), thus restricting and frustrating officer's ability to impose a sense of coherence on atypical experiences (Dunning, 2003). It follows that if it is to contribute to effective preparation for and increase the probability of officers finding benefit in critical incident experience, the maintenance of organizational coherence will play a pivotal role in managing critical incident stress risk. In other words, an organizational (management) failure to distinguish "routine" and "critical" incidents can result in the police agency making inappropriate assumptions regarding the readiness of their officers for the more challenging events they may be called upon to respond to, increasing officers' stress risk in the process (Alexander & Wells, 1991; Paton, 1994; Paton & Violanti, 2007).

This has several implications for understanding the relationship between decisions made by the organization to conduct its core business and the potential for these decisions to influence critical incident stress risk, particularly with regard to understanding how these decisions may impact on officers' resilience or their vulnerability. For example, the adoption of this perspective makes it apparent that decisions about the content and medium of delivery of training can influence critical incident stress risk (Paton, 1994). It is the responsibility of training programs to prepare officers adequately for routine operational trauma exposure; to provide the capacity for officer's to shift conceptually into a non-routine disaster context; and to maintain coherence between organizational expectations and occupational experiences, thereby minimizing the occurrence and impact of daily chronic stressors (Dunning, 2003).

Operational and Organizational Risk

Investigations of stress and well-being within police are beginning to acknowledge the powerful influence of daily experiences on officers' stress risk (Kohan & Mazmanian, 2003). The evaluation and acknowledgment of daily occupational stressors provides a fresh insight into officer's stress reactions and, subsequently, into the factors that influence stress vulnerability (Burke & Paton, 2006a; Hart, 1999; Hart, Wearing & Heady, 1995; Kohan & Mazmanian, 2003). The climate created by the police organization, and its subsequent effect on the daily experiences of officers, has the potential to promote vulnerability and disrupt the processes of resilience and growth unless organizational coherence is maintained.

Defining the experience of organizational systems and procedures through the eyes of the officers themselves has led to a distinction being drawn between hassles (e.g., having an arrest fall through on a legal technicality, red tape) and uplifts (e.g., saving the life of a member of the public, recognition for good work, being given responsibility for operational decision making, working in autonomous teams), with each making different contributions to negative and positive outcomes respectively (Hart et al., 1993; Hart et al., 1995; Hart & Cooper, 2001). Both operational and organizational experiences can be subdivided into positive ("uplifts") and negative ("hassles") dimensions (Figure 2.1; Tables 2.1 and 2.2).

This distinction is important. Each holds the potential to influence well-being in different ways (Hart et al., 1995; Hart & Cooper, 2001; Tedeschi & Calhoun, 2003). Positive operational experiences have been identified as playing a significant role in sustaining a sense of coherence between the occupational roles, identities, and expectations of officers (Dunning, 2003; Haarr, 2005; Paton, 2005). Negative organizational experiences, on the other hand, have been implicated in the breakdown of organizational coherence and can have a profound impact on a police officer's professional identity (Paton & Burke, 2007) and can lead to adverse psychological outcomes due to a perceived fracture in the psychological contract between the officer and the organization (Haarr, 2005; Paton, 2005).

In this context, it is not surprising that studies that have purposefully focused on the organizational determinants of stress and well-being have consistently found that organizational processes are just as, if not

TABLE 2.1
THE SUBSCALES OF THE POLICE DAILY UPLIFTS SCALE

Subscale	Description
Operational Uplifts	
Offenders	Deals with the potential positive aspects of the job such as successful resuscitation and delivering a baby
Victims	Examines the potential positive aspects of helping the public, from the perspective of the officer
Rosters	Officers perceptions of shifts and assigned working hours
Organizational Uplifts	
Decision Making	Examines officer perceptions of positive decision making and responsibility
Workload	Examines officer perceptions of the amount of work they must accomplish on a shift
Co-workers	Deals with the potential for positive interactions and perceptions of coworkers
Administration	Examines officer perceptions of potential positives from the correct application of policies, rules and operational guidelines
Amenities	Deals with the perceptions of adequate provision of amenities and facilities for officers.
Supervision	Examines the adequacy, quality and level of staff supervision, from the employee perspective.
Promotions	Examines officer perceptions of opportunity for and fairness in the promotions process
Family	Examines the perceived impact of the job on family

Adapted from Hart, 1996.

more important in determining employee well-being than the operational content of the job. This relationship has been found for both occupational and traumatic stress (Burke & Paton, 2007; Gist & Woodall, 2000; Hart, 1999; Hart et al., 1995; Hodgins, Creamer & Bell, 2001; Stephens & Long, 2000).

The realization that organizational practices sustain bureaucratic and political objectives as much they do the pursuance of core policing activities highlights the potential for this aspect of police work to shatters officers assumptions and contributes to their experiencing adverse psychological outcomes (Violanti & Paton, 1999). This was evident in the comments made by officers described in Chapters 3 and 4. That is, organizational characteristics can facilitate or hinder

TABLE 2.2
THE SUBSCALES OF THE POLICE DAILY HASSLES SCALE

Subscale	Description
Operational Uplifts	
Frustration	Examines the potential feelings of frustration on the job from events such as hoax calls and abuse from offenders/victims and/or their family and friends.
External	Deals with the potential for officers to experience unfair criticism from, and to be the subject of unreasonable expectations from the public, other health professionals, law enforcement and justice officials.
Victims	Examines officer perceptions of the situations they may face when attending to a victims of crime.
Activity	Deals with the potential on the job hassles of interruptions at meal times, quick changeovers and pace changes.
Complaints	Deals with the handling of complaints by the department, and those made by the public.
Danger	Examines the potential dangers faced by officers on the job.
People	Examines officer perceptions of the inherent responsibility for other people and their lives.
Workload	Examines officer perceptions of the amount of work they must accomplish on a shift.
Driving	Deals with the demands of driving and sharing the road with possible offenders faced by officers on the job.
Organizational Hassles	
Communication	Examines aspects of officer-officer and officer-department communications.
Administration	Examines administrative procedures such as paperwork, policies, regulations and operational guidelines.
Supervision	Examines the adequacy, quality, and level of staff supervision, from the employee perspective.
Ratings	Examines rating system of the organization.
Coworkers	Examines officer perceptions of coworkers who may not be "up to scratch."
Morale	Examines perceptions related to the overall morale of the station and work environment.
Individual	Examines officers' perceptions of their place in the service and their feelings about the job.
Amenities	Deals with the perceptions of adequate provision of amenities and facilities for officers.
Equipment	Examines perceptions of equipment availability and adequacy.
Promotions	Deals with studying and examinations for work purposes.

Adapted from Hart, 1996.

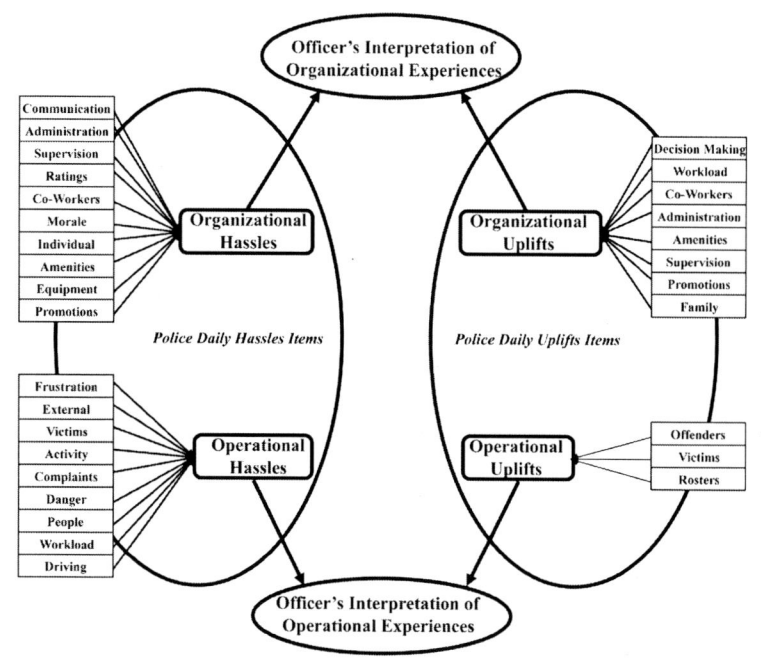

Figure 2.1. The police daily hassles and uplifts scale (adapted from Hart, 1996.

employee adjustment, functioning, and well-being by focusing officer interpretation more on administrative matters (hassles) and less on understanding new challenges and working out how to adapt to them (Burke & Paton, 2006; Paton et al., 2003; Paton & Burke, 2007).

CONCLUSION

The study by Burke and Paton (2006b) illustrated that when the causality of positive and negative outcomes is investigated, organizational factors represent a stronger predictor of occupational and traumatic stress than event demands. This is because, in contrast to the manner in which lay persons experience traumatic events, police officers generally experience them in the context of performing routine duties associated with their chosen profession, and in the context of an organizational environment that influences patterns of interactions with such events (Gist & Woodall, 2000). Furthermore, while the predictive value of the organization has previously been identified only as playing a possibly peripheral role, growing recognition of its salience as a source of vulnerability or resilience has cemented its place as a factor with a pivotal role to play in understanding and managing critical incident stress risk.

As a consequence, the structure and culture of the organization are being recognized for their ability to exercise a powerful influence over the way in which adverse events are experienced by police officers. The climate of an organization represents a means for facilitating capabilities to promote coherence and meaning on to atypical events (Pollock et al., 2003b), alongside its training and development policies. Thus, the organization itself provides the context within which officers interpret their experiences.

The actions taken and promoted by the police organization, particularly in the provision of operational guidelines, must make sense to officers in terms of their occupational expectations and experiences. A breakdown in organizational coherence can place unexpected restrictions on officers and frustrate their actions, increasing the likelihood of their having to reconcile their interpretations of operational experiences with organizational construal of incidents, thus increasing their stress risk. Therefore, in order to ensure that police officers believe their actions can provide a substantial benefit in operational circumstances, thereby justifying their professional identities and alleviating stress vulnerability from perceived unpredictability and contradiction, the maintenance of organizational coherence is vital. For the reasons outlined in this chapter, the police organization merits being identified as a domain with highly significant implications for understanding the life trajectories of police officers.

In this respect, police organizations have a number of responsibilities to their officers in terms of protection from vulnerability factors and the enhancement of resilience. The police organization has a responsibility to develop polices, procedures, and practices designed, as far as possible, to facilitate officers' ability maintain a sense of coherence between organizational expectations and occupational experiences, thereby minimizing the occurrence and impact of daily chronic stressors. The impact of organizational factors at all levels of occupational experience illustrates the potential for management to instill preventative mechanisms in employees at each of these levels—neglect at any level will increase employee vulnerability.

The adoption of the life-course perspective increases awareness of the fact that organizational responsibility for managing critical incident stress risk must change in response to career-related factors and shifts in the environment of policing that arise over time. With regard to career-related factors, issues are illustrated with reference to the impact of entry into the police profession (Chapter 3), officer's early career experiences (Chapter 4), and the life of the experienced officer (Chapter 9). The implications of major shifts in the environment of policing are discussed in Chapters 7 and 8 using the emergence of terrorism as an example. However, before officers can be affected by career and environmental transitions, they must first be successful in realizing their ambition of becoming a police officer. This process is the subject of the next chapter.

Chapter 3

FROM CIVILIAN TO RECRUIT: SELECTING THE RIGHT STUFF

INTRODUCTION

The life-course perspective presented in Chapter 1 introduced a need for the conceptualization of critical incident stress risk to accommodate significant transitions in the life trajectory of police officers. One such transition is described by the decision to become a police officer and, in so doing, embark on a journey characterized by a very unique life trajectory.

The act of becoming a police officer represents the outcome of a series of considered decisions on the part of the aspiring officer. Factors such as, for example, their past experiences, family history, personality characteristics, and personal motivations and expectations interact to influence the decision to apply to enter the police profession. Having made the decision to apply, whether the aspiring recruits can further their ambition is a function of their capacity to satisfy the selection criteria and procedures adopted by the police agency.

The police agency perspective on selection is captured in the processes they put in place to ensure that the characteristics and motivations of applicants will facilitate recruits' ability to fit into the unique environment of the police agency (i.e., fulfill their organizational role by being committed members of the police organization) and to act in ways that promote its goal of protecting and serving the community (i.e., to perform their operational and societal role). In other words, the ability of the applicant to progress to becoming a police recruit is a function of whether applicant and agency needs can be reconciled in ways that provide a sound foundation for the development of a satisfactory level of **Person** (the aspiring officer) and **Environment** (matching the selection criteria set by the police agency to qualify as an applicant) **Fit**. In practice, this describes the degree to which officer and agency characteristics are deemed to complement one another.

This process is not, however, characterized by equality. The process of ensuring Fit involves more change on the part of the officer than the organization (see Chapter 4), but the ease or otherwise of this transition is strongly influenced by the outcome of the selection process and officers' early experience in the organization. In this chapter, the focus is on the first stage of this process. It examines how police agencies acquire the raw material they hope to mold into effective police officers.

This chapter introduces the argument that a comprehensive understanding of police officer's critical incident stress risk requires starting our exploration of this phenomenon at that point where people, and the prior experience, life history, personal characteristics, motivations, and aspirations that they bring with them, first interacts with the police agency and police work; that is, at the point where people enter their chosen profession. Of particular interest is the fact that those aspiring to become police officers may also bring with them prior experience of traumatic events (see Chapter 1) that could influence their motivations, expectations, and reactions to the challenging events that are an inevitable aspect of contemporary police work (Paton & Smith, 1999).

The point of entry represents the first time that the goals, expectations, and experiences of aspiring officers come in contact with the reality of policing and the organizational context in which their lives will evolve over the several decades of their professional life. It defines the point where aspiring officers begin the process of realizing their ambition to become police officers by learning how to become an effective officer and learning how to fit into the culture of the police agency. While the role of factors such as personality has received considerable attention in this regard, other factors, such as people's expectations and prior experiences, have been less extensively canvassed.

In addition to discussing the selection process itself (e.g., the role of personality assessment), this chapter also examines the less familiar territory of the experiences that recruits bring with them in order to understand how officer-agency dynamics unfold over time to influence critical incident stress risk and its management. It is important to accommodate the fact that people elect to enter police work. This confers upon factors such as, for example, people's motivation to join, the expectations that fuelled the formulation of their career aspirations, and their experiences prior to joining, a capacity to influence the quality of the Person-Environment Fit (P-E Fit). In particular, this chapter asks whether the interaction between personal characteristics and experiences and the organizational context (i.e., the degree of P-E Fit) that describe officers' early experience could influence the future consequences of the critical incidents that officers will inevitably experience over the course of their career. By way of introduction to the examination of these issues, the chapter first offers a brief discussion of some of the key component of the selection process.

SELECTION

Police officers are regularly required to respond to and manage events that can be physically and psychologically challenging. The unique nature of their work, the characteristics of the agencies in which they work, and their relationship with the community they protect and serve makes personnel selection and screening an important activity. While selection procedures are not regulated, and are by no means universal, they are employed, in part, to select into the profession people whose individual characteristics are believed to indicate they are more likely to be resilient to constant exposures to traumatic events (Goldfarb & Aumiller, 2004). Thus, right from the start, recruits are acknowledged as having the characteristics necessary to be successful police officers, and thus the potential to cope in effective and positive ways with the unexpectedness inherent in policing. There are well documented relationships between personality, individual coping mechanisms, and satisfaction outcomes within police personnel (e.g., Burke, Shakespeare-Finch, Paton & Ryan, 2006; Kaczmarek & Packer, 1997, Thompson & Solomon, 1991). Personality and dispositional characteristics such as extraversion, hardiness, and self-efficacy have also been identified as contributing to officer's resilience and their ability to impose meaning on challenging critical incident experiences (Affleck & Tennen, 1996; Linley & Joseph, 2004; Paton, 2005; Thompson & Solomon, 1991).

In addition to selecting for operational capability, police agencies are also seeking to select people who will fit into an often highly bureaucratic agency that is organized along paramilitary lines, be able to interact effectively with people from all walks of life, and be able to remain calm in crises and handle pressure well. If such people can be identified using standardized selection measures, then job performance in high-stress occupations may be improved, the adverse effects of high-stress work environments mitigated, and the performance of a highly demanding organizational role handled more effectively. To achieve this objective, agencies have typically relied on personality assessment.

Personality testing as a selection mechanism for entry into the police force first emerged in the United States. Other Western countries soon followed suit. Today, most countries employ some form of personality testing to "select out" people who are deemed to possess characteristics inappropriate for fulfilling the role of a police officer in contemporary society. Over time, police agencies have progressively moved toward using personality assessment for developing "selecting in" procedures to identify those attributes that distinguish one candidate over another as being a potentially more effective officer. This approach assumes that there are traits, habits, reactions, and attitudes that distinguish an outstanding officer from a satisfactory one. Bartol (1996) argues that this is not possible and that screening out, on the basis of personality, is far more effective than screening in. However, the very notion of personnel selection, and the basis of much research in the field of Industrial/Organizational psychology, supports the notion that suitable employees can be "selected in" based on some aspects of their personality. If consistent differences in critical incident stress risk can be linked to personality dimensions, this stability would confer upon selection strategies based on personality assessment a capacity to play a role in the management of critical incident stress risk by facilitating the "selection in" of officers with a "head start" with regard to their capacity to deal with critical incidents.

The selection of employees based on aspects of their personality became dominant in policing in the United States during the 1960s. However, it was not until the meta-analytic reviews of Barrick and Munt (1991) and Tett, Jackson, and Rothstein (1991) that beliefs about the validity of personality assessment were widely recognized for their usefulness as a predictive tool for personnel selection.

The widespread use of personality assessment within policing in the

U.S. was a direct result of the President's Commission on Law Enforcement and the Administration of Justice (1967) in the United States recommending the use of psychological tests to determine the emotional stability of all police officers. According to Bartol (1996), it was their hope that police departments would, as a result of personality testing, reject candidates who demonstrated racial and ethnic prejudices prior to being hired, thus alleviating one of the major forms of contention in police behavior of the time. In 1968, the National Advisory Commission on Civil Disorder called for the widespread use of screening methods that would improve the quality of law enforcement officers, making them "more emotionally suitable" (Bartol, 1996, p. 74) for the job. This work was aided by the emergence, at the time, of consensus regarding the taxonomy of personality–the five factor model.

Personality is commonly defined as the enduring patterns of thoughts, feelings, motivations, and behaviors that are expressed in different circumstances. Generally, contemporary researchers agree that there are five robust factors of personality and that these serve as a useful and meaningful taxonomy for classifying personality characteristics. The Five Factor Model (Costa & McCrae, 1989) describes five broad dimensions (commonly called the Big 5 personality factors). These are Extraversion, Neuroticism (or emotional stability), Conscientiousness, Agreeableness, and Openness to Experience (or culture). Research on the five-factor solution has generally confirmed the characteristics of the factors, and the dimensions appear to be fairly stable over an extended period of time during adulthood (Soldz & Vaillant, 1999). In addition to requiring a reliable means of assessing personality, it is important to be able to anticipate how personality factors could be linked to key aspects of the police role. Following a brief introduction to the Five Factor Model, the relationship between personality and policing will then be discussed.

Dimensions of the Five Factor Model

People scoring high on Neuroticism (i.e., who are emotionally labile) tend to experience negative affect (e.g., being nervous, sad, hostile, insecure, and self-conscious). They are constantly worried about their health, chase unrealistic ideas, may be unable to control their impulses, and adapt poorly to stressful situations (which increases vulnerability to adverse stress outcomes). It should be noted that some researchers refer to this construct as emotional stability. This clearly describes an attribute of personality that would reduce the capacity of someone to discharge the duties of a police officer. In contrast, individuals scoring high on Extraversion usually are sociable, talkative, and open toward other people. They tend to be adventurous and outgoing. This characteristic would increase the probability of the person being able to respond effectively to atypical events and to provide support for others. This personality characteristic thus captures attributes that would be important for aspiring police officers who will be required to work in high demands situations as members of cohesive work units. Introverts, on the other hand, describe themselves as withdrawn, calm, discreet, and rather cautious.

The dimension of openness to experience relates to characteristics such as appreciation for new experiences, preference for variety and change. People scoring high on Openness report being curious, creative, imaginative, and predisposed to making independent judgments (Costa & McCrae, 1989). Individuals high on Conscientiousness are characterized by a tendency to be habitually reliable, careful, hardworking, well-organized, and purposeful (which would help the person fit with the administrative and organizational facets of their role). Agreeableness is proposed to be the opposite pole of antagonism. It characterizes people as being friendly, understanding, caring, empathic, altruistic, and good-natured. Those who score high on this dimension report a high degree of interpersonal trust, willingness to cooperate, and compliance. They are also characterized by their need for harmony. These characteristics would help the person fit into the team environment that is so important in policing, and facilitate officers' ability to work well with others in circumstances where an ability to deal effectively with the unexpected would be important. It is evident from this brief introduction that the Big 5 personality characteristics have the potential to inform understanding of an applicant's potential to "Fit" in the police agency. This begs the question of whether personality can indeed predict performance on the job. The task of providing answers to this question has, however, proved challenging.

Personality and Police Performance

Sced (2004) suggests that the selection of honest, reliable, and productive officers is vital to maintain the integrity and effectiveness of the police organization. Consequently, all police applicants undergo rigorous screening procedures prior to entry into the training system. Whether these procedures contain screening in and/or screening out tools varies. In countries like Australia and the United States, there is no consistent approach to the selection, or nonselection, of police officers. Despite the lack of consistency between and within countries, personality assessment has been used to predict everything from police academy performance to liability for corruption to the ability to cope with stress. However, these studies have yielded mixed results. This is likely an issue of constancy. Not only is there no consistency in how personality assessment is used to select police officers (i.e., selecting "in" or "out"), there are no consistent guidelines as to which personality measurement instrument to use for this purpose. Consequently, a wide variety of measures are used within and between countries. By far the most widely used is the MMPI-2, but the CPI, IPA, NEO-PI, and 16PF have all been used as selection tools within policing.

The argument that police officers possess a unique personality is not a new one. Early literature in the field describes the characteristics of police officers extensively, yet few meaningful comparisons have been made with the wider population. Notwithstanding, identifying the characteristics that comprise the "police personality" has been a goal of several researchers. This objective derives from the clinical goal of establishing whether certain characteristics predisposed police officers to experience distress on the job, and if certain qualities predicted higher levels of stress in police officers (e.g., Beutler et al., 1988; Brown & Campbell, 1994). Factors implicated in this context have included:

- Type A personality (Davidson & Veno, 1980; Fenster & Locke, 1973; Kirmeyer & Diamond, 1985);
- Optimism/pessimism (Alkus & Pedesky, 1983; Schier, Weintraub & Carver, 1986; Violanti & Aron, 1993);
- Extraversion/introversion (Costa, Somerfield, & McCrae, 1996; Hart et al., 1995; Krohne, 1996);
- Authoritarianism (Coleman & Gorman, 1992; Genz & Lester, 1976; Jensen, 1957);
- Hardiness (Kobassa, 1979);

- Cynicism (Abraham, 2000; Chandler & Jones, 1979; Neiderhoffer, 1967; Regoli, Poole, & Hewitt, 1979; Skolnick, 2005; Wilt & Bannon, 1976).
- Self-confidence and self-esteem (Hewitt & Flett, 1991).

Hewitt and Flett (1991) found that officers characterized by greater levels of self-confidence in their abilities, and who held themselves in high regard were generally more satisfied in the profession. Similarly, Schier et al. (1986) found that those holding a more positive outlook on life were more hopeful about the future and were happier individuals. While cynicism amongst police has been identified as problematic (Brown & Campbell, 1994; Lotz & Regoli, 1977), Niederhoffer (1967) argued that rather than being an aspect of personality, the cynicism observed amongst police officers is actually a coping mechanism employed to enable officers to deal with the hostile and violent experiences they encounter on the job. In this sense, it has been recognized as a feature of policing that can underpin the development of positive outcomes for officers (Brown & Campbell, 1994). In fact, there is an argument that while characteristics such as cynicism and authoritarianism may not be desirable attributes for a police officer, they offer some level of protection to the officer and are not necessarily the cause of stress outcomes for police (Carver, Scheir, & Weintraub, 1989; Davidson & Veno, 1980; Reiser, 1974).

Kaczmarek and Packer (1997) argue that an individual's perception of job stressors is directly influenced by his or her locus of control, and that these stress perceptions then influence job satisfaction. They identify an internal locus of control as a desirable characteristic for a general duties officer due to its value as a mechanism for coping with stress. Spector (1982) proposed that individuals' with an internal locus of control, as compared to an external locus, would perform better on tasks requiring initiative and autonomy as they tend to look to themselves for direction. This trait then is arguably an important one for police officers to possess, and is often implicated as an aspect of conscientiousness (Costa & McCrae, 2003).

In contrast, characteristics such as neuroticism increase the likelihood of people using ineffective coping strategies that lead to increased levels of distress (Shakespeare-Finch, 2006). Similarly, Kaczmarek and Packer (1997) suggest that extraversion is related to more positive, active coping, while neuroticism is related to more negative, avoidant strategies. Thompson and Solomon (1990) also report a consistent relationship between neuroticism and psychological distress, and found that extraversion had a protective effect on police officers who had been involved in body recovery duties.

The traits of introversion and extroversion have been studied extensively in the police population. Extraversion, amongst police, has been linked to the seeking of social support (e.g., Anshel, 2000) which has strong links with job satisfaction (Crank, Regoli, Hewitt, & Cuthbertson, 1995). Similarly, officers who have been found to be more optimistic, also have higher levels of self-esteem and self-confidence, and experience less strain in stressful situations (Lefcourt, 1992; Kobassa, 1979). While this research has sought to uncover the existence of a general relationship between personality characteristics and facets of stress risk, other researchers have proposed the existence of a distinct "police personality." This debate has not been restricted to police officers. Rather it reflects the belief that a "rescue personality," exhibited by those who choose to work in protective service professions (e.g., police, ambulance, fire) exists.

The problems associated with choosing selection measures are compounded by the complex challenge that police work poses for selection. On the one hand, it is important to select officers who will fit in the bureaucratic and autocratic management structure prevailing within most police agencies (see above). On the other hand, selection has to consider the need to select those capable of demonstrating innovative and autonomous thinking required to respond effectively to complex, often rapidly escalating critical incidents. Attempting to reconcile these different demands is a significant challenge for selection procedures, and one that may be more effectively dealt with by adopting more comprehensive assessment center procedures (Paton & Jackson, 2002). Notwithstanding, personality assessment will play a role in this process, and this calls for more systematic consideration of the relationship between personality and performance, particularly with regard to whether or not officers can be described by the possession of a unique set of personality characteristics. An important issue here concerns whether the characteristics that contribute to being an effective police officer differ from the mix of characteristics found amongst the general public.

Comparing Police and the Public

While each of the personality assessment instruments introduced above has been used to predict officer performance, their use as comparative tools to examine differences between police and the general population is scarce. This is surprising, given the widely held belief that police officers differ systematically from the general population. It is held that it takes a "special kind of person" to be involved in police work. Consequently, marked personality differences between police officers and members of the general public would be expected.

Mitchell (1983) argued for the existence of a distinct rescue personality, characterized by a high level of empathy, performance, and dedication. Mitchell and Bray (1990) describe emergency response workers as inner-directed, action-oriented, obsessed with high standards of performance, socially conservative, traditional, highly dedicated, and easily bored. Additional characteristics identified included having a desire for control of both the situation and the self, and enjoyment from being needed. However, this description reflects the belief that all aspects of the stress process are encapsulated within the person and emerge as a result of their interaction with a challenging event.

The idea of their being some unique rescue personality was one of the fundamental tenets of the intervention designed by Mitchell, known as Critical Incident Stress Debriefing (CISD), developed to address the "emotional devastation" that may occur as a result of emergency work (Wagner, 2005). The approach relies on the assumption that rescue workers are an homogenous group of individuals, thus making a "one-size-fits-all" approach appropriate as a means of operational stress intervention. This assumption is problematic.

Gist and Woodall (1998) argue that personality homogeneity or a unique rescue personality is not supported by the available literature. Gist and Woodall argue, with regard to overall concept of the rescue personality, that those individuals who elect to enter emergency professions make that choice based on aspects of the job, and that there is no one "type" of person who is attracted to the job. On this premise, it is unlikely that a cluster of characteristics that will serve to justify the use of some prescriptive personality profile capable of ameliorating critical incident stress will exist. Gist and Woodall also argue that police officers, and other emergency workers, have an expectation of involvement in the kinds of challenging events that prompted speculation about the existence of a unique personality and that these experiences enhance their organizational coherence and perceptions of fit. In other words, any similarity between officers could reflect common purpose and/or experience rather than any underlying personality similarity per se. Consequently, it can be argued that it is the quality of the interaction (fit) between diverse personal characteristics, operational expectations, and organizational qualities that facilitate one's organizational commitment, job satisfaction, and critical incident stress risk rather than some unique personality or personality profile.

The next section of this chapter discusses the personality characteristics of individuals entering police work. It examines whether evidence to support a "rescue personality" exists. A problem that arises when examining this issue is the self-fulfilling prophecy. If police agencies believe that there is a link between a personality characteristic and performance, this characteristic is likely to be over represented in the population. Consequently, any relationship between personality and performance could be an artifact of the process (particularly given the lack of longitudinal prospective analyses of relationships between personality and performance) rather than a real effect.

Discussion of this issue draws on data from a police service whose officers have not undergone stringent, standardized personality testing (Burke, 2008). Thus, while personality profiling is not specifically conducted with this population, officers are selected on the basis of their apparent ability to cope with stress in a constructive way, with their potential to use initiative and autonomous thinking being measured using the locus of control construct rather than any standardized personality measure. This population affords a unique opportunity to examine the personality profiles of people who self-selected to enter police work. A focus on this population permits examining the characteristics of recruits who have *not* been subjected to standardized psychometric personality testing.

THE PERSONALITY PROFILE OF POLICE RECRUITS

In many states and countries, officers enter policing having been selected because their individual personality characteristics are held to indicate that they are likely to be resilient to the effects of operational stress and trauma (Goldfarb & Aumiller, 2004). That is, their psychological profiles reflect agency beliefs that officers with specific personality characteristics can effectively cope with the type of operational environment policing entails. The police population that are the subject of discussion in this section, because they have not been subjected to standardized personality testing (with locus of control being the only factor assessed), provide a rare opportunity to determine whether people who effectively self-select for police work are defined by the existence of a unique, homogenous personality profile.

Drawing upon data obtained from 158 police recruits, Burke (2009) examined this question in two ways. The first involved comparing the personality profile of a group of police recruits with the general population. The second compared recruits who had prior traumatic experience with those who had no such experience to assess whether any differences in personality profile could be discerned. To do so, Burke placed recruits into either a "trauma" or "no trauma" group on the basis of whether or not they had experienced a traumatic event (consistent with the *DSM-IV-TR* (APA, 2000) definition of a traumatizing life event) prior to their joining the police. Accordingly, 58 percent of the recruits ($n=93$) were placed in the trauma category. The remaining 67 recruits comprised the "no trauma" group.

Comparing Recruits and the General Population

A comparison between the personality profile of the police recruits and U.S. adult population norms (Figure 3.1) revealed that officers had comparable levels of neuroticism, openness, agreeableness, and conscientiousness, with a difference being evident only for extraversion (which was higher in the police recruit sample). It is worth noting, however, that the higher level of extraversion could represent an artifact that can be traced to cultural differences in the weighting attributed to it, with the possibility of normative levels of extraversion being higher in Australia (from where the data used for comparison was drawn–this was necessary to ensure that the population had not been subject to personality assessment and to ensure that any relationships between personality and self selection to join the police could be assessed) than in U.S. populations. While normative data for the NEO-FFI is not available for the Australian population, cross-cultural studies, conducted with the longer NEO-PI, suggest that Australians characteristically present with a level of extraversion that is typically

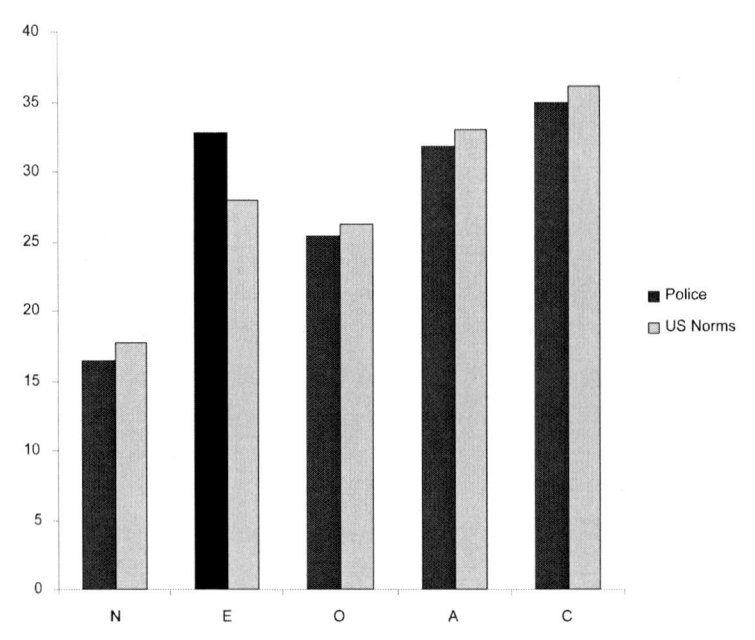

Figure 3.1. Comparison of personality profiles for Australian police recruits and U.S. adult population norms (adapted from Burke, 2009).

higher than their U.S. counterparts (McCrae & Terracciano, 2005). Thus the observed difference may be more an artifact than an indication of any real distinction. Accordingly, the assumption of this difference between police and the general public being significant must, of course, remain tentative until a more searching analysis of this proposition is undertaken. On the basis of the data discussed here, the distribution across the personality dimensions fails to provide unambiguous evidence for the existence of a unique cluster of personality characteristics amongst people who effectively self-select to enter police work.

Before proceeding to the next line of inquiry, some comment on the possible existence of elevated levels of extraversion and its implications is warranted. Similar to the heightened extraversion found in this population, Thompson and Solomon (1991) observed a trend towards heightened extraversion in U.S. police officers and suggested that these elevated levels had the potential to mitigate harm from the exposures to stress and trauma characteristic of the occupation. Consequently, additional work is needed to elucidate this issue. Thompson and Solomon also found significantly lower levels of neuroticism in their officers and concluded that this was indicative of greater emotional stability compared with the general population. This result was not replicated by Burke (2009). The latter study suggested that the current population of police recruits and the general population have comparable levels of emotional stability and that the personality profile of police recruits and the general public are broadly similar across all dimensions of personality.

It is important to remember that the sample from which Burke's (2009) data were obtained had not been subjected to selection using any of these personality dimensions, reducing the risk of any relationship reflecting the operation of a self-fulfilling prophecy. Burke's approach provided an opportunity to examine whether the personality of recruits who self-selected to enter police work could be described according to the presence of some distinctive personality profile that might have influenced their decision to apply. With the possible exception of their possessing elevated levels of extraversion, no evidence of any unique personality profile was found. This is not, however, the only way to examine the issue of their being a unique police personality.

If police officers could be defined by the presence of a unique personality profile, this could also be examined by comparing recruits who had prior trauma experience with those who had not. This approach is based on the assumption that prior traumatic experience would have acted as a kind of filter, resulting in only those with the 'right stuff,' from a personality perspective, deciding to enter police work. Comparison of the personality profile of members of the 'trauma group' with their 'no trauma' counterparts failed to reveal any significant differences. These data are depicted in Table 3.1.

Not only were no differences evident between recruits and the general population (see Figure 3.1), comparison of the personality profiles of recruits who had experienced traumatic events prior to entering police work with those who had not failed to identify any specific influence for personality. Further support for this view emerged when Burke (2009) examined the relationships between personality and the Impact of Event Scale (IES) and Postraumatic Growth (PTGI) scores of those with prior traumatic experience (Table 3.2).

Burke's (2009) correlational analyses of the relationship between personality and measures of traumatic stress symptoms and posttraumatic growth failed to provide strong evidence for the existence of a

TABLE 3.1
COMPARISON OF PERSONALITY PROFILES
FOR "TRAUMA" AND "NO-TRAUMA" GROUPS

	No-Trauma Group Mean (SD)	Trauma Group Mean (SD)	t	p
N	16.43 (6.93)	16.34 (6.35)	.003	.96
E	32.44 (4.37)	33.05 (5.58)	.55	.46
O	25.18 (5.57)	25.55 (5.68)	.18	.67
A	31.87 (5.12)	31.76 (5.02)	.02	.90
C	35.22 (5.68)	34.70 (5.20)	.37	.55
n	66	92		

N = 158
N = Neuroticism; E = Extraversion; O = Openness to Experience; A = Agreeableness; C = Conscientiousness. (Adapted from Burke, 2009).

TABLE 3.2
COMPARISON OF RELATIONSHIPS BETWEEN PERSONALITY AND MEASURES
OF TRAUMA OUTCOMES FOR TRAUMA GROUP OF POLICE RECRUITS

Trauma Group	IES Total	PTGI Total
N	.27*	.15
E	.09	.24*
O	.04	.31**
A	-.04	.18
C	-.05	.03

(N= 66). N = Neuroticism; E = Extraversion; O = Openness to Experience; A = Agreeableness; C = Conscientiousness. (Adapted from Burke, 2009).

specific relationship between personality and posttrauma outcomes. A significant correlation emerged between neuroticism and IES scores (as would be expected). However, a positive, though nonsignificant, correlation was evident between neuroticism and PTGI scores (Table 3.2). This was an unexpected finding. Extraversion and Openness to Experience held positive correlations with PTGI scores, but did not reveal any significant influence on IES scores. Furthermore, extraversion and openness did not, as would have been expected, reveal a negative relationship with the IES. Taken together, while not allowing an unambiguous conclusion to be drawn regarding the existence of a "rescue personality," the data reported here fail to support the existence of such a phenomenon.

Personality is not the only personal attribute that recruits bring with them into their new career. Chapter 1 introduced several life trajectory issues that could influence the decision to become a police officer. These include the aspiring officer's developmental and family history, the motivations and expectations that underpin his or her career choice, and his or her prior life experiences. The implications of these issues have not generally been considered in the process of selecting officers. The next section seeks to rectify this omission.

DECIDING TO ENTER POLICE WORK: MOTIVATIONS AND EXPECTATIONS

Policing is a high demand profession and one, it is assumed, that people would not elect to join without considered deliberation. Given that the high demand and high-risk nature of the issues likely to be encountered is widely known, the motivations that drive people to apply to enter the police profession could have an important bearing on their subsequent critical incident stress risk. This makes it pertinent to consider the history, motivations, and expectations that aspiring officers bring with them. Drawing on the work of Burke (2009), this topic is discussed in this section.

Factors motivating a decision to join, and the consistency or otherwise between officer's expectations about the job and their actual experience of police work during their training and operational duties were examined using interviews (Burke, 2009). Burke invited recruits to discuss their "reasons for joining" (*Why policing*) in order to gain insights into the factors that influenced their decision to join the service and to examine whether prior experience, occupation, or exposure to the police influenced this decision. In doing so, she identified two distinct latent themes: motivators and satisfiers. Motivators comprised the themes of "family association" and "attraction to power." The second theme, Satisfiers, described the degree of consistency between what individuals saw as attractive about the profession prior to joining, and their achievement of these things in the police role. Two manifest themes of "prior experience" and "people" made up this domain.

Collectively, these deliberations contributed to officers entering police work with expectations. These expectations motivated their

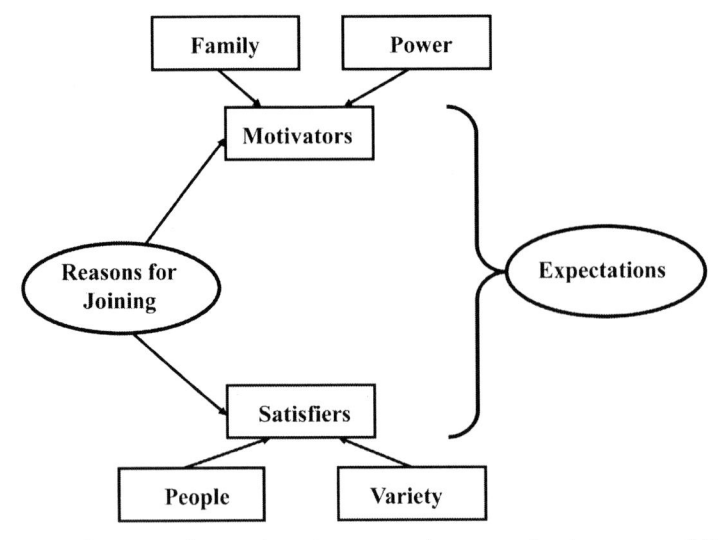

Figure 3.2. The latent and manifest themes making up the category of Reasons for Joining (Why policing?) and their influence on officer expectations (adapted from Burke, 2008).

choice of profession. This means that the Person element in the P-E Fit equation being characterized by belief about what police work would entail.

Motivators

Family

Several, predominantly male, officers brought with them a family history of policing, and perceived their entering the police profession in terms of the maintenance of a family tradition. Officers talked about growing up in a policing context, and tended to cite strong relationships with serving or retired officers. Roger explains, "Oh, my Dad, and 3 of my uncles . . . all cops. I grew up with a great deal of respect for one of my Uncles, and I guess really, it was just kinda a natural thing . . . yeah, it was expected to some extent, but then I'm not sure there was really ever anything else I was serious about doing anyway."

Officers believed their family history provided them with important insights into the job, and that provided them with realistic expectations of what the job entailed, particularly with regard to what they would experience. This suggests that family context contributed to their expectations and the schema they brought to their commencement of their police career. However, the expectations implicit within these family-derived schema were not always met. For example, Stuart mentioned his expectation of the content and scope of the training received at the police academy was very different to what actually occurred. Hence, while he believed at the outset that he was well prepared for what he would face on the job from talking to family members, inconsistencies between these assumptions and the reality of the training received (e.g., lack of mortuary experience) resulted in a need for him to adapt. This is not the only way in which the family can influence stress at this stage in the officer's career.

Some officers believed that family history exerted extra pressure on them to succeed. Importantly, from the perspective of preparing officers for dealing with organizational and operational challenges, this pressure to succeed was measured predominantly by their reactions to events, as opposed to any external performance indicators.

While not emphasized by those electing to be interviewed, there are some grounds for believing that recruits enter professional life with knowledge of the traumatic content of their chosen profession, with this knowledge deriving, at least in part, from a family history of policing. Burke's (2009) finding thus introduces a need to consider how family experience and the context of developing within a specific family context can influence the schema or interpretive processes recruits bring to bear on their experience of the job, at least during the early stages of professional life (see Chapter 1). The possible role of family history as an influence on the schema or interpretive styles that officers develop has not previously been recognized and represents an area worthy of future study. The second factor influencing motivation to enter police work was power.

Power

Several officers described how their career aspirations were influenced by the power and respect associated with being a police officer. Alongside this, a number also talk about the power inherent in the uniform, and its visibility. The content of this theme affords the opportunity to speculate on its role in building expectations into officers' operational schema that describe their beliefs about their operational effectiveness in their professional role. A belief in the power inherent in the role is consistent with the performance expectations that manifest themselves in the form of the helper stereotype (Short, 1979). While normally held to develop as a consequence of the interaction between training and operational activity (Paton & Stephens, 1996), the idea being advocated here is that this important attributional style, which has been identified as a critical incident stress risk factor, may have its origins at much earlier point in an officer's career. These expectations could also influence the origins of several of the operational hassles (see Chapters 2, 4 and 9) that have been identified as critical incident stress risk factors. The developmental characteristics could also influence coping strategies (see Chapter 4 and 9). Knowledge of such motivators can inform understanding of the degree of P-E Fit likely to emerge in the early stage of the officer's career. It is evident that motivators can generate expectations about policing. The degree to which expectations was something that underpinned the content of Burke's second motivational theme.

Satisfiers

Officers who cited satisfiers, Burke's (2009) second major theme, as reasons for joining, tended to have had some contact with the police in a professional work environment, or had had a positive experience with police as a previous victim of crime. These officers tended to see their contact as positive regardless of outcome (i.e., whether the crime was solved or not). Satisfiers reflected the degree of consistency between officers' expectations of the job and their perceptions of the degree to which these expectations were realized in their training. While these issues were discussed in relation to their reasons for joining the profession, they also appear to be acting as reasons for the maintenance of employment. Satisfiers comprised two themes, prior experience and people.

Prior Experience

This category encapsulated officer's experience of positive contact with police officers prior to joining. They thus had, or believed they had, some insight into police work. For example, one officer recounted a situation in which she had contact with a police officer when she was a child. She believed that the positive nature of this encounter as a young child laid the foundation for her thinking about joining. This account reiterates the potential for earlier life experience to be influential in deciding to enter police work (see Chapter 1).

People

The second satisfier category described officers' desire to work with people as a primary reason for joining the profession. Several officers expressed this motivation in terms of a belief that they would be able to help people (i.e., victims of crime) and, for some, this was an extension of experience gained in a previous role. Thus, some officers joined the service after having spent time in occupations involving a high level of contact with the general public and people in need (e.g., teachers, nurses, custom's officer). These officers believed that their previous occupational experiences would help them be effective police officers, and that they would, to a certain extent, be able to rely on the same skills, instincts, and affinity, at the same time as being able to build on these and learn new skills as officers. For example, Chad discussed how his previous occupation had involved working closely with police, but that he had felt he had little control and opportunity to see jobs through within his previous occupation. "I thought I might be able to get some of that control and responsibility, and be able to really follow things through in the police . . . and I thought . . . I'd be able to use the instincts I'd developed already and really hone my investigation skills. It's really just a more complex version of what I was already doing." Justine recounted how her contact with officers as a citizen, in her previous prior occupation, influenced her decision to join. "I figured I could do a better job for more people if I changed jobs. I didn't have the control I needed (over the outcomes) in my last job, at least as a police officer I have some level of discretion."

Similarities between the expectations expressed in these quotes and the characteristics of the helper stereotype (see above) provide additional insights into how life experiences that precede a person's decision to become a police officer could influence the development of an attributional style that has implications for critical incident stress risk (Paton & Stephens, 1996). That is, if motivations to help and "put things right" are not realized, the potential for adverse stress outcomes is increased. This is more likely in the context of hassles such as dealing with the criminal justice system over which officers have no control (see Chapters 4 and 9). These beliefs may also influence how coping strategies develop (see Chapters 4 and 5), particularly with regard to their influence on officer's realization that they may be unable to exercise control over several operational and organizational experiences. That is, starting with a belief in an ability to exercise control, the need to adjust to being more constrained in this regard than anticipated not only adds an adaptive pressure, it may also increase the likelihood that officers adopt dysfunctional strategies (see Chapters 4, 5 and 9). If the latter can be traced to pre-employment and early career expectations, a need for the inclusion of more reality orientation in selection and early training experience is called for.

What these accounts do highlight is the fact that officers do not enter police work with neutral expectations. The contents of this section have introduced the possibility that critical incident stress risk may be influenced not only by (expected) encounters with traumatic events but also by inconsistencies between expectations and the reality of organizational experience. Importantly, the themes that emerged from Burke's (2009) interviews represent issues that tend not to be given prominence within selection processes. Nor are the expectations of officers considered as having any bearing on how academy training could act to influence subsequent critical incident stress risk. Consequently, it can be argued that officers' expectations prior to joining must be considered when examining how they adjust to their police role, particularly if officers' expectations of police work were not realized on their becoming operational police officers.

While additional work will be required to examine this issue in detail, the discussion presented here suggests that expectations and motivations formed prior to becoming an officer can interact with early training experience to influence the development of interpretive styles or schema (e.g., the helper stereotype) that can affect future critical incident stress risk. It is also possible that these expectations can impose adaptive demands on officers that remain undetected by current approaches to selection and development. This contention is explored further when officers' expectations of their job role is discussed in relation to the process of socialization in Chapter 4. Another reason for exploring how pre-employment experience influences adaptation and interpretation can be traced to the fact that officers may in fact bring prior experience of traumatic events with them as they embark on their new career as a police officer.

PRE-EMPLOYMENT TRAUMATIC EXPERIENCE

When working with police populations, exposure to traumatic events need not be something that occurs only after an individual becomes a serving officer. Given the prevalence of traumatic experiences within the general population (e.g., Norris, 1992), individuals may enter their chosen profession with a history of experiencing the kinds of events (e.g., physical or sexual assault, road traffic accidents) they will have to confront and respond to as serving police officers. This makes it pertinent to ask what implications this has for officers' future well-being.

Stephens, Long, and Flett (1999) suggested that professions such as policing attract individuals who have experienced traumatic life events and that this prior exposure increases their risk of developing stress related pathologies in response to subsequent on-the-job experiences. Pre-employment traumatic experience could thus act as a vulnerability mechanism, especially if events experienced on the job mirror personally tragic or traumatic experiences that preceded their employment, predisposing the officer to ineffective coping and increased distress. It is, however, possible to anticipate an alternative outcome under these circumstances.

For example, prior exposure to traumatic events and the successful resolution of their psychological consequences could mean that recruits enter their police career having developed a more diverse repertoire of coping strategies, making them better equipped psychologically to deal with the demands of the job, increasing stress resilience and facilitating officers' capacity to cope with and adapt to highly challenging operational experiences (Huddleston, Paton, & Stephens, 2006). It could also result in officers having some degree of personal insight into the types of events they will face as operational police officers, particularly if these experiences were influential in motivating their career choice. The potential for prior experience to influence vulnerability or resilience introduces the potential for it to influence risk, with the way in which prior experiences were resolved and the experience interpreted playing a pivotal role in this regard. These factors must be accommodated in the analysis of the relationship between past experience and future risk.

If officers bring a history of prior traumatic experience with them into a highly challenging profession, understanding how prior experiences, which could influence future traumatic stress risk either positively or negatively, and whose nature and implications could be assessed within a selection process would have significant implications for police agencies. For example, agencies may deem it necessary to select out those with unresolved issues that could put them, their colleagues, and the public at future risk. However, if prior (effectively resolved) traumatic experiences increase resilience, agencies could use this knowledge to proactively select officers and to ensure that the training and support programs offered facilitate officers' ability to build on their past experiences to develop their future capacity to adapt to challenging incidents. This could make a significant contribution to their ability to protect and serve the public, themselves and the agency.

From pragmatic and methodological perspectives, it is important to examine the relationship between critical incident experience and growth/adaptive outcomes from the point of entry into police work in order to capture how pre-employment experiences influence well being (Paton & Smith, 1999). This approach can also provide a more objective starting point from which to assess the progressive influence of operational and organizational influences on mental health, and to assess the specific impact of traumatic events that characterize officers' transition through their career. This section introduces this issue by illustrating the degree to which officers bring with them a legacy of traumatic experiences.

Prior Traumatic Experience

Given that some 69 percent of members of the general population may experience a traumatic event at some point during their lives (Norris, 1992), there are no a priori grounds for assuming that those individuals who elect to enter police work are immune from having had such experiences. The first question concerns whether recruits enter police work with prior experience of traumatic events. If they do, it then becomes pertinent to ask whether this affects their psychological well-being at this time. With regard to question of whether recruits bring with them a legacy of traumatic experiences, the answer is yes.

Buchanan et al. (2001) found that 70 percent of police officers had been involved in a trauma event prior to joining the police.

Huddleston et al. (2006) found that some 85 percent of the 315 police recruits they surveyed had experienced at least one traumatic event prior to their entering police work. Some 54 percent had experienced at least two traumatic events, and 26 percent had experienced three or more events prior to entering police work. Burke (2009) observed that some 84 percent of recruits had prior traumatic experience, with 33 percent reporting having experienced at least one traumatic event, 24 percent having experienced two, and 28 percent reporting having experienced three or more traumatic events.

While it is difficult to determine an appropriate yardstick against which to gauge the relative incidence in any specific population, comparison with Norris (1992) conclusion that, in the population as a whole, 69 percent had lifetime experience of traumatic incidents, the above data suggests that the percentage of recruits enter police work having experienced one or more traumatic events is high. The percentages of officers reporting involvement in each of the events measured by the Traumatic Stress Schedule (TSS) from studies by Burke (2009) and Huddleston et al. (2007) are shown in Table 3.3, alongside the lifetime frequencies for each event reported by Norris (1992).

With regard to the specific nature of the experiences that recruits, reported the results of Burke's (2009) and Huddleston et al.'s (2007) assessment of prior experiences is listed in Table 3.3. The nature of

TABLE 3.3
PERCENTAGE OF RECRUITS WHO HAD EXPERIENCED
SPECIFIC TYPES OF TRAUMATIC EVENTS AT POINT OF ENTRY

Event	Prior Experience Burke (2009)	Prior Experience Huddleston et al. (2007)	Lifetime Frequencies (Norris, 1992)
Military Combat	18%	3%	9.2%
Robbery	9%	11%	24.9%
Physical Assault	44%	20%	15%
Forced sexual encounter	8%	6%	4.4%
Fire	3%	10%	11%
Disaster	10%	11%	13.3
Tragic Death	38%	40%	30.2%
Motor Vehicle Accident	22%	20%	23.4%
Other experience	26%	35%	15.2%

(Adapted from Burke (2009) and Huddleston et al., (2007)) compared to lifetime incidence in the general population (Norris, 1992).

these experiences meant that many recruits had personally experienced events similar to those they could encounter as police officers or be called upon to deal with while acting in this role. Moreover, it must be borne in mind that those entering police work are more likely to have accumulated their experiences in the first 20–30 years of life rather than over the lifetime reflected in Norris's (1992) data.

While experiencing relatively lower levels of robbery, recruits in both studies brought with them relatively higher levels of personal experience of being physically assaulted, sexually assaulted, and experiencing tragic or violent death. These data indicate that the recruits surveyed in these studies entered police work with relatively high levels of experience of the kinds of trauma they could encounter as serving officers. A key question, in the context of the present study, concerns whether these experiences affected their mental health at point of entry.

When Burke (2009) examined the IES-R scores of recruits who had reported a prior traumatic experience, the overall mean score indicated low-moderate levels of posttraumatic stress symptoms that could be attributed to recruit's past experience. The mean score for recruits at point of entry was 16. Further examination of the data indicated that 29 percent ($n=46$) of the participants had total IES scores >20 (total scores ranged from 0 to 57), indicating heightened levels of posttraumatic stress symptoms amongst these recruits. It should be noted here that a score of 20 or more on the IES-R is considered to be indicative of potentially problematic levels of pathology. Huddleston et al., (2006) found a mean IES-R score of 10.9 for recruits who entered police work with prior traumatic experience, with 11 reporting scores above 20.

These data suggest that prior traumatic experience can result in officers entering a high-risk profession with a persistent symptomological legacy of these experiences. This makes it pertinent to ask whether psychological status at the point of entry into police work influences the consequences of exposure to similar kinds of events as serving officers. Increase vulnerability of increase resilience? The question of whether any legacy of traumatic experiences recruits bring with them into their new career influences their subsequent well-being is dealt with in Chapter 4.

Chapter 4

FROM RECRUIT TO OFFICER: TRANSITION AND SOCIALIZATION

INTRODUCTION

Following the successful negotiation of their academy training, the next transition point in the life course trajectory of a police officer involves their making the transition to becoming operational. The transition from recruit to serving officer is a process characterized by, it is hoped, progressive improvements in the degree of Fit between the police agency and the officer. It commences with recruitment and selection processes used to capture core competencies and the personal characteristics and attitudes that are deemed to provide the raw material required to produce an officer capable of functioning effectively in both operational and organizational contexts (see Chapter 3). Subsequently, the development of P-E Fit is a function of the quality of the transactional process involving officer and agency that is mediated through the process of socialization and acculturation.

The period of transition from recruit/trainee to officer describes that period when officers are, for the first time, fully immersed within the culture of the organization and experience how the procedures and expectations (of themselves, their colleagues, their senior officers, etc.) interact with the performance of their operational role to influence the quality of their experience as police officers. The organizational culture also describes the context in which, as a result of officers developing and changing their interpretive schema as they experience organizational responses to events, officers future adaptive capacities are nurtured or constrained (Paton & Burke, 2007).

While the organization presents a relatively stable and consistent (from the officer's perspective) context for this process, the same cannot be said of the officers themselves. During this early stage in their career, officers are characterized by considerable diversity with regard to, for example, their prior experience of traumatic events and the degree to which their expectations of police work are matched by the organizational and operational reality they have encountered (see Chapter 3). This diversity makes socialization a dynamic process. An important source of this diversity can be traced to the legacy of pre-employment traumatic experience that officers bring with them into their police career. This chapter first considers how pre-employment traumatic experiences interact with operational experiences. The first question that emerges here concerns whether and to what extent officers' prior experience of traumatic events influences risk during this transitional period.

Chapter 3 introduced the fact that many recruits bring with them into their new career as police officers a legacy of experience of traumatic events as well as various levels of posttraumatic stress symptoms. This makes it pertinent to question whether this influences how recruits make the transition from recruit to officer, and whether this transitional process influences critical incident stress risk and their future well-being as serving officers. This chapter examines the initial impact of such experience on officers as they make the transition from recruit to serving officer. It also considers how the process of becoming a police officer, and the progressive immersion into the organizational culture and procedures that accompanies it, can influence critical incident stress risk. The latter may be particularly important from the point of view of understanding how socialization into the police agency can influence future critical incident stress risk.

PRIOR TRAUMATIC EXPERIENCE

By following recruits from point of entry through their training and into the early stages of their careers as serving officers, it is possible to examine the degree to which early experience and psychological status at point of entry into policing influences subsequent critical incident stress risk. This was the objective of the Huddleston et al. (2006) study introduced in Chapter 3. For most of the 315 officers they sur-

TABLE 4.1
A COMPARISON OF THE NUMBER OF PRE-EMPLOYMENT TRAUMATIC
EXPERIENCES AND RESIDUAL POSTTRAUMATIC STRESS SCORES
(IMPACT IF EVENT SCALE) OF OFFICERS DISENGAGING IN DURING
THEIR FIRST YEAR WITH THOSE REMAINING IN EMPLOYMENT

	Number of Pre-Employment Traumatic Experiences	IES Score @ Point of Entry
Disengage During 1st Year	2.29	23.0
Remain in Employment	1.82	10.9

Adapted from Huddleston et al., 2006.

veyed, traumatic stress symptoms (IES) at point of entry did not affect their status when assessed at 12 months. However, a more complex picture emerged when the focus was on the small number of recruits who presented with levels of IES that could suggest the existence of more significant posttrauma pathology. Huddleston et al. identified 11 recruits who presented IES scores of 20 or over. The experiences that these officers brought with them into their police career may well have influenced their well-being during their first year of police work.

During the first year, seven of these 11 officers left the police. Table 4.1 provides a comparison of those who left versus those who stayed with regard to their pre-employment exposure and their IES scores. These seven officers differ from the majority in several ways. One relates to the number of pre-employment traumatic events experienced. The seven recruits who disengaged during their first year had experienced an average of 2.3 events, compared with 1.8 for the majority (i.e., those who scored < 20) who remained in employment.

More significant was the finding that that the mean IES scores of the seven was 23 (i.e., that would place them in the pathological category), compared with 11 for those who scored <20 and who remained employed at 12 months. These data suggest that high levels of posttraumatic stress at point of entry may increase risk for adverse stress outcomes. However, this is not inevitable. Data from the other four members of this initial "high risk" group revealed a different outcome. The four officers in this group reported mean IES scores of 24.6 at point of entry. At the 12 month data collection period, this had dropped to 13.5.

Prior Trauma and Vulnerability

While not permitting the drawing of unambiguous conclusions, there is no strong evidence to suggest that pre-employment traumatic experiences and associated posttraumatic stress symptoms that persisted at point of entry into police work increased operational traumatic stress vulnerability during officers' first year of operational duties. This was certainly true with regard to the majority of the officers Huddleston et al. surveyed (i.e., those whose entry IES score was < 20). With regard to those whose entry score was 20 or over, the fact that some left and some remained suggests that the level of traumatic stress symptoms per se cannot be used to predict future vulnerability. Notwithstanding, it is not possible to dismiss the possibility with regard to those presenting with initially high symptoms and who subsequently left before commencing operational duties.

Since it was not possible to conduct exit interviews with those officers with high pre-employment traumatic experience and IES symptoms, it is not known whether it was interaction between their earlier traumatic experience and some aspect of their early career experience that influenced their decision to disengage. That is, decisions to disengage during training may have been made for reasons unrelated to their prior trauma experience (e.g., family factors). Until exit interviews are conducted in future studies, the suggestion that it was linked to their psychological status at point of entry can only be regarded as tentative. It is, however, clear that high levels of pre-employment traumatic symptoms do not result in the automatic decision to disengage. For the four members in the 20+ IES Score group who remained operational, other factors must have been at work to result in the substantial reduction in their scores during their first year.

While high levels of traumatic stress symptoms at point of entry may increase vulnerability, the manner in which it interacts with other kinds of experience within the police role may moderate any relationship with subsequent risk. This could include, for example, opportunities to develop understanding of prior experiences, access to social support, or the capacity to use training and operational experiences to render prior experiences coherent and meaningful.

Prior Trauma and Resilience

Prior experience may have contributed to the motivation of these officers to enter police work. Police officers choose to enter a profession that explicitly increases the likelihood of their exposure to traumatic and threatening events that will be similar to those they experienced prior to entering police work. Exercising their professional responsibilities and competencies affords the opportunity to interpret their involvement, in some contexts at least, as opportunities to help people (who are faced with significant adversity) in ways that could have salutary and beneficial consequences for them and the communities they have elected to serve. Some measure of support for this possibility comes from anecdotal accounts offered by the four officers originally in the high trauma group who remained and who, despite exposure to several traumatic events during their first year, experienced a significant decline in their IES scores from point of entry to the 12-month data collection point (Huddleston et al., 2006). These officers commented on how the training they had received in the academy helped them impose meaning on their pre-employment traumatic experiences in ways that served to increase their well-being.

At present, the review of prior trauma experience is neither a component of selection nor incorporated within training to broaden officers' capability to impose meaning on operational events or of increasing stress resilience. If the contention that training can assist officers to impose meaning on pre-employment traumatic experiences is correct, it raises the possibility that incorporating residual traumatic stress assessment into the training process and adapting training to include sessions on making prior experiences meaningful in the context of the police role could make a valuable contribution to developing officers' adaptive capacity. While such an approach has not been tried within the context of the initial training period offered to recruits, evidence that training and support practices can facilitate officers' adaptive capacities is evident from studies of training offered to serving officers (Alexander & Wells, 1991; Paton, 1994).

In addition to assisting those officers who bring these valuable experiences into police work, this process could assist others vicariously. Thus, training could be influential in ensuring resolution of prior experiences and help render them coherent in regard to the relationship between their experience and the impact of criminal and traumatic acts on citizens. This last comment introduces a need to consider how pre-employment and operational traumatic experiences interact to influence risk.

PRIOR AND EARLY CAREER TRAUMATIC EXPERIENCE

Of those officers who continued in employment, what implications did their early career experience have for their well-being? When reassessed after 12 months (i.e., after five months of training and seven months of operational duties), some 27 percent of these officers reported experiencing one operational traumatic event, and 47 percent reported experiencing two or more events during this period (Huddleston et al., 2006). That is, some 74 percent had some operational experience of traumatic events during their first year as serving police officers. Given this level of exposure, it is pertinent to ask whether officer's pre-employment traumatic experience and its psychological legacy at point of entry influenced their subsequent critical incident stress risk. Discussion commences with those who did not experience a critical incident during their first year.

The Number of Operational Critical Incidents

According to Huddleston et al. (2006), officers who reported no traumatic incident exposure during their first year (26%) reported a mean IES score of 4.1. In the absence of any specific critical incident experience, it is necessary to account for their reporting IES scores at this time. One possibility is that this reflects the continuing influence of pre-employment exposure. Another possibility is that vicarious exposure to colleagues' experiences or their training experiences influenced prevailing levels of posttraumatic stress symptoms. This could have resulted from, for example, hearing of the experiences of colleagues or the accounts of operational events in training scenarios or from instructors that vicariously sustained or instigated a psychological response or reactivity. These possibilities remain tentative until more searching analyses of early experience are undertaken. Of those who did report experiencing a critical incident, a different picture emerges when on- and off-duty experiences are compared.

On Versus Off-Duty Experiences

Huddleston et al. (2006) research suggests that on-duty critical incident experience represents a more potent influence on well-being than off-duty events. Their comparison of officers reporting only one off-duty event (10%–mean IES score of 4.75) with those reporting one on-duty incident (mean IES score of 7.26) supports this view. This difference could result from one of several possibilities.

One is that off-duty and on-duty events differ with respect to the nature of the traumatic incidents experienced and/or have a differential influence on the magnitude of their symptoms, with on-duty events being more threatening or challenging. An alternative explanation is that duty-related experiences occur within an organizational context that makes a unique contribution to the variance in traumatic stress scores for on-duty events but not off-duty events. Determining whether this is indeed the case is a question that identifies an interesting line of future inquiry. This issue is explored in more detail below. What of those who experienced more than one duty-related critical incident? It would appear that the number of events experienced within the first year of policing has implications for officers' well-being.

The 47 percent of officers who reported having had two or more traumatic experiences reported mean IES scores of 13.28 (cf. 7.26 for those experiencing one incident). It may seem logical to attribute this to the cumulative or stair-stepping consequences of exposure to multiple events (Williams, 1993). However, before this can be accepted as fact, it is important to consider the possibility that some of the variance in traumatic stress symptoms could be attributed to cumulative exposure to organizational characteristics (e.g., hassles and uplifts) or to interaction between critical incident experience and organizational experience.

The discussion of officers' initial experience of the organizational bureaucracy and its procedures (see also Chapters 2 and 3 and below) identified how adapting to the bureaucratic reality of organizational life was a significant stressor. Critical incident experience brings officers into contact with organizational systems and procedures under challenging circumstances. If the reality of the organizational aspects of this experience is inconsistent with their expectations, this could result in both the critical incident and the organizational experience threatening the officer's psychological equilibrium (Paton, 2006; Paton

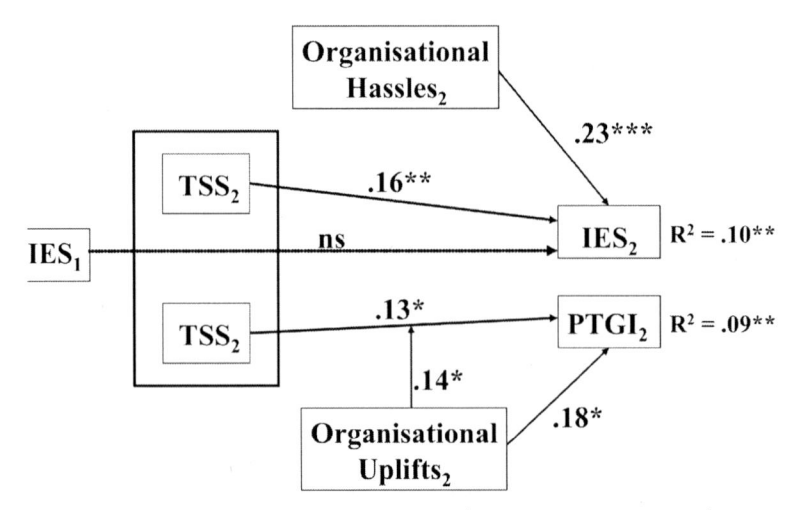

Figure 4.1. The relative contribution of traumatic (Traumatic Stress Scale) and organizational experiences (Police Daily Hassles and Uplifts Scale) to posttraumatic stress (Impact of Event Scale and Posttraumatic Growth (PTGI). Subscript 1 = Point of entry data; Subscript 2 = 12 month data. (adapted from Huddleston et al., 2006).

& Burke, 2007), with both incident and organizational experiences making independent contributions to the observed critical incident stress. Evidence supporting this explanation was forthcoming from a more detailed analysis of officers' critical incident experience (Figure 4.1).

Hassles and Uplifts and Posttrauma Outcomes

Huddleston et al. (2006) found that duty-related traumatic experiences during the first year of operational duties did influence IES scores at 12 months (Beta = .16, $p<0.01$). However, they also noted that organizational hassles (e.g., lack of consultation, poor communication, red tape) exercised a stronger influence on IES scores (Beta = .23, $p< 0.01$). They found that traumatic experiences during the first year of operational police duties and organizational hassles accounted for 10 percent of traumatic stress symptoms at 12 months. Huddleston et al. also found that duty-related traumatic experiences predicted posttraumatic growth scores (Beta = .13, $p< 0.05$). Again, organizational variables were also influential in this regard. Organizational uplifts (e.g., having responsibility, empowerment, recognition of good work) had a direct (Beta = .18, $p < 0.05$) influence on PTGI scores.

Organizational factors were a stronger predictor of outcome. Traumatic experiences during the first year of operational police duties and organizational uplifts accounted for 9 percent of posttraumatic growth at 12 months (Figure 4.1).

Because these data were collected during the early career period, officer's experience of organizational hassles and uplifts reflect the period of their socialization into organizational life. That is, officer's perceptions of organizational procedures appeared, even at this early stage in their career, to be able to influence critical incident stress risk. What is clear is that critical incident stress risk commences at point of entry and will continue throughout the officer's career. Risk management programs must be implemented over a corresponding period. How this might be accomplished is discussed in more detail in Chapter 10. Traumatic stress outcome is not the only issue affected.

Huddleston et al. (2006) reported similar outcomes when general mental health status and self-reported physical health status were examined. General mental health status (measured using the HSCL-21) at point of entry was a significant predictor of mental health status at 12 months (Beta = .17, $p < 0.01$). However, organizational hassles scores (Beta = 0.23, $p < 0.001$) was a better predictor of general mental health than point of entry stress. Uplifts did not influence general mental health. Time 1 HSCL-21 scores and organizational hassles accounted for 9 percent of the variance in general mental health at 12 months.

With regard to self-reported physical health, health status at point of entry predicted health at 12 months (Beta = 0.38, $p < 0.01$). Duty-related traumatic experience during the first 12 months did not influence health, nor did organizational hassles. However, positive organizational experiences (organizational uplifts) did influence health status (Beta = 0.15, $p < 0.01$). Physical health status at point of entry and organizational uplifts accounted for 19 percent of the variance in health status at 12 months.

These data indicate that, with regard to both traumatic stress symptoms and posttraumatic growth, organizational factors are significant predictors and, in both cases, exercise a stronger influence on each outcome than traumatic experiences per se. With regard to traumatic stress scores, these data are consistent with those of earlier studies (Paton et al., 2000). The importance of organizational factors is reinforced when other anecdotal sources are included. For example,

Huddleston et al. (2006) discussed how, when officers' ratings of factors that contribute to negative perceptions of police work were examined, organizational factors were implicated there more often than operational factors. Organizational hassles were the most frequently presented issue amongst those officers who had utilized psychological assistance under the New Zealand police trauma police (Disengagement Summit (NZ Police), 1998).

In summary, predictors of traumatic stress symptoms are organizational hassles and traumatic incident experiences. Predictors of posttraumatic growth are organizational uplifts and traumatic incident experiences. These findings have implications for managing traumatic stress risk. First, because stress symptoms and PTG outcomes are influenced by different factors, different strategies will be required to manage each. Second, the prominent influence of organizational factors means that support practices that focus on managing experience from the perspective of the person must be supplemented by organizational changes that minimize hassles and increase uplifts.

Analyses of this transitional period in the life of a police officer have raised some interesting issues regarding the relationship between challenging experiences and psychological growth. Of particular interest was finding that officers' interpretation of their organizational experience had an influence on PTG and that this was independent of traumatic experience per se. To examine this is in more detail, Burke (2009) compared posttraumatic growth (PTGI) scores in groups that differed with regard to their pre-employment and operational experiences of traumatic incidents (Table 4.2).

The Influence of Pre-Employment and Operational Traumatic Experience on Posttraumatic Growth (PTG)

Burke's (2008) findings (Table 4.2) can be subdivided according to whether officers had (groups 3 & 4) or had not (groups 1 & 2) experienced traumatic events prior to entering police work. These data provide tentative support for the contention that pre-employment traumatic experiences can "prime" officers' capacity to interpret critical incidents encountered early in their career in ways that increase the likelihood of their experiencing posttraumatic growth. Furthermore, the fact that no significant differences were evident between the scores for members of group 3 and group 4 (both groups had pre-employ-

TABLE 4.2
THE CONTRIBUTION OF "NO-TRAUMA," "PRE-EMPLOYMENT TRAUMA,"
AND "OPERATIONAL TRAUMATIC EXPERIENCE" TO
POSTTRAUMATIC GROWTH (PTGI) SCORES

GP	Traumatic Experience	N	PTGI Score (at 12 months operational experience)
1	No Trauma at Point of Entry & No operational trauma	18	13.44
2	No Trauma at Point of Entry & Operational trauma	15	14.8
3	Trauma at Point of Entry & No operational trauma	14	38.77
4	Trauma at Point of Entry & Operational trauma	12	34.50

Adapted from Burke, 2008.

ment traumatic experiences, but members of group 4 also had operational critical incident experience) raises the possibility that pre-employment traumatic experiences could exercise a more significant influence on officers' ability to realize posttraumatic growth outcomes than their operational critical incident experiences, at least during the first year of police work (based on the premise that their schema are primed to make sense of what they encounter on duty).

Of particular interest was the finding that those officers comprising Group 1 (Table 4.2) recorded PTGI scores despite having experienced neither pre-employment nor operational traumatic events. Several possibilities can be offered to account for this observation. One is that growth could result from vicarious experiences (e.g., from training, accounts provided by other officers). A second derives from the fact that all officers undergo a major life transition by commencing police work, with this transition to life as a police officer being responsible for their experiencing a sense of growth. The assumption that this growth reflects that officers have experienced their socialization and acculturation into police life makes it important to consider how positive change from events appraised as challenging but that cannot be defined as traumatic influence officers' quality of life.

While additional work is required to examine these issues in more detail, this interpretation has implications for the assessment of posttraumatic outcomes. It implies that, when assessing posttraumatic growth associated with officers' operational traumatic or critical incident experiences, given that realization or recognition of positive or growth outcomes associated with a specific operational experience may take weeks or months to manifest itself (Linley & Joseph, 2004), it will be necessary to control for other life events occurring within the same time period that could have had salutary consequences for them (e.g., successfully making the transition to being a serving officer, getting promoted into a position of increased responsibility, etc.). It is also important to ascertain whether officers appraise these life events as challenges from which they can learn and grow as a consequence, and to recognize that critical incident and organizational experiences may be making independent contributions to critical incident stress risk.

This possibility highlights a need to accommodate the demands associated with adjusting to work when attempting to build a comprehensive understanding of traumatic stress processes. Furthermore, as evinced by the fact that officers' perceptions of their early experience of organizational procedures (i.e., hassles and uplifts) represents an important aspect of their socialization experience, the process of making the transition to operational life and adjusting to the work environment and its demands will define the context in which officers experience, respond to, and develop from their subsequent experience of critical incidents (see Chapter 1). To understand this process and its potential to impact on critical incident stress risk, it is necessary to understand the socialization process that describes how recruits adjust to their operational role and the organizational context in which they will work.

ADJUSTING TO WORK IN A POLICE AGENCY

To understand how socialization and acculturation influence adjustment to police work and organizational life, it is essential to consider the relationship between the person and his or her environment, as well as the degree to which the two fit or fail to fit together (Blau, 1981). The fit between the person and the environment depends on how well: (a) officers' skills and abilities match the practical job demands and requirements, and (b) their psychological and social needs and expectations are consistent with those required for effective performance in the organizational (tasks, climate, etc.) environment. A good fit between officer and environment is not something that happens automatically. The diversity of experience, competencies, and personal characteristics that officers bring with them, as well individual differences in their adaptive skills, makes this a fairly dynamic process.

Socialization describes a process which involves officers actively negotiating their P-E Fit. Over time, interaction between officer and organization transforms recruits into participating and effective, or ineffective, members of the police work culture. An important issue in this context concerns how socialization into the police work culture can influence officers' definitions, interpretations, and responses to stress and how this influences their subsequent critical incident stress risk (see above).

The process of socialization can be challenging, particularly during the first few months when officers are striving to understand and impose meaning on their workplace experiences (Nelson, 1987) and to reconcile their existing expectations and goals with the emerging reality of police work (see Chapter 3 and below). This involves officers negotiating the transitional phase of learning the job, fitting in and coming to terms with the diverse ways that organizational structure and procedure affects them, both positively and negatively, and their work. Positive socialization experiences that facilitate the ability of the officer to negotiate this adjustment process will increase fit, reduce vulnerability, and increase adaptive capacity and resilience. In contrast, socialization that fails to facilitate adequate levels of fit can leave new officers feeling alienated, increasing the risk of their experiencing adverse stress outcomes.

When considering these processes, it is important to remember that officers do not enter police work as a blank slate upon which the organizational culture can be written. People's prior life and developmental experiences (see Chapter 3), including prior exposure to stress and trauma, will influence how they approach and deal with the socialization experience. Socialization is thus a transactional process. Consequently, when considering the relationship between well-being, socialization, and adjustment in new police officers, it is necessary to consider personal experiences, individual predispositions and characteristics and how their interaction with organizational characteristics, and processes and practices influence the progressive development of P-E Fit.

Socialization

Socialization into a police organization and into the role of police officer involves both formal (e.g., training) and informal (e.g., interaction with senior officers) processes. Interaction between the officer and these diverse processes describes the context in which the transition from recruit to operational officer takes place. Prominent influences on the quality of the socialization experience are the training officers receive and the degree of coherence between recruits' expectations of police work and the reality they encounter. To gain first-hand insights into how these factors influenced officers' socialization, Burke (2009) interviewed officers at a point some 12 months into their career. These interviews furnished the insights presented in this section which examines the socialization process from the perspective of the officers themselves. In particular, it examined their perceptions of their training, the positive and problematic aspects of their transition to operational policing, and explored how each was influenced by officers' expectations about the work they would perform and the organizational context in which they would work. The implications of inconsistencies between expectation and reality are discussed throughout, as are the ways in which officers responded to these unmet expectations. This category was split into two subcategories of Academy Training and Transition. Their relationships within the socialization process are shown in Figure 4.2.

Academy Training

Early career training is designed primarily to prepare officers for the operational and organizational situations they will face as serving officers. Officers' perception of the effectiveness of their training, and of the role they would ultimately play as police officers was directly influenced by their expectations of the job role prior to their embarking on operational duties. It is also important to appreciate that early career training provides officers with their first experience of the autocratic, hierarchical, often paramilitary, nature of the management of most police services.

Their period at the academy introduced recruits to the hierarchical nature of organizational life. Thus, from the very early stages of their career, officers were made aware that there is little opportunity for empowerment within this environment. The issue of empowerment,

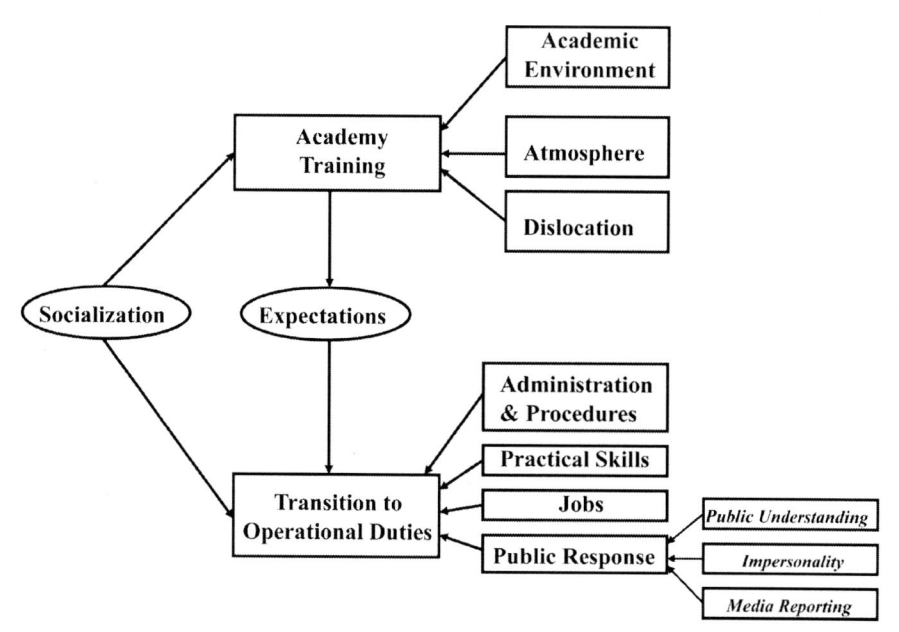

Figure 4.2. The relationship officer expectations and socialization in the police agency (adapted from Burke, 2009).

or the lack of it, has important implications for understanding how organizational culture impacts on critical incident stress risk. Consequently, understanding structural and procedural impediments to empowerment, and how these are perceived by officers, has important implications for the development of resilient officers and agencies (see Chapter 10). Officers' training experience can reinforce this sense of disempowerment in several ways.

After a few months, when another course of trainees arrives at the academy, the previous intake moves slightly up the organizational food chain. With this elevation up the hierarchical ladder, recruits come to be held, by academy staff and training officers, in slightly higher regard than their new junior counterparts. However, this does not equate to any increase in a sense of autonomy or authority. Rather, it acts as an overt socialization tool that indoctrinates trainees into the stratified organizational structure of the service and reinforced the perception of how hierarchical position equates to power.

Burke (2009) captured officers' perceptions of their training experiences in several latent themes linked to this structured, authoritarian environment (Figure 4.2). The first theme, *academic environment*, describes how the setting in which early career training were conducted impacted on officer's perceptions of his or her work and organization. The second theme, *atmosphere,* provides insights into an officer's feelings of depersonalization and constant surveillance by superiors. The third theme, dislocation, described an officer's feelings of dislocation from the outside world.

Academic Environment

The pressure of an academic-based workload was identified as one of the most stressful aspects of training, particularly with the regard to the pressure to maintain a level of performance that was subject to formal assessment. However, this introduction to the demands of police life was overshadowed by their early experience of the autocratic, hierarchical nature of organizational life.

Atmosphere

The paramilitary structure of life in the police academy created an authoritarian environment in which adherence to rules at all times was a prominent stressor. Non-compliance was met with strict penalties and punishment. It is in this context that the authoritarian, paramilitary style and hierarchical structure of the police agency becomes apparent. ". . . It's a quasi-military environment, and everyone down there is referred to by their rank, and there's a lot more brass walking around, so you're always aware and on your toes and making sure you do everything right" (Eric). The continuous use of negative reinforcement to deal with the consequences of rule infringement provided further insights into how officers are socialized into an autocratic work environment. "You know, sometimes a bit more positive reinforcement might have been better, but you kinda knew you weren't in trouble if they didn't say anything. . . . So if you weren't getting yelled at you were alright, but not having that positive reinforcement was a big thing. . ." (Tamryn). Another officer discussed his frustration with the authoritative nature of the police hierarchy during training at the academy "The most annoying thing about the academy is that you get treated like nothing, and I think that frustrates quite a few people. . . . You know it's drilled into you that you're at the bottom, the bottom of everything, and then you graduate and the next day the first thing you're supposed to do in any situation is to take charge" (George).

These perceptions of structures and procedures fuel a sense of disempowerment. Even when complying, rule-based approaches to training that lack any positive feedback or encourage responsibility do not encourage any sense of empowerment. These insights illustrate how an autocratic, top-down management structure is perceived as disempowering. These observations also provide insights into how culture influences how organizational procedures come to be perceived as hassles (see Chapter 2).

A cultural predisposition towards disempowering officers, at least during training, can be discerned in the fundamental paradox between the objectives of the training process and the nature of the autocratic, paramilitary training environment. For example, the training goal of teaching someone to be an independent learner and to rely on his or her instincts and initiative, which is advocated in both academic and practical senses, is in direct contrast to the authoritarian nature of the police academy (and perhaps more poignantly, the police organization) within which officers early socialization takes place as a result of the emphasis on hierarchy and the autocratic adherence to rules that characterizes the organizational aspects of academy life. Recruits experience of these aspects of academy life results, to some extent, in the perception of mixed messages being sent regarding expectations and behavior, initiates feelings of stress and impersonalization amongst the trainees, and decreases their sense of empowerment.

Transition

Officers' discussions of the transition from training to operational duties was dominated by issues associated with their expectations of policing and their perception of the level of preparedness their training played in this process. "(Training prepared us) pretty much as well as it could, there's heaps you don't know, I mean there's so much you don't get taught, but there's too much to teach, you can't teach every situation" (Amanda). This comment reflects a general belief regarding deficiencies in training being reflected in inconsistencies between recruits' expectations and their experience of the reality of life in a police organization. Four latent themes were identified: the first related to administration and procedures, the second to practical and operational skills, the third to the types of jobs they would be required to attend as police officers, and the fourth discusses the officers' expectations of how the public would respond to them.

Administration and Procedures

This theme described officers' perceptions of the administrative duties involved in policing and the degree to which they felt their training had prepared them for this aspect of their work. Important here was their perception that a lack of training contributed to their problems with administration. Officers felt unprepared for the amount of time it took to process a simple offense and were critical of the training they had received in the compilation of offense reports and the accompanying paperwork. Chad reported that "I'd have to say the academy training was a little bit deficient, especially regarding offence reports, we didn't do a lot on offence reports and I've learned since that they're how you're judged, because that's the work that everybody else sees."

In addition to highlighting an inconsistency between training and officers' actual experiences, the last comment illustrates how officers come to realize how their performance is evaluated on the paperwork completed rather than their actual operational performance. If this occurs in relation to a critical incident, it is possible to anticipate how perceptions of this kind of organizational hassle would influence stress risk. This observation illustrates the issue raised in Chapter 2 regarding the officer's realization that organizational systems and procedures sustain the bureaucratic and political imperatives of the police agency as much as they do the pursuance of core policing activities. A failure of bureaucratic processes to support core operational functions can represent a source of disequilibrium for officers (see Chapter 2), with it being this aspect of work that shatters assumptions and contributes to the experience of adverse psychological outcomes (Violanti & Paton, 1999).

Inconsistencies between senior officers with regard to how administrative and procedural guidelines should be interpreted were identified as another problematic aspect of the socialization experience. "There's inconsistencies from different people, you know I'll ask one person and then I'll need to ask other details along the same line of inquiry and that person isn't there so I ask another person. So I give them the full picture and so they say "Oh no, don't do what they said, do it this way" and after getting that about 5 or 6 times about one particular job, you get frustrated, it all leads to the same end result, but I'm not used to being out of my depth." Chad's frustration at the lack of uniformity in the advice and preference for how procedures should be completed illustrates how individual differences in senior officers' preferences can add to the demands officers experienced.

Practical Skills

Because it is more consistent with their expectations of the work of a police officer, it was not surprising that officers held generally positive views about the value of the practical component of their training. Notwithstanding, all called for more training in operational skills, particularly with regard to the scenarios used to add realism to the training experience.

Several officers cited the positives of scenario training but argued that the scenarios themselves needed to reflect real-life situations, and be less story-like. According to Harry, "The scenario training was pretty good. I'd like to see more of the scenario training. . . . I s'pose there has to be linear scenarios, there has to be a start and there has to be a middle and there has to be a definite end for it, and the clues that you pick up at the start have to steer you towards that end. But I'd like to see more of the scenario training." The organization of scenarios in a "linear" fashion, with an end already determined is not indicative of the unpredictability of actual operational situations when dealing with real people. One officer said "I learnt more probably in the first 2 weeks [of operational duties] than what I learnt at the academy, it was a major thing where you don't have the power, what do you do then? We weren't taught what to do in those situations" (Carol). The importance of observations such as this can be traced to the fact that officers are more likely to find themselves in situations in which their (expected–see Chapter 3) level of control could be called into question. This, in turn, can influence the development of coping strategies, and thus stress risk (see below). This was particularly so with regard to some of the more challenging aspects of operational life.

A minority of those interviewed by Burke (2009) identified deficiencies in their preparation for seeing people with injuries and in accidents. One officer recounted his reactions to having to do a mortuary admission within his first few weeks of operational duties. "Like when someone's severely injured and they're in a lot of pain, and also the body . . . the bodies and stuff cos we have to do a lot of mortuary admissions there has to be a police officer present . . . and so we get sent to them . . . and previously I'd never seen a dead body in my life and I saw 3 in a week. So that's probably one thing that stands out, they need to do something there. Yeah, you used to go and watch a post-mortem, but they don't do it anymore" (Stuart).

Overall, most officers could see the relevance, importance, or necessity of the majority of what they were taught at the academy. However, they would have appreciated more practical, operational, and skills-based training. The importance of the latter stems form the role that realistic training simulations play in developing schema capable of imposing meaning and coherence on (future) operational experiences (Paton, 1994). The greater the discrepancy between the schema developed in training contexts and the demands of critical incidents, the greater becomes officers' critical incident stress risk (Paton, 1994). This supports officers' call for more simulation-based training designed to expose them to more challenging situations, thus proactively increasing the range of operational situations they will be able to adapt to in future.

Simulations promote the integration of theory and application (essential for broadening the range of experiences officers can make sense of prior to their experiencing them for real by allowing them to extract and apply lessons learned from others' experiences within the training program) through experiential learning (Paton & Jackson, 2002). This creates a training context that develops officers' capacity to apply knowledge to goal-directed actions, and receive feedback to facilitate the identification of residual training needs. Simulations also afford opportunities for officers to develop, review, and rehearse operational and stress management skills under realistic circumstances, practice dealing with high-pressure situations in a safe and supportive environment in the roles they will adopt in operational contexts, receive feedback on their performance and identify areas for personal development, understand their reactions under high-stress conditions, and rehearse strategies to minimize negative reactions (Paton & Flin, 1999). Failure to do so within the academy environment represents a lost opportunity, given the difficulties of finding time for extensive periods of training when officers are operational.

Jobs

The jobs theme described officers' perceptions of the degree of consistency between their expectations about the nature of the work they would perform and the reality encountered. Officers expected that they would be involved in many more serious incidents and that they would be busier–citing frustration at the amount of down time on shift, and the number of tedious jobs they had to attend. While they were quick to dispel the myth that a police officer's job was like that portrayed in the popular media, many expected the job to resemble the "cop shows" on TV with respect to the types of incidents they would be involved in. "You don't think that you get that involved in like domestic arguments all that sort of thing. . . . I thought it would be more like you know, stealings you know, And you know that sort of stuff you see on TV" (Rick). In a similar vein, Irene said, "I honestly thought we'd be busier, like from one major job to another and it'd be really high stress type of thing, but its not."

Officers also recounted their shock at seeing how some people live their lives from their exposure to a side of society that is generally hidden from the majority of the public and one which most acknowledged they did not realize existed to the extent that they observed. Harry stated, "Just working at Woolworths and going home everyday, you don't see what's going on in the homes, you don't see the domestic violence, you don't see the assaults, car accidents, and unless you stumble across one, you're not gonna see it, it's [life outside policing] a really distorted view of what's going on." This highlights another adaptive demand that officers had to come to terms with.

Some officers reported being thrown in at the deep end, while others said that they wanted to be given more responsibility earlier in their career. The specific issue raised was primarily dependent on the size of the station to which the officer was assigned. Those working in smaller regional stations tended to be given a higher level of responsibility and autonomy earlier than their counterparts in larger metropolitan stations due to the former having substantially less staff. However, the support provided to the new officers particularly in terms of seasoned officers being on hand to act in a teaching/mentor/advisory capacity was more evident at the larger stations than the smaller. This again reflects differences in levels of staffing between regional and metropolitan stations. Both types of experience, greater responsibility and different levels of support and mentoring, have implications for understanding critical incident stress risk (see Chapter 10).

The significance of these issues, and a major reason for arguing for their inclusion in future research agenda, is the fact that differences in empowerment (e.g., being given responsibility, autonomy) and the availability of support were evident in the month to six weeks immediately following graduation. The importance of identifying these issues as having fundamental implications for the quality of socialization can be traced to their role in facilitating stress resilience. These issues are discussed in detail in Chapter 10. However, given the significant role these factors play as predictors of critical incident stress risk, the fact that socialization experiences can be differentiated in this way highlights a need for the development of contingent approaches to stress risk management from an early stage. It will not be possible to adopt a one-size-fits-all approach to intervention.

These insights into the relationship between training and socialization, particularly with regard to the degree to which officers had to impose meaning on their work experiences in situ, illustrate how the schema that officer's brought with them (e.g., that underpinned their expectations) had to change and new schema had to be developed on the job. The degree to which schemas have to change and the ease with which new schema can be developed will influence critical incident stress risk (Paton, 1994). The ways officer and organization can interact to influence the ease or otherwise of schema change or development is discussed in more detail in Chapters 7–10.

Public Response

This theme encompassed officers' perceptions of how the public reacted to them and the disorientation caused, in many cases, by their having to adjust to the beliefs and expectations the public held about the police. Assuming an underlying motivation to protect and serve, the need to reappraise this aspect of their schema, and impose coherence on the inconsistencies that emerged from their experience provides further insights into how socialization could influence critical incident stress risk, particularly with regard to the lack of attention paid in academy and early career training to providing realistic insights into this aspect of policing. While officers acknowledged that they expected some negative treatment from members of the public, they did not anticipate the scope of these negative reactions, nor the expectations to be inconsistent with their powers. This theme comprised three subthemes (Public Understanding & Expectation, Media Reporting, and Impersonality).

Public Understanding and Expectations

This subtheme reflected officer's perceptions of the degree to which the general public held inaccurate beliefs about the police role. "They [the public] don't understand . . . the kind of powers you have, like what you can do in certain situations, and they think that you're not doing anything, its just the simple fact that you don't have the power to do it" (Carol). Officers felt that the general public had very little idea of what the job entailed, but believed that offenders with whom they had regular contact knew more about the police role and their powers.

Several officers reported having negative encounters with the public that reflected public misconceptions about the role of police. One officer said "you get people who think that they know everything and that all you want to do is pull them into jail. I don't think that people realize that the last thing we want to do is to put someone away because you know it's just not in our best interests to get people locked up, you know it's better off if we can sort it out before it goes that far but a lot of people won't understand that. They think that your presence automatically means that someone's gonna get in trouble" (Chad). However, several officers discussed positive encounters with the general public. Rachel said she found it funny that "people talk to you about everything, everything under the sun. You're the source of all knowledge about everything."

Impersonality

Many officers believed that members of the public only saw the uniform, and thus that is what they respond to. Several officers reported feeling that this dehumanized them to a certain extent because people didn't see that there was actually a person behind the uniform. Chad said, "you do see it in people eyes . . . they do see you as a police officer first and then as a person and when you say something like just in normal conversation and you can see their minds tick away." Some officers were beginning to find that being a police officer was beginning to define them as individuals in other contexts, Eric recounted this experience, "It's really funny, every time you go to a party . . . you're always introduced as Eric who's a policeman." While describing this as frustrating, officers accepted that this was something that they would have to get used to if they continued their career in the police.

A corollary of this impersonality was a growing tendency for many officers to decline to disclose their occupation to people they didn't know well. "I certainly wouldn't slip it into the conversation [that I'm a police officer], I wouldn't tell people because I do think police officers are somewhat isolated and I can see why that happens. I think there is a culture or subculture if you like which is good and bad but its about their [police officer's] survival as individuals, so I think its probably necessary to some degree" (Frank). One officer talked about his frustration at feeling the need to adhere to this nondisclosure because of the way people reacted to police, "It's dehumanizing in a way, because it implies that all police officers act in exactly the same way, and people believe that, they see you in the uniform and nothing else" (Karl). "People watch you, even when you know, you've just got the t-shirt on going home, people can see that you're a copper and you've got to be aware of what you're doing more than ever, and you can't ever just be you anymore, you've always got to be mindful that you're a cop" (James). These comments reiterate the issue discussed in Chapter 3 regarding isolation.

Media Reporting

This subtheme describes officers' beliefs regarding how the negative reactions they received from the general public could be attributed to the negative portrayal of aspects of police work in the media, and the media's tendency to focus on negative things which they deemed to be newsworthy, while either not reporting, or not finding out the full story. "I think negative publicity . . . it's really just choosing a negative view on a given set of facts and for people to believe that which they mostly do 'cos that's the way its portrayed in the media then people are going to swallow it hook line and sinker" (James).

Taken together, the content of these interviews identified how several components interact to determine officers' expectations about policing and their role. Officers' motivations for joining the profession, their perceptions of the effectiveness of training as a preparatory mechanism, and their experience of the transition from trainee to operational officer all interact to influence officers' experience of the socialization process and their progress towards an effective level of person-environment fit that is the fundamental objective of socialization.

Officers talked in detail about how the job differed from their expectations. Even those who felt they had a degree of insight from previous contact with police officers, in a variety of forms including family relationships, were surprised and disturbed by some aspects of the job. Clearly neither officer's pre-employment history and experience nor their training provided a wholly effective foundation for the everyday operating contexts in which they subsequently found themselves working. The experience of inconsistencies between expectation and reality led officers to describe the transition from trainee to officer as a kind of "culture shock." For example, "I said to my sergeant the first few weeks, I felt like an absolute fish out of water, like I just thought oh my god I know nothing, because its so different to the environment down there [at the academy compared to operational policing] and its so different to what you expect or you think its gonna be" (Jim). Many described questioning their judgment about becoming a police officer because the job differed so much from their expectations. "I was really stressed, really annoyed, and I was asking myself whether I'd done the right thing and whether in fact I even wanted to work for these people" (Justine). These observations illustrate how working in a new occupational context that fails to match expectations can be a source of distress.

The expectations officers have of what the job would entail can be conceptualized in terms of the development of a schema about policing and their role as a police officer. These expectations represent a schema molded by little or no involvement in the profession to this point. If these expectations are not met in reality, attempts to reconcile experiences that are incompatible with these representations can increase stress and threaten perceived and actual feelings of control.

On the other hand, while increasing stress in the short term, schematic disruptions can facilitate the adaptive capacity of these officers if the schema and reality can be reconciled (Fredrickson et al., 2003; Paton, 2005). This reiterates the need to consider patterns of interaction between the officer and the organization. From the perspective of the development of schema and thus the way in which officers impose meaning and coherence on all facets of their work experience, organizational culture, and procedures, and the way they are transmitted and sustained by the actions of senior officers, will play a significant role. Meaning making is imposed through, for example, training, performance appraisal, and officers' perceptions of the attitudes and actions of senior officers. The issues discussed above identify several areas in which academy and early career training can be improved. How these various influences can be reconciled to facilitate critical incident stress resilience is discussed in more detail in Chapter 10.

Burke (2009) also discussed how officers' accounts of their training experience indicated that it played a role in the development of coping strategies. While acknowledging that the situation was stressful and invoked feelings of pressure and stress, they felt that this was inevitable, and that it was better to focus on dealing with other things (like assignments) than to place energy into trying to change something that they could not control. This is perhaps best exemplified by Eric, "I didn't like it, didn't like it at all. . . . I felt stressed and pressured most of the time. But I knew that they were doing it to teach us, to get us into the right frame of mind . . . getting us ready to think, feel and be, a cop." Because stress risk will be influenced by the coping strategies adopted by officers, the final issue to be discussed in this chapter concerns the coping strategies officers bring with them into the role, and how the socialization experience influences this important influence on risk.

COPING

When she examined the coping strategies used by recruits, Burke (2009) found that, on commencing training, the coping strategy used most was positive reinterpretation, followed by planning, acceptance, and active coping. On completion of their training, she found that positive reinterpretation remained the most widely used strategy, followed by instrumental social support, planning, acceptance, and active coping. This pattern was similar for both male and female officers.

At time of entry into policing, the two least reported strategies were behavioral disengagement and religious coping respectively. This reversed posttraining, with religious coping reportedly used least, followed by behavioral disengagement. While Burke found no significant change in use of religious coping, denial, or alcohol/drug disengagement when comparing officers at point of entry and again at 12 months, she did find significant changes on all other dimensions of coping. Each saw a significant decrease in the reported usage of the specific coping strategy, with the exception of instrumental social support which showed a marked increase, and behavioral disengagement which showed a slight but significant increase.

Burke's (2009) analysis of early career police officers revealed greater use of adaptive coping at baseline, a pattern which was maintained to the posttraining phase. This indicates the predominant use of coping mechanisms likely to support adaptive outcomes following challenging experiences. The high use of adaptive strategies such as positive reinterpretation and acceptance at both times suggests that officers possess and use the capacity to reframe negative events in a more positive light. This would certainly be advantageous given the types of events officers are likely to face operationally in the future. In addition, the use of other adaptive strategies such as active coping and planning is potentially beneficial in an operational context, enabling officers to proactively approach challenging events and situations in ways that increased the likelihood of their experiencing adaptive outcomes. Burke argued that this pattern reflected a mixture of pre-existing predisposition to using certain coping strategies, with the use of such strategies being reinforced and encouraged during training. Burke also suggests that prior traumatic event experience, or experience of highly stressful life events, could have facilitated officers' ability to identify strategies that are adaptive and effective in dealing with the psychological consequences of challenging events, thus enhancing the repertoire of available coping resources. This is another area in which additional work will be required before this issue can be adequately elucidated.

While Burke found differences in the coping profiles of each gender at the baseline phase, these were not preserved when she revisited this issue in the posttraining phase. She argued that this could reflect the training officers receive at the police academy. Given the heavy emphasis on effective ways of coping with adverse events in the training curriculum, it may be that officers are reporting how they expect themselves to respond to certain events. At the posttraining phase, the officers studied by Burke had limited operational experience. Thus the greater consistency between genders may be a result of prospective reporting, rather than a true reflection of the coping strategies they would use in operational situations.

Another possibility for the emerging consistency in coping strategy use across the genders is social desirability. In particular, female officers do not want to be seen as soft, or as different to their male counterparts with regard to their response to the challenging experiences they encounter. Nor do they want their ability to cope with challenging circumstances to be called into question. This may constitute an additional socialization pressure, and one that is specific to female officers. Thus, female officers may be reporting strategies that match those taught at the academy, and that emulate the masculine police culture in order to facilitate their socialization. Similarly, male officers may have perceived that they were expected to respond in a certain way. More detailed answers to this question must await further research.

The preceding discussion raises additional questions about coping. In particular, given the possibility that the reported pattern of coping styles could reflect a social desirability bias, it is pertinent to ask whether this pattern of adaptive coping will be maintained throughout officers' professional careers. Furthermore, Burke's (2009) finding that a strategy more likely to increase vulnerability to adverse stress reactions, behavioral disengagement, trended in the direction of increasing use and highlights a need to consider the wider implications of maladaptive coping. Finally, Burke's discussion of how patterns of coping in female officers could have been influenced by the nature of their socialization experience highlights a need to consider this issue in more detail. The issues of maladaptive coping and the socialization of female officers are dealt within the next and the subsequent chapter.

Chapter 5

MALADAPTIVE COPING DURING THE POLICE CAREER

INTRODUCTION

The efficacy of police coping throughout various chronological stages of a career has an impact on whether or not trauma and stress will continue to plague their lives. Police officers often comment that they feel helpless and ineffective in dealing with the vast amount of crime in this country. Peck (1984) stated that coping behavior can be attributed in part to stress-related reactions to the person's perceived inability to act upon social conditions and events causing traumatic stress.

POLICE COPING EFFICACY

Most people can find alternative ways to cope with situations other than suicide. Police officers as a group, however, tend not to cope well with psychological distress, and often turn to maladaptive coping strategies (Violanti, 1993a). Coping skills may be defined as behavioral reactions to distress, and two primary categories of coping strategies have been identified: emotion and problem-focused strategies (Lazarus, 1981). Hovanitz (1986) reported that emotion focused strategies are generally less successful than problem-focused strategies. In a recent study, Lennings (1994) found that police officers tend to use problem-solving coping strategies less than nonpolice persons (Toch & Grant, 1991). This was seen as unusual, since police generally perceive themselves as problem solvers. Although police may use some problem-solving techniques, it appears such techniques are primarily defensive in nature, and may lead to inaccurate appraisals of a stressful situation (Fridell & Binder, 1992).

Violanti (1993b) found that police officers primarily turned to two types of coping when confronted with stress: "escape avoidance" and "distancing." Escape avoidance involved avoidance of people and the use of alcohol or drugs, and distancing involved emotional escape from the situation. Distancing is distinctly different from escape coping; one can distance oneself psychologically from a situation but may not be able to escape or avoid the consequences of that same situation. Highly distressed officers likely use escape avoidance and distancing to deal with the lack of personal control in their work. Distancing may lead to depersonalization, which has been noted as a prominent feature of individual police behavior and culture (Pogrebin & Poole, 1991). For the police, these strategies may be maladaptive, as evidenced by increasing alienation, stress, and reliance on alcohol to manage the stress (Violanti, Marshall, & Howe, 1985).

The police training environment may contribute to the inefficacy of police coping abilities. Violanti (1993a) suggested that the use of distancing, self-controlling, accepting personal responsibility, and escape-avoidance were employed significantly more by recruits under high distress. Escape-avoidance and distancing have an especially strong maladaptive potential. It is also possible that the training academy experience may increase the use of such strategies. If counterbalancing socialization does not occur after the recruit leaves the academy, the possibility exists that such strategies might well carry over into the work environment. A lower stress training environment may allow for a wider choice of behavior conducive to proper coping and adjustment to police work.

The research suggests that police get into trouble at least some of the time because of perceived appraisal strategies. Either they are unaware of people's feelings and situations, unaware of their own anxiety in a situation, or have made a judgment based upon a inflexible plan that is rigidly followed (Fridell & Binder, 1992; Pogrebin & Poole, 1991). Even maladaptive coping techniques, however, may breakdown over time in officers. Given evidence of the lack of viable coping alternatives in police work, and the primary socialization of officers into potentially maladaptive coping strategies, it is possible that suicide may become a final coping alternative. Perhaps training officers in problem solving, emotion focusing, and decision-making strategies may provide them with coping alternatives to suicide.

Coping Impact: "Acting Out" the Police Role

Dependence on the police role may affect the ability of officers to deal with distress inside and outside of police work. Cognitive, social, and inflexible styles associated with the police role hinder efficacious coping with stressful interpersonal interactions and precipitate risk factors associated with the potential for suicide.

Adherence to the police role not only limits cognitive abilities but also the use of other social roles for the amelioration of distress. Adherence to the police role may affect the self-representational structure of officers, which defines the self as having purpose and meaning in the social environment. When meaning is lost, or the officer becomes isolated through role restriction, the potential for suicide may increase (Violanti, 1997; Turner & Roszell, 1994). These findings suggest that the influence of the police role as a primary self-representation role may deprive officers of the use of other life roles in dealing with trauma. This leads to speculation that not only are the police officers' cognitive self-representations constricted by virtue of the police role, but that they also have decreased flexibility to use other life roles for the amelioration of distress. As a consequence, police officers may deal with most life situations, good or bad, from the standpoint of their work role. This raises the question of the impact of the police role on life relationships that may precipitate psychological distress—personal, police peer, and societal relationships.

ALCOHOL ABUSE

Precise figures for alcoholism among police officers are not available, but reports indicate that more than 25 percent of officers have serious problems related to alcohol abuse (Kroes, 1986). In the Chicago police suicide study, alcoholism was documented in 12 of 20 suicides. In addition, these 12 officers had extensive medical records, six (30%) had average records, and two had limited medical records. The majority of medical complaints were stomach flu, nervous problems, high blood pressure, heart trouble, back trouble, kidney disease, bursitis, and alcoholism. Discipline records revealed that seven of the 20 had serious discipline problems, seven had normal discipline records, and six had no discipline problems (Cronin, 1982).

Alcohol is an important problem in police work, and may lead to other work problems such as high absenteeism, intoxication on duty, complaints by supervisors and citizens of misconduct on duty, traffic accidents, and an overall decrease in work performance (McCafferty et al., 1992). Skolnick (1972) commented that police officers are by no means abstainers and that they usually drink together to avoid public criticism. Unkovic and Brown (1976) found that 8 percent of their category labeled "heavy drinkers" were police officers. Van Raalte (1979) reports that 67 percent of his police sample admitted drinking on duty. He also cites several instances of intoxicated off-duty officers injuring others with a firearm. Hitz (1973) found police mortality ratios for alcohol-related cirrhosis of the liver to be significantly higher than the general population. Alcohol use among police may be underestimated. Many officers, fearing departmental discipline, are unwilling to officially report their dependence. Police organizations appear ambivalent towards drinking problems, placing blame on the individual officer and not the police occupational structure. Other departments may "hide" problem drinkers in positions where they will not adversely affect police operations (Kroes, 1986). Besides alcohol, drug use may be an increasing problem in policing. McCafferty et al. (1992) commented that drug abuse is becoming a problem for police departments as more officers begin to use drugs, or are hired with the habit already established. A police officer with a weapon who is abusing drugs is a risk to himself, his family, his fellow police officers, and the public.

Alcohol abuse by itself can cause many problems for police officers, but synergistic effects can worsen the situation. Alcohol use has been found to be a factor in suicide, and police use of alcohol may be precipitated by stress. Violanti et al. (2004) found a significant positive relationship between alcohol use and PTSD among police officers. Beutler, Nussbaum, and Meredith (1988) found increased time in police service to be associated with maladaptive responses by officers. Even early in the police career, officers tended to respond negatively to the demands of police work by addictive alcohol use. Romanov, Hatakka, Keskinen, Laksonen et al. (1994), in a study of over 21,000 adults, found increased alcohol use to lead to a 2.5-fold risk of suicide.

Alcohol abuse has long been characterized as a problem among police officers (Richmond, Wodak, Kehoe, & Heather, 1998). The police culture reinforces the use of alcohol as a social and psychological device for coping with the stresses of the job (Violanti, 2003). Epidemiologic Catchment Area (ECA) survey findings suggested that the rate of comorbid psychiatric-alcohol disorders significantly exceeds rates that would be expected by chance alone. Lifetime prevalence of mental disorders was found to be nearly twice as high among alcoholics than in the general population. A 13-nation study conducted by Lester (1995) suggests a positive association between increased alcohol use and increased suicide. Alcoholism is the second most common diagnosis among suicides, occurring more often in men than in women. Volpicelli, Balaraman, Hahn et al. (1999) pose an interesting hypothesis that alcohol use or abuse generally occurs after rather than prior to trauma. Alcohol may relieve symptoms of PTSD because it compensates for deficiencies in endorphin activity following a traumatic experience.

It is not uncommon to find a synergistic effect of alcohol use and PTSD on suicide ideation. Joiner and Rudd (1995), for example, examined the effects of depression with six other psychological problems and found that many factors working together increased the severity of suicidal ideation. Other researchers have found that depression and anxiety interactively increase the likelihood of suicidal ideation (Rudd, Dahm, & Rajab, 1993). Depression and alcohol abuse may also increase suicidal ideation (Bongar, 1991). Many persons diagnosed with PTSD have comorbid difficulties (Green, Lindy, & Grace, 1989). For example, in a study of Vietnam veterans with PTSD, Roszell, McFall, and Malas (1991) found that nearly 50 percent indicated a current sense or belief of foreshortened future, and over 64 percent had a current coexisting diagnosis of major depression (93% were currently diagnosed with some form of mood disorder).

SUICIDE

Suicide is frequently thought of as an ultimate coping response to an intolerable condition. Suicidal police officers may, if effect, exhaust all available coping strategies to deal with the stress of their jobs. The result may be what Schneidman (1986) termed "constriction" of thought, a condition of limited response to a situation. Officers in a state of constriction can only perceive two alternatives: remove the intolerable condition or die. Since it is unlikely that the conditions of exposure in police work will change, the suicidal officer may choose death.

Epidemiological evidence suggests that there is an elevated rate of suicide within law enforcement. Violanti, Vena, and Marshall (1996) found that male police officers had a suicide rate of 8.3 times that of homicide and 3.1 times that of work accidents. Compared to male municipal workers, male police officers had a 53 percent increased rate of suicide over homicide, a three-fold rate of suicide over accidents, and a 2.65-fold rate of suicide over homicide and accidents combined. Vena, Violanti, Marshall, and Fiedler (1986) found male officers to have an age-adjusted mortality ratio for suicide of approximately three times that of male municipal workers in the same cohort. Lester (1995) found that seven of 26 countries for the decade of 1980–1989 had police suicide rates above the general population. A mortality study of police officers in Rome, Italy found the suicide ratio among male police officers to be 1.97 times as high as the general male Italian population (Forastiere et al., 1994).

Gershon, Lin, and Li (2002) provided recent evidence of job-related problems among police officers that may be related to suicide. Officers had an approximate four-fold risk of being exposed to traumatic work events, a three-fold risk of exhibiting PTSD symptoms, a 4-fold risk of alcohol abuse, and a four-fold risk of aggressive behavior. Charbonneau (2000), in a study in Quebec, Canada, found police suicide rates to be almost twice that of the general population. Rates were elevated mostly among young officers (20–39 years of age). Hartwig and Violanti (1999) found that the frequency of police suicide occurrence in Westphalia, Germany has increased over the past seven years, particularly in the 21–30 and 51–60 years of age categories. Most of suicides were male officers (92%). Cantor, Tyman, and Slatter (1999) found the high rate of suicide among Australian police attributable to stress, health, and domestic difficulties. Occupational problems were more intense than personal ones. Helmkamp (1996), in a study of suicide among males in the U.S. Armed Forces, found military security and law enforcement specialists had a significant increased rate ratio for suicide. Darragh (1991) conducted an epidemiological analysis on factors based on 558 consecutive cases of self-inflicted death in the United Kingdom, which revealed a dramatic increase in suicide

Trauma and Police Suicide

While being emotionally impenetrable is considered necessary by officers in police work, it may also increase the likelihood of suicide when the "armor" is suddenly shattered by stress and traumatic events. Feelings of vulnerability may affect coping ability, but it is not yet understood precisely what those effects are. It is known that people experience differential vulnerability, as some cope satisfactorily with trauma while others do not (Fowlie & Aveline, 1985; Frye & Stockton, 1982; Foy, Sipprelle, Rueger, & Carroll, 1984). Police Officers expect not to feel vulnerable; when they do, it brings feelings of shame, fear, and a heightened sense of danger.

Suicide may become an option as the officer attempts to adapt to shattered perceptions of invulnerability. The denial of mortality becomes progressively more difficult for officers, and the effect of confrontation with hostile people takes its toll. To overcome emotional numbing associated with trauma, the officer seeks increased stimulation. The result may be outrageous behavior, involvement in casual sexual affairs, impulsiveness, and aggressive actions. Suicide may result from the lack of an outlet for these behaviors and a final coping strategy for unendurable psychological pain (Mcafferty et al., 1992).

TRAUMA AND POLICE SUICIDE IDEATION–The complexity of the relationships between precipitants of ideation, suicidal ideation, and completed or attempted suicide make it difficult to predict outcomes (Fremouw et al., 1990; Bongar, 1991). Violanti (2003) found that increased exposure to certain types of traumatic events in police work significantly increase the risk for high PTSD symptomatology, which in turn increased the risk for comorbid increased alcohol use and suicide ideation. Officers seeing someone die, for example, had an approximate significant 3.5 times higher odds ratios (OR) (OR=3.37) of developing high-level PTSD than those not exposed. Other traumatic exposures, such as the homicide of a fellow officer (OR=2.65) and miscellaneous disturbing traumatic incidents (rape victims, mistreated children, elderly abuse, etc., OR=2.84) also increased the odds of high level PTSD symptoms. High levels of PTSD, in turn, increased the odds for suicide ideation significantly, almost six times higher (OR=5.72) and the use of alcohol to levels approximately 2.5 times higher (OR=2.5). Taken together, the comorbid risk of high PTSD and alcohol use increased the odds of suicide ideation approximately 10 times higher those officers who had lower levels.

Thus, posttraumatic stress symtomatology appears to produce many negative consequences, including increased alcohol use and suicide ideation among police officers. Being the target of, exposed to, as well as witness to events that can precipitate a sense of horror, helplessness, and hopelessness, it is not surprising that police officers have been empirically found to suffer the mental injuries associated with traumatic stress (Violanti & Paton, 1999). However, with support from those around them, most officers manage to come to terms with the traumatic event and get on with their lives and careers (Carlier et al., 2000; Carlier, Lamberts, Gersons, & Berhodlt, 1997). For those officers who cannot cope adequately, symptoms of PTSD may become overwhelming. In some cases, officers might conclude that life is no longer worth living, thus triggering suicide ideation (Violanti, 2003; Carlier et al., 2000).

The reality of psychological wounds in the workplace has also been one of effects that resulted from 911 terrorist attacks and the recent war in Iraq. Since these events, the police and others have been put under additional strain due to personnel shortages resulting from military deployment and homeland security measures (Violanti, 2003).

PTSD has been previously associated with increased suicidal ideation. Marshall, Olfson, Hellman, Blanco, et al., (2001) found that persons diagnosed with PTSD had a three-fold risk of suicide ideation compared to those without PTSD. The high risk of ideation remained even when depression was controlled. Freeman, Roca, and Moore (2000) found that combat veterans with PTSD had significantly more suicide attempts and self destructive behaviors. It is also possible that chronic exposure to stress may lead to symptomatic emotional numbing in officers that may make death easier to accept as a coping solution (*DSM-IV,* American Psychiatric Association, 2000). McCafferty et al. (1992) commented:

> It would be impossible to adequately prepare an individual in the police academy for the stress encountered on the street. There is almost continual psychologic pressure in police work because the officer must be prepared even if nothing is happening. The constant reminder of the badge and the weight of the pistol on the hip serves notice that at any

moment a police officer may be called upon to use deadly force to cope with a sudden life-threatening situation. There is constant exposure to hostility, anger, aggression, depression, and tragedy in the various events and confrontations that occur daily in a police officer's life. The constant exposure to these sorts of stress requires the officer to use all of his adaptive mechanisms to cope . . . the ultimate result in some individuals is despair, alienation, isolation, a sense of futility, and hopelessness. . . .

FAMILY DISRUPTION

Police officers appear to have problems coping with relationships. One reason for relational difficulties may be an emotional detachment from others. The role of a police officer calls for depersonalization—interpersonal relationships, on the other hand, call for human emotion (Violanti, 1997). Police officers are socialized into not expressing emotion, to put up an emotional barrier to protect themselves from the human misery they witness. When officers are off-duty, however, they cannot turn their emotions back on. They remain stuck in prescribed "tough guy" roles that are seen as necessary to be an effective police officer (Madamba, 1986). As a result, the personal relationships of police officers are not personal at all; they are more like a transaction on the street. Significant others soon become less important to the police officer. Compassion is subdued in favor of the police role, which takes precedent over most other emotional feelings. In some respects, the police role becomes a safe place to hide but at the same time does not allow for an outlet of emotions. The inability for police officers to use other roles to cope with problems with a family person, friend, or lover may be behind many police relationship problems.

INTERVENTION STRATEGIES

Because maladaptive coping strategies are likely the result of a complex interaction of many factors, all major components of the work environment must necessarily be involved in prevention efforts. Braverman (1995) pointed out that prevention in the workplace goes far beyond initial screening and profiling of individuals employed. Instead, one should focus on systemic-level assessment of risk and development of policies and procedures to mitigate potential problems. A prevention approach should focus on building a person's work and life competencies, thereby enhancing their resilience to stressors. It should be realized that maladaptive behavior does not result from a single major crisis but from the accumulation of apparently minor life events (Loo, 1995). The establishment of cost-effective, confidential, and successful early intervention system designed to identify and assist police officers with problems can be a first step toward prevention.

Trauma Risk Management

The risk management approach is built on the premise that if the factors that predict the psychological outcomes associated with critical incident exposure can be identified it may be possible to manipulate them in ways that afford opportunities to make informed choices regarding the psychological consequences of responding to challenging events (Paton, Violanti, Dunning, & Smith, 2004). According to this conceptualization, knowledge of these factors and how they interact can be used to estimate stress risk and inform the development of risk management policies and practices that can be implemented to increase personal, group, and organizational well-being and adaptation (Paton, Violanti, & Smith, 2003). However, for this risk to be managed, there must exist a capability to make choices regarding outcomes by exercising control over the causes of adverse stress reactions or over the factors that influence how these experiences are interpreted. Vulnerability makes a significant contribution to this risk (Paton et al., 2003), making its management an important component of a risk management strategy. As Violanti and Paton (2006) suggest, fundamental to the effective management of this risk is identifying the vulnerability factors that mediate the relationship between the critical incident experience and its psychological consequences that are under organizational purview. Realizing the benefits that can accrue from the adoption of this perspective requires that risk management considers two separate, but related, processes. The first is concerned with developing a coherent and comprehensive model of traumatic stress vulnerability that includes individual, team, and environmental factors. The second concerns the mechanisms that integrate these resources within an organizational sense of community.

Alcohol Abuse

Alcohol abuse is likely an approachable target for intervention. Based on early prevention strategies, a police department should set two goals for dealing with alcohol abuse (Violanti, 1999). First, it should seek to maintain lower alcohol consumption levels among those who already manifest high levels. If officers express an intention not to increase alcohol consumption, and do so in the context of making other changes in their lives that would sustain that practice, then prevention is achieved. Second, departments should encourage the minimization of factors leading to alcohol use among members. Stress is one example. Stress management programs hit at the heart of alcohol-related problems and are essential in a comprehensive approach to mental well-being at work. Research has demonstrated that an early prevention approach has the long-range potential to reduce alcohol abuse. Police departments should take note that it is economically and practically easier to "prevent" than to cure and proactively seek early prevention of alcohol abuse among its members.

Suicide Prevention

Traditionally, police officers view themselves as rugged, stand alone, individuals. Law enforcement officers routinely deal with the problems of others yet often deny or attempt to bury their own. Within the police culture, officers who are experiencing psychological problems can be viewed as weak and sometimes a "bad fit" for the profession (Hackett, 2004). This attitude has been responsible for officers remaining silent and not seeking the psychological assistance they may need. It is often not until the officer's individual situation reaches crisis proportion, such as in a suicide, that a department will acknowledge there may have been a problem. While personal intervention is certainly necessary in preventing suicide, police departmental changes and training can effectively add to any prevention protocol.

SUICIDE AWARENESS TRAINING–Training should be broken down into segments:

- The statistics around police suicide–Compare and contrast law enforcement suicide to line-of duty-death.
- Those affected by suicide–Family, friends, coworkers, the entire agency, and the community.

- The motivations for a law enforcement suicide—Critical incidents, relationship problems, substance abuse, to gain attention, to escape an intolerable situation, etc.
- Explore the common myths regarding suicide such as it usually happens without warning; low risk after mood improvement; once suicidal; always suicidal, intent on dying.
- The verbal and behavioral clues of suicide—Comparing and contrasting the moods and behavior of the employee. Is he/she acting out of place as compared to usual conduct? Why is his or her work suddenly substandard? Why are they suddenly not getting along with coworkers? Temper outbursts or possible withdrawal.
- Major predictors of suicidal behavior include a prior suicide attempt, family history, a major relationship break down, internal investigation, focal point of a criminal investigation, the plan, availability of means, lethality of method.

THE INTERVENTION ROLE OF THE POLICE SUPERVISOR

The law enforcement first-line supervisor, when properly trained, is in an excellent position to monitor his or her subordinates for signs of distress, trauma, and life problems (Hackett, 2004). Generally, the supervisor is in daily contact with subordinates and can spot check the overall emotional wellness of line officers on a regular basis. These spot checks can be done during briefing sessions, evaluation periods, meal breaks, or any impromptu meeting that may occur during the work shift. Kates (1999) discusses critical incident stress exposure and the correlation of the exposure to the onset of severe posttraumatic stress disorder. The signs and symptoms of an individual in crisis as a result of critical incident stress can mirror the warning signs of suicide. The supervisor is in a position to insure proper critical incident debriefing procedures and follow up care is given those employees potentially affected by a traumatic event. The ability and skill to recognize suicidal symptoms and behavior in subordinates comes through structured training, caring, and compassion. Further, good supervisors realize the personnel that make up a law enforcement agency are the most important and valued resources. With training in suicide prevention and intervention tactics, the law enforcement supervisor could literally save the lives of those he or she leads.

Supervisors need to closely observe and learn the personality characteristics of those they are assigned to lead. One-on-one meetings should be conducted between the supervisor and his/her subordinates on a regular basis. This is an excellent means by which clues of possible depression, anxiety, or a host of other psychological maladies can be noted and a possible intervention started. It is highly recommended that departments incorporate supervisory training narrowly and specifically related to the warning signs of those officers that may be considering suicide. Although the reasons for maladaptive behavior are complex, the supervisor is in an excellent position to identify and lead those employees in crisis to treatment. Not only is it important for supervisors to recognize such behavior, they should know the intervention steps necessary for those in need of treatment. All law enforcement agencies should have a mental health professional identified and trained in dealing with law enforcement psychological trauma. Furthermore, supervisor behavior has an important role to play in the development of stress risk management strategies capable of accommodating repetitive exposure to challenging events (see Chapter 10).

PEER SUPPORT PROGRAMS IN LAW ENFORCEMENT

The prevention of maladaptive behavior requires a strong support system. To the police officer, no one is better qualified to understand "the job" more than another police officer (Hackett, 2004). Peer support program seem to work very well for suicide intervention. Peer support within law enforcement agencies is hardly a new concept. Law enforcement officers have always confided in their peers when the going gets tough. Each agency seems to have those individuals who are natural, often informal leaders in which others are drawn to during difficult times. These trusted coworkers are usually natural listeners and very adept at communication skills. Most of all, they are trusted, approachable, and compassionate. In a nutshell, they have that ability to help others through difficult times and get them back on track.

Peer support and counseling can most accurately be described as a process whereby officers who feel a need to communicate their feelings about the job, their home life, or a combination of the two, may do so with other officers that are trained to assist. In structured law enforcement peer support programs, peer counselors are formally trained by mental health professionals in topical areas such as counseling skills, crisis theory and intervention, early warning signs of prolonged or acute stress, suicide assessment, alcohol and substance abuse, and matters of confidentiality. Overall, the peer counselor's mission is to provide a confidential outlet, then decide if further referral to a mental health professional is necessary.

From the perspective of taking a proactive, preventative approach to managing risk, developing high quality peer relationships is an activity that plays a pivotal role in this process (see Chapter 10). A need to re-examine how peer and supervisor relationships influence the life arises as a result of demographic influences on how trajectories are described. It is to a discussion of how one such demographic change, the gender distribution of police officers, influences life trajectories that this book now turns.

Chapter 6

GENDER DIFFERENCES IN POLICING

INTRODUCTION

Up to this point, discussions of the transitions and trajectories that comprise the police career have been treated as being broadly applicable to all officers. In Chapter 4, Burke's (2009) work introduced the possibility that gender could interact with the socialization experience (i.e., the process of acculturation) in ways that could have different implications for male and female officers. This makes it pertinent to consider how being a female member of a police organization can affect the life-course trajectory and its interface with critical incident stress risk. This is the subject matter of this chapter.

According to Patterson (2001), the study of the influence of demographic patterns on the exposure to traumatic incidents and their consequences in law enforcement in general is an underresearched area. He examined the effects of demographic characteristics on exposure to traumatic incidents in a sample of 233 police officers and found correlational evidence of a relationship between demographic variables and traumatic incidents. This suggests that the comprehensive understanding of critical incident stress risk requires that demographic factors be added to the research agenda.

Female gender has been identified as a risk factor for developing posttraumatic stress disorder (PTSD) in several studies, but its role in the course of PTSD, or as a factor capable of specifically influencing vulnerability, has not been elucidated completely (O'Toole, Marshall, Schureck, & Dobson, 1998). Kessler et al. (1995) found a lifetime prevalence of 10.4 percent PTSD for women and a prevalence of 5.0

percent for men in the general population. These results are consistent with the findings of other studies that described the risk of PTSD to be almost twice as high in women as in men (Halligan & Yehuda, 2000, Breslau, Chilcoat, Kessler et al., 1999). Community studies have also revealed higher rates of PTSD in women than in men (Davis & Breslau, 1998). Andrews, Brewin, and Rose (2003), referring to the meta-analysis of Brewin, Andrews, and Valentine (2000), also report that in civilian samples, women are at higher risk than men. Gender thus becomes a factor deserving of attention in police populations.

The question is then, what is it about gender that night influence critical incident stress risk? Is it gender per se, or is it an artifact of gender such as the types of incidents that female officers are more likely to experience? Answers to questions such as these will have an important bearing on how knowledge of the relationship between gender and posttrauma outcome is utilized with critical incident stress risk management programs. For example, can male and female officers be differentiated with regard to the kinds of incidents they attend, or more specifically the kinds of incidents they are deployed to attend? If the kinds of incidents officers are deployed to can be differentiated along gender lines, this opens up opportunities to explore another way in which thinking (and decisions) implicit within the way in which the police culture manifests itself could affect risk.

Patterson (2001) discussed how female officers reported exposure to more traumatic events than their male counterparts. Patterson assumes that the gender differences in terms of psychological reactions are associated to the degree of identification with victims, frequency of exposure to victims, and coping styles. This reiterates the need to include gender as a specific issue in risk management programs in police agencies.

Fullerton et al. (2001) claim that only few studies have investigated the reasons why female gender is a risk factor regarding PTSD without controlling the type of trauma, which was found to be different in women and men and to influence the rates of PTSD. Hence, the important feature seems to be the specificity of a potentially traumatic incident, not only the amount of exposure. Freedman, Gluck, Tuval-Mashiach et al. (2002) state that research on exposure to specific events indicates that men are exposed to combat, muggings, or beatings, more often, while women experience higher rates of rape and sexual assault. Breslau, Chilcoat, Kessler et al. (1999) also found women to be exposed to rape and other sexual assault more often, as well as higher rates in men of military combat, being shot or stabbed, mugged, or threatened with a weapon and beating. In addition to these findings, their results indicated higher prevalence of men being exposed to serious car accidents, other serious accidents, and witnessing acts of violence like killing or serious injury. Since they did not find gender differences in the total number of potentially traumatic events people were exposed to, the conclusion was drawn that women are more vulnerable to developing PTSD as a consequence of traumatic experiences. Others, however, suggested that the higher prevalence of PTSD in women reflects a higher rate of exposure to incidents that are more challenging in type and severity (Breslau et al., 1999). Freedman, Gluck, Tuval-Mashiach et al. (2002) emphasize that research on gender differences in terms of prevalence and intensity of PTSD is indistinct and not sufficient. Nevertheless, the fact that female gender has been implicated as a risk factor for PTSD in several studies calls for its inclusion in research into critical incident stress risk and in risk management strategies used to mitigate this risk. Consistent with the environmental theme adopted in the present text, it is argued that a comprehensive understanding of the role of gender as a risk factor cannot be fully achieved unless it is discussed in the context of the organizational culture in which female officers work.

POLICE CULTURE AND WOMEN OFFICERS

> When intervention programs focus exclusively on the individual and his behavior, they ignore the fact that these behaviors occur in a social and cultural context. (Syme, 1991, p. 11)

Critical incident stress risk in police officers derives not only from the high level of exposure to critical incidents characteristic of the profession, but also from the culture and organizational structure of the police occupation. Both represent important antecedents of critical incident stress risk in traumatic situations. It is, however, also important to acknowledge that culture and critical incidents are linked in many other ways. One relates to the fact that recognition (by police officers themselves, the public, the media, etc.) of policing as an occupation that is fundamentally one of the most dangerous in our society is fundamental to sustaining its unique culture (Woody, 2005).

To understand occupational exposure to traumatic incidents amongst police officers, and to use this knowledge for prevention programs, interpreting officers' experiences in the context of the police occupation and its culture is vital. As introduced earlier, culture can be defined as a pattern of basic assumptions, invented, discovered, or developed by a given group, as it learns to cope with its problems of external adaptation and internal integration (Schein, 1990). Because the assumptions that are embodied in culture have worked well enough to be considered valid in the past, they are deemed important enough to be taught and transmitted to new members as the correct way to perceive, think, and feel in relation to the issues and problems that arise in a profession. This is accomplished through the process of socialization in general and through mechanisms such as training and performance management in particular. It was in the context of the process of socialization that led Burke (2009) to argue that while socialization led to progressively greater levels of similarity in male and female officers over time, female officers may have experienced more acculturation stress and, at least during the early stages of their career, some of this similarity could represent some kind of social desirability.

According to Schein, culture has three levels: artifacts (e.g., uniforms, badges of rank, awards for bravery), espoused values (e.g., to emotional disclosure), and basic underlying assumptions (e.g., autocratic operational management). He states that culture is an outcome of shared experiences (e.g., through training, interaction with peers and senior officers). The basic element is the attempt to resolve fundamental problems of adapting to the external world and achieving internal integration and consistency (e.g., the similarity reported by Burke—see Chapter 4). This results in a "collective pool of knowledge that determines what is appropriate behavior, directs understanding and gives guidance on how to resolve problems" (Kampanakis, 2000, p. 2).

Culture is sustained by socialization and organizational systems and procedures. The first step in the socialization process is recruitment and selection of new group members (see Chapter 3). Candidates who already have the appropriate set of assumptions, beliefs, and values are more likely to become new members of the organization (Kampanakis, 2000). Culture also can be defined as "a body of knowledge that emerges through the shared application of practical skills to concrete problems encountered in daily routines and the normal course of activities" (Kampanakis, 2000, p. 3). Experiences shared by group members result in knowledge how to act and how to think about work.

The police occupation has specific cultural values like masculinity and patriarchal attitudes, control of affective responses to distressing circumstances, effectiveness and competitiveness, and helper stereotype and authority, which have a significant influence on the impact of traumatic experiences within this work environment. Police culture is characterized by political conservatism, cynicism, a sense of suspicion, isolation from social life, a peculiar sense of colleague solidarity, a code of silence, racial prejudices, and categorizing citizens as either rough or respectable (Kampanakis, 2000).

Pieper and Maercker (1999) stated that specific cultural values were the root cause of the fact that, for a long time, police officers had to cope on their own with the traumatic experiences they experienced through their work. The link between this expectation and the stereotypes listed above can be drawn. The image of a "real man," especially within this occupation, is determined by components like feeling no fear, no pain, no helplessness, no grief, and no trauma. This was encapsulated with the "helper stereotype" (Short, 1979) that described officers as powerful, resourceful, and able to put things right no matter what. To be strong and independent represents the typical ideal of a personality for this occupation. Over time, constructions of masculinity and police culture exercise a reciprocal influence on each other. Consequently, it is not clear if masculinity is due to the police occupation or if it is just used or cultivated by police (Behr, 2002).

The occupation of policing has traditionally been considered to be a masculine domain (Blok & Brown, 2005). The distribution of full-time sworn personnel in local police departments (population served–all sizes, U.S. 2000) confirms the tradition. Female officers represent the minority, and account for some 10.6 percent of officers (Sourcebook of Criminal Justice Statistics 2003, p. 48). However, in large city police departments, there are signs that a trend towards increased female representation is becoming evident, with female sworn personnel in 1990 accounting for 12.1 percent and in 2000 some 16.3 percent (population served–total, U.S. 1990 and 2000, Sourcebook of Criminal Justice Statistics 2003, p. 53) of serving officers.

Blok and Brown (2005) state that changes have occurred in how police services deploy male and female officers. While they state that officers of either gender are likely to be deployed to the majority of incidents, women officers were more likely to be deployed to sexual offences. This supports the contention introduced above that decisions about the deployment of officers may be based on implicit cultural assumptions about the relationship between gender and incident type.

Patterns of deployment along gender lines, whether conscious or otherwise, have other implications. For example, with regard to the overall trend towards interpersonal and communication skills and away from physical skills pre-eminent in more traditional models of policing. In their study based on the responses of 101 operational uniformed police constables and 150 members of the public, Blok and Brown (2005) found few gender differences. For example, women rated themselves as having more skill than men in deployments for domestic violence, missing adults, indecent assaults, and delivering death messages. Furthermore, women officers are more likely to follow protocol in their approach to policing than are men. What implications do these findings have for understanding critical incident stress risk and its management?

Women Officers and Critical Incident Stress Risk

Freedman et al.'s (2002) study did not indicate gender differences in the total amount of lifetime exposure to potentially traumatic incidents. Therefore, they assumed that gender differences in the incidence of traumatic stress reactions to critical incidents could be explained by the gender specific attributes of those responding or by differences in the types of critical incidents that male and female officers responded to. Especially in the police occupation, gender specific attributes or rather stereotypes are significant features. Niland (1996) states that "policing is one of the world's most masculinised occupations" (p. 2). One gender specific prejudice illustrated by Niland is the "women as risks" argument, which means that male officers put themselves under risk when they rely on someone who is "not physically able to support them in dangerous situations and protect them in return" (p. 3). Women do not fit naturally in a masculinized context, which hinders their integration and thereby limits access to social support from colleagues. Furthermore, working in such a context tends to put female officers in the position of the "weak one." This may have the effect of creating a self-fulfilling prophecy in case of trauma and therefore may intensify any adverse impacts that could arise form their critical incident experiences. This is valid for secondary traumatic stress as well, which represents a significant source of stress risk for police officers.

Concentrating on secondary traumatic stress, Patterson (2001) presumed that gender differences in psychological reactions are associated to the degree of identification with victims. Proceeding on the assumption that women are exposed to rape and sexual assault more often, while men experience higher rates of physical violence like stabbing, beating, mugging, or shooting as research indicates, one could suppose female officers to be more affected by victims of sexual violence and male officers by victims of physical violence. On the other hand, being confronted by traumatic incidents is only one side of the coin. Reactions of significant others also play a role after experiencing trauma.

Gender and Social Support

To perceive social support influences the impacts of a trauma and the coping process, Allen (1995, p. 186) argues, "the availability of social support and the capacity to make use of it can protect traumatized persons from developing PTSD." According to Baumann, Humer, Lettner, and Thiele (1998), social support improves well-being in general. Although social support can be seen as a protective factor, it may also be a stressor itself. Hence, Baumann et al. discuss that the concept of social support needs to be supplemented by social burden or stress.

One hypothesis that can be proposed when considering social support assumes that there is a direct positive effect of social support on health and well-being. In contrast, the indirect hypothesis supposes that social support influences health, because it lessens the negative effects of stress. Inadequate support, overprotection, or unintentional side effects are seen as negative social support. The distinction between negative and positive effects of social support is not possible all the time, because both aspects may interact. Thus, a clear categorization of social support in either protective or vulnerability factor is not possible. Nevertheless positive social support may help a person to cope effectively with traumatic experiences. The question is then one of whether the kinds of gender-event differentiation introduced above can influence the quality of female officers experience of incidents and their psychological consequences.

Andrews, Brewin, and Rose (2003) focused on gender differences in social support. As they state, "women's higher risk might involve differences in both the levels and benefits of support received by men and women in response to trauma" (p. 421). They elucidate to have found that even though male and female victims of violent crime reported a similar level of received positive support and an equal support satisfaction, women had a greater likelihood to report negative reactions from family and friends. That is, they will experience fewer opportunities to engage those close to them for discussing their experiences. Some of this can be attributed to a desire not to expose loved ones and close friends to the more traumatic, threatening, or distasteful aspects to the job (see Chapters 4 and 9). This is, however, not the only possible reason for this.

To explain these findings, Andrews et al. (2003) refer to Turner and Rozell (1994) who illustrated that women's higher levels of negative responses from family and friends might be due to their greater social involvement. That would mean that the more people one is interacting with, the greater the possibility of being a recipient of negative responses or the more likely one is to be called upon to provide support for someone displaying a negative response to an experience. One could also assume that avoidance as part of the coping process after experiencing a trauma is hindered by social contacts, since interaction usually includes inquiring one's well-being, as well as emotional expressions. Therefore, even relatively minor points or innocuous remarks might remind a person of his or her traumatic experience or the feelings associated with it. Social interaction can stress an officer, since it means contact with persons and therefore it is harder to control affective responses as well as to maintain avoidance.

While it can be hypothesized that differences in the nature or use of social networks could influence stress risk in different ways for male and female officers, additional work is required to determine whether differences in the nature of the incidents that each gender attends adds further complexity to this process. It is possible to speculate that such differences could affect the quality of support available from one's colleagues. For example, limited experience of particular kinds of events would reduce the ability of female officers to receive constructive advice or support from their male counterparts. Answers to this question must await further research.

An occupational culture both confers benefits on officers and imposes constraints on them. In practical terms, a police officer gains benefits from and is protected by the police culture yet is also vulnerable to the risk of adverse effects, such as loss of social resources such as would arise if the characteristics of the culture influence the quality of support and nature of social support available (Paton & Stephens, 1996; Woody, 2005). To be identified as not being fully part of the organization implies that identification might be less strong in female officers, thereby reducing the influence of the effects of police culture. However, while this can mean that the negative (from a critical incident stress risk perspective) may be diminished, the positive effects (e.g., cohesion) may also suffer. What this discussion does reveal is that there is a rich vein of complex and dynamic issues to be mined in future research.

Along with the officer's professional life, other sources of influence exist as well, such as from family, friends, and subculture memberships. This multiplicity of different values and beliefs from influential sources will produce conflicting expectations and demands on the officer (Woody, 2005). The gap for women officers is even greater, with being a woman in private life on one hand and part of a traditionally masculine occupation on the other. If not resolved effectively, the associated conflicts can lead to high levels of stress. The possible disruption between the police culture and other subcultures, like the officer's family, can have devastating effects on nearly all types of personal interactions as well as intrapersonal consonance (e.g., inability to have healthy relationships, or emotional disturbance). With respect to its influence on coping with a traumatic experience, this kind of disruption is likely to increase the likelihood of adverse posttraumatic stress outcomes.

Being a women officer can be both an advantage and disadvantage. Less identification with the occupational image may support the personal distance and thereby help managing traumatic work encounters. The limited social support, on the other hand, however, can aggravate the coping with trauma on the job. Overall the contents of the preceding discussion suggest that being a women officer is something of a double-edged sword.

Despite it having been a male-orientated profession since its inception, the contents of this chapter reflects the growing presence of female officers in contemporary police agencies and this introduces a transition stimulus for police agencies. For female officers, the transitions that contribute to their life-course trajectories will, as a result of their career development taking place in a male-dominated professional culture, differ in some respects from the course followed by their male counterparts. However, because trajectories are interconnected and have reciprocal effects on one another (see Chapter 1), the trajectories of male officers will also be affected and the gradual shift in culture that will ensue will affect the career trajectories of all future officers.

The change wrought by this demographic shift is taking place at a relatively slow pace. This need not always be the case for changes that can occur in the environment of policing. The events of 9/11 describe how a crisis event created far-reaching implications for police agencies and the life-course trajectories of the officers who work in them. The enduring legacy of 9/11 for officers and agencies is examined in Chapters 7 and 8 respectively.

Chapter 7

THE CHANGING NATURE OF EXPOSURE DURING THE POLICE CAREER: TERRORISM AND TRAUMA

INTRODUCTION

While events such as commencing employment and becoming a sworn officer represent fixed transitions, the trajectory of police life can be affected by events that emerge from significant changes in society. Some of these can have profound and enduring consequences for the trajectories of serving and for future officers. A good example of one such change was 9/11. The emergence of terrorism on the landscape of policing has had significant implications for agencies (see Chapter 8) and officers. It is the implications that it has had for the latter that is considered in this chapter.

Terrorism today represents a significant risk factor for psychological trauma in police work. It is, however, possible to influence the outcome of terror trauma in officers; as such events have the potential to either impact posttrauma pathology or positive outcomes. Acts of terrorism represent a significant risk factor for psychological trauma (Galea et al., 2002; Shuster et al., 2001), and the protective services and disaster mental health professionals who respond to them are not immune from this consequence (Brown, Mulhern, & Joseph, 2002; Creamer & Liddle, 2005; North et al., 2002). Law enforcement officers are in the front line for exposure to acts of terrorism. However, the fact that response to terror events can result in both posttrauma pathology and positive outcomes (North et al., 2002) begs the question of whether it is possible to influence this outcome. This chapter utilizes a risk management paradigm which may be used to minimize the pathogenic impact of terror events on law enforcement officers and uses this to frame recommendations for strategies to promote an adaptive response to this growing threat to contemporary policing.

The pursuit of this goal requires several inputs. One involves identifying the specific physical, social, and psychological challenges that officers will have to respond to. Another is concerned with identifying factors that determine whether outcome of responding to these challenges is characterized by deficit or pathological outcomes or by resilient and adaptive outcomes.

Terrorist stress risk factors can rarely be identified from the event (e.g., detonating a weapon of mass destruction, flying a plane into a building) per se. They can, however, be discerned in the hazardous event characteristics (e.g., confronting biohazard agents, dealing with human remains, handling infectious materials, making complex and urgent decisions under conditions of uncertainty) that officers confront when performing their professional role. The nature of the police role precludes preventing exposure to terrorist events as a mitigation strategy, but managing this risk by altering the consequences of exposure to such events presents a viable alternative. The fact that officers will be called upon repeatedly to deal with terrorist events, and may experience prolonged periods of involvement under hazardous conditions makes a proactive approach important. This chapter outlines approaches to proactive primary prevention to mitigate traumatic stress risk by identifying those factors that influence posttrauma outcomes by reducing those that lead to the experience of deficit outcomes and increasing those that facilitate a resilient and adaptive response. Developing a comprehensive understanding of the issues that need to be accommodated is aided by conceptualizing the response to critical incidents and acts of terrorism as a sequential process whose nature, and whose implications for officers' critical incident stress risk, changes over time.

TERRORIST RESPONSE AS A SEQUENTIAL PROCESS

Officers' experience of terror events will evolve over time as they progress through a series of stages, each with its own unique demands and characteristics, and thus implications for trauma risk. These stages are the alarm/warning and mobilization phase, the response phase, and the process of reintegration into routine work following the termination of their deployment (Hartsough & Myers, 1985). The following is a discussion of these stages. In terms of the career-wide impact of these stages, they may be considered transitory for each experienced terrorist event. The accumulation of trajectories brought on by these events (either positive or pathogenic) may depend heavily on the reaction of peers, the police organization, and the timing and intensity of the terrorist events.

Mobilization–Response to Terror Events

The alarm phase describes the period of comprehending and adjusting to the occurrence of a terrorist event. During this phase, officers are tasked with, for example, accessing intelligence about what has happened, differentiating fact from inference, and making sense of the confusing and often ambiguous information. In addition to coming to terms with the reality of a terror attack, acute stress reactions can also be attributed to the demands associated with adapting plans to deal with urgent, emergent and evolving emergency demands (Brake, 2001; HBWMD, 2001; Kendra & Wachtendorf, 2003), and negotiating operational arrangements with other agencies and jurisdictions (Brake, 2001; Department of Homeland Security, 2003; Grant et al., 2003). Irrespective of the quality of planning for terrorist events, the translation of plans into operational reality remains a contentious issue (Department of Homeland Security, 2003; Grant et al., 2003; McKinsey, 2002), with the different statutory and regulatory frameworks that prescribe how agencies (e.g., law enforcement, military) define and engage in the response being prominent contributors to this discrepancy (Brake, 2001). It is not response as normal, but responding in conditions of uncertainty in a physically, socially, and organizationally complex environment.

Terror events can also create highly dangerous operating environments. A prominent source of stress risk is the complexity of consequences created. For example, a biohazard attack (e.g., pollution of water supplies, release of a biohazard such as smallpox) may have commenced prior to its existence being identified, present diffuse beginnings and ends, spread in ways dictated by local conditions (e.g., building density, topography, and prevailing weather), create relatively prolonged periods of impact, and result in a complex social environment characterized by confusion and uncertainty in the general public (Department of Homeland Security, 2003; Fisher, 2000; HBWMD, 2001; Lasker, 2004). Public uncertainty regarding what they should do to protect themselves can increase their reliance on officers for information. However, under these circumstances, they may not have recourse to the normal means of reassuring citizens (Fisher, 2000; Lasker, 2004).

Stress risk is increased if deployment precedes a full appreciation of the nature or implications of a terror event. Given the complexity and uncertainty associated with terrorist events, this is likely to become the norm. The consequences of operating in an environment defined by this uncertainty can be gleaned from looking at previous work on response to acts of terrorism. For example, police officers deployed immediately to the site of the Lockerbie disaster found it difficult to comprehend the carnage and death encountered (Mitchell, 1991). While performing similar duties in a similar environment, officers deployed after the cause of the event had been identified (a terrorist bombing) reported significantly lower levels of stress. Being able to define their situation as a criminal investigation allowed the second group of officers to apply professional schema (e.g., conceptualizing the work of handling human remains as an evidence gathering procedure) to render the experience more meaningful. The organizational role is to facilitate this capacity to impose meaning on threatening and challenging demands to limit the likelihood that officers will be overwhelmed by the scale, uncertainty, or the horror in the situation they must contend with (Paton, 1994).

For officers, the uncertainty (e.g., regarding what has happened, its consequences, whether future acts will occur etc.) surrounding terror increases the likelihood that they will have to deal with concerns for their families (HBWMD, 2001). This marks a significant departure from other emergency events and makes a substantial contribution to the stress risk associated with acts of terrorism.

Managing traumatic stress risk during this phase involves guarding against mobilization plans being based on assumptions derived from routine emergencies or on unrealistic or untested plans (Carafano, 2003; Department of Homeland Security, 2003; Lasker, 2004; Paton & Flin, 1999). They must be derived from accurate analyses of community (e.g., accommodate the need to reconcile different actions) and professional (e.g., concerns for self and family, having to adapt plans to accommodate emergent issues) response needs and expectations, and be designed to accommodate the unique demands (e.g,. a biohazard response) likely to be encountered. Developing effective stress management plans also requires an understanding of how these issues influence risk during the response phase.

Stress Risk During Response to Acts of Terrorism

Despite a long history of responding to emergency events, the psychological contexts (e.g., with regard to vulnerability and assumptions of safety) and demands associated with terrorist events present protective services officers with a unique set of problems (Carafano, 2003). For example, one significant departure from "routine" events is the unique capability of terror events to create a sustained climate of fear. They can also involve hazard agents (e.g., biohazard and radiological agents) that are difficult to detect, that can create significant acute and chronic health problems, and generate consequences that may persist for long periods of time. Given the novelty, complexity, and uncertainty associated with terror events, stress risk is inevitably heightened. If the nature of the factors that determine whether risk is resolved in a pathological or adaptive manner is known, it may be possible to use this knowledge to manage stress risk emanating from this source. However, some of the factors that influence how risk is resolved are less amenable to such intervention.

Officers' history of traumatic experience prior to their employment falls into this category (Violanti & Paton, 2006), as do transient factors such as health status, fatigue, and occupational stress. Sources of post-trauma vulnerability derived from biological and genetically-based predispositions (e.g., heightened autonomic and physiological reactivity), and historical antecedents (e.g., pre-existing psychopathology), do not lend themselves to intervention (Scotti, Beach, Northrop, Rode, & Forsyth, 1995). However, though not amenable to direct intervention, knowledge of these factors can be incorporated into the risk assessment process using a vulnerability coefficient (Violanti & Paton, 2006) that can be used to assess for tertiary intervention. However, vulnerability emanating from psychological factors (e.g., social skills deficits that limit use of social support, inadequate problem-solving behavior) are open to change through development (Scotti et al., 1995).

Vulnerability is also affected by the fact that the schema or mental models that underpin how people interpret and comprehend complex experiences have been rendered less applicable by the growing threat of terrorism (Daw, 2001).

Zimbardo (2001) stated that the fear generated by terrorism undercuts the sense of trust, stability, and confidence in one's personal world. The fact that the 9/11 attacks were deliberate human acts made them particularly distressing for Americans and contributed substantially to their loss of perceived safety and security. This lost sense of safety and security may be accompanied by feelings of helplessness and anxiety (Figley, 1985). In addition, unlike natural disasters, the fear and feelings of vulnerability generated by terrorism have the capability to spread to general as well as local populations, and persist for considerably longer periods of time. Public uncertainty, and the very real possibility that members of the public will act in ways that are inconsistent with the assumptions of public response encapsulated in formal response plans (Lasker, 2004), will contribute additional demands to the response context and create an additional source of uncertainty for officers. One reason why public response can differ from that assumed in formal plans arises from the diverse ways in which fear is manipulated as a weapon of terrorism.

The fear instilled by terrorism works by introducing a new mind set dominated by preoccupation with the fear of reoccurrence. Once victimized, it is relatively easy to see oneself in the role again; the experience is now "available" and one sees oneself as "representative" of those victimized (Maercker & Muller, 2004; Kahneman & Tversky, 1973; Lasker, 2004; North et al., 2005). The assumptions that had formerly enabled people to function effectively can no longer be relied on as guides for behavior (Janoff-Bulman & Freize, 1983). Consequently, everyone, police officers and citizens alike, must explore a new way of being (Daw, 2001) and knowledge of terrorists, their culture, language, and psychology must be encapsulated in schema that can assist adjusting to this new reality. Because it is difficult to anticipate how fear will affect public response, the climate of fear represents another source of uncertainty in the response environment.

The new interpretive mechanisms that derive from this climate of fear will have important implications for police officers who may have to confront the consequences of terrorism and respond to meet the challenges it poses to themselves and the communities they serve. At present, more work has to be done to understand how public interpretation will influence the response environment. However, Lasker's (2004) work warns of a need to gain a better understanding of public behavior. While it is currently difficult to accommodate implications of these kinds of interpretive process in a risk management program from the point of view of developing specific strategies, the uncertainty associated with this aspect of response can be accommodated within residual risk assessment (Violanti, 2006). It is, however, possible to attend to managing risk from the more tangible aspects of the demands posed by acts of terrorism. How this might be accomplished is discussed in the context of the characteristics of terrorist events that officers must confront and the personal and organizational competences mobilized to manage the response (Alper & Kupferson, 2003; Grant et al., 2003; Kendra & Wachtendorf, 2003; Paton & Hannan, 2004; Simpson & Stehr, 2003).

Event Characteristics

Because the causes of acts of terrorism can always be attributed to deliberate human action intended to cause harm, they threaten perceived control, a prominent stressor in police officers whose training is designed to promote control (MacLeod & Paton, 1999; Myers, 2001). The magnitude of the death and injury encountered, coupled in many cases with uncertainty regarding cause of death or whether those they come into contact with are infectious, provides a further source of stress risk (Jackson et al., 2003).

Stress risk can be particularly pronounced when performing body recovery and identification duties (North et al., 2002). For large scale events, like those presented by the aftermath of the World Trade Center collapse, the time frame for body recovery can be prolonged (Simpson & Stehr, 2003). Working in close proximity to dead or seriously injured victims, particularly if coupled with a perceived lack of opportunity for effective action, results in officers facing constant reminders of their (perceived) inability to deal with this loss and suffering. The ensuing reduction in officers' sensitivity to the needs of others as they attempt to shut out these signals can reduce their willingness to utilize support resources (Paton & Stephens, 1996; Raphael, 1986), and increase their risk of experiencing posttrauma stress reactions.

The scale of events such as the attack on and subsequent collapse of the World Trade Center in 2001 presents officers with a set of circumstances in which the demands will, often by a substantial amount, exceed the resources available to respond to them effectively. Such events can also present new demands for which appropriate response resources are not available. Perceptions of having insufficient, inadequate, or inappropriate resources to perform response tasks can fuel a sense of inadequacy and increase stress vulnerability (Carafano, 2003; Paton, 1994). This is true even when it was the sheer scale of the event, rather than any lack of capability on the part of the officers themselves, that limits any scope of effective action (Paton & Stephens, 1996). Terror events can also affect role demands as, for example, officers have to deal with the response environment being simultaneously a disaster area, a crime scene, and a mass grave (Simpson & Stehr, 2003).

Uncertainty regarding, for example, the duration of their involvement or additional attacks heightens officers' stress risk, as does their exposure to personal danger. With regard to sources of danger, exposure to events that pose unseen threats (e.g., highly toxic chemical, biological, or radiation hazards), by making it more difficult for emergency responders to directly observe what they need to take protective actions against, contribute substantially to stress risk. Environmental factors such as heat, noise, or poor visibility affect stress risk (Vrij, van der Steen, & Koppelaar, 1994). The need for protective clothing contributes to stress risk directly (e.g., its use is necessitated by the use of biological or chemical contaminants) and indirectly (e.g., increased heat stress from wearing protective clothing and from additional problems with operating equipment (Carafano, 2003)). Increased danger also emanates from the fact that, when responding to terror events, the scene could become an intentionally hostile environment for them (Department of Homeland Security, 2003; FEMA, 2004; Maniscalco & Christen, 2002). That is, they must attend events knowing that they may be being deliberately targeted. In addition to this constituting a personal threat, added stress is likely to result from their not being able to help those affected immediately and only being able to do so when its has been deemed safe for them to act.

This brief discussion of the hazards that offices will encounter reiterates the fact that terror events present an operating context that can be qualitatively and quantitatively different from that characterizing their routine work. The importance of this issue stems from the fact that the psychological foundation upon which officers' competencies are based derives from their "routine" training and experience. Officers' needs have been underestimated because expectations have been based largely on the training they have received and any experience of responding to routine events or possibly from some experience of responding to natural and manmade disasters. These experiences provide the raw material that is formed into the schema or mental models officers use to anticipate what they may have to deal with and that are brought to bear on how they respond, physically, socially, and psychologically, to events. However, past experience may not be accurate predictors of conditions officers could encounter in a determined, protracted terrorist campaign, thus calling the effectiveness of officers' mental models into question (Brake, 2001; Carafano, 2003; Kendra & Wachtendorf, 2003; Paton, 1994).

The schema or mental models that guide response to terror events reflect officers' socialization into their profession and organization, their training, the experiences they accumulate over time, and the operating practices that prescribe how they respond to routine emergencies. These become implicit, or taken for granted, aspects of the mental models used by officers to make predictions about future events, organize experiences, and make sense of the consequences of events and their reactions to them. However, their importance as determinants of well-being and performance effectiveness tends to remain unrealized until officers encounter events that challenge these implicit assumptions (Paton, 1994) and that can occur when schema developed through routine training and experience are applied to more complex terrorist events. Consequently, training for terrorist events must confront these assumptions and facilitate the development of interpretative competencies capable of accommodating the reality of the response environment. In addition, they must accommodate the legacy (e.g., increased levels of fear in the community, changes in security precautions, perceiving the world as increasingly threatening) of terrorism into their thinking (see above).

Interpretive processes influence outcome in other ways. For example, the scale and complexity of terrorist impact can limit opportunities for effective action. Stress risk increases if any failure is attributed to personal inadequacy rather than to environmental constraints beyond an officer's control (MacLeod & Paton, 1999). However, training that develops realistic outcome expectations, an ability to differentiate personal and situational constraints, and interpretive processes that review experiences as learning opportunities to enhance future competence reduces stress risk (Dunning, 2003; Paton, 1994). Positive interpretation (e.g., interpreting body recovery duties in terms of their role in assisting families to begin the grieving process and not as performance failure on the part of the officers themselves) can also facilitate adaptation to the demands associated with body recovery duties (Deahl et al., 1994; Thompson, 1993).

In general, training that develops a capability for operational mental models (essential to response planning and organizing action) to impose coherence upon atypical and challenging experiences and to accommodate the demands encountered should be an essential component of stress risk management (Dunning, 2003; Paton, 1994; Paton & Hannan, 2004). A capacity for reframing can be developed using simulations. Simulations provide opportunities to conceptualize and review response activities, construct realistic performance expectations, increase awareness of stress reactions, and to use feedback about stress reactions and how to manage them to rehearse strategies to progressively develop a capacity to adapt to and cope with complex operational demands (Crego & Spinks, 1997; Paton & Jackson, 2002).

Developing these more sophisticated psychological structures requires that simulations are constructed using information derived from two sources. One concerns the systematic analysis of the competencies required for effective response to terrorist events. The second involves designing simulations capable of reconciling event characteristics (e.g., exposure to biohazards, personal danger, dealing with human remains and cross-cultural aspects of death and loss) with the competencies required to manage them (e.g., hazard identification and interpretation; adapting plans; team and multiagency operations; information and decision management) in ways that promotes adaptive capacity (Paton & Hannan, 2004).

Traditionally, the causes of traumatic stress reactions have been attributed to the horrific and threatening event characteristics (e.g., handling human remains) to which officers are exposed. While this aspect of a terror event will remain a prominent predictor of traumatic stress risk, it is not the only one. Organizational factors and the response protocols they prescribe also play a significant role as predictors of stress risk. What evidence supports a role for organizational factors as predictors of posttraumatic stress risk?

Organizational Factors

Officers' perception of organizational culture is a significant predictor of posttrauma risk (see Chapters 2, 3, 4, 8, and 9). Core aspects of organizational culture such as, for example, inadequate consultation, poor communication, a predisposition to protect the organization from criticism or blame, and excessive "red tape" can exercise a pervasive influence on stress risk (Gist & Woodall, 2000; Paton & Flin, 1999). Furthermore, stress risk is also increased if the response paradigm (e.g., command structure, level of autocracy, degree of devolved authority) is inappropriate and derived from those used for routine work (Carafano, 2003; McKinsey, 2002; Kendra & Wachtendorf, 2003; Paton & Hannan, 2004). However, culture that supports autonomous response systems, a flexible, consultative leadership style, and practices that ensure that role and task assignments reflect incident demands can facilitate resilience and reduce the risk of adverse stress outcomes (Gist & Woodall, 2000; McKinsey, 2002; Paton, 1999; Paton, Violanti, & Smith, 2003). Incident management practices should also address issues relating to the decision making and interagency collaborating that represent significant sources of demand on officers.

The dynamic and complex nature of terrorist events generates a need for a level of creative decision making that exceeds that required for response to "routine" emergencies (Jackson et al., 2003; Kendra & Wachtendorf, 2003). Stress risk is also heightened by having to deviate from the standard operational procedures associated with routine work and producing contingent solutions to novel problems. The capacity to do so can be facilitated by the associated stress, particularly if officers are trained in crisis decision making.

For trained personnel, crises enhance alertness and thinking skills (Flin, 1996). However, putting this to good use requires a capability to operate in environments characterized by information overload. Situational awareness, the capability to extract or operate on limited cues within a complex environment, and using them to construct mental models of complex events that allows naturalistic decision making can mitigate stress risk (Carafano, 2003; Endsley & Garland, 2000;

Paton & Hannan, 2004). In the complex interagency context of terror response, agencies need to be able to access, interpret, collate, and use information to manage complex events (Alper & Kupferman, 2003; FEMA, 2004; Grant et al., 2003; Jackson et al., 2003; McKinsey, 2002; Paton et al., 1999). That is, the information they require to manage the response will be sourced within a complex multiagency environment.

The Interagency Environment

A central characteristic of the response to acts of terrorism is the need for a multiagency and multijurisdictional response (Brake, 2001; Department of Homeland Security, 2003; FEMA, 2004; Grant et al., 2003; Jackson et al., 2003; Kendra & Wachtendorf, 2003). The complex nature of terrorist events brings together agencies that typically have little, if any, functional contact with one another under routine circumstances, reducing opportunities to allow shared understanding of their respective roles to develop. For example, response to terror events could include hazardous materials response teams; urban search and rescue teams; community emergency response teams; antiterrorism units; special weapons and tactics teams; bomb squads; emergency management officials; municipal agencies; and private organizations responsible for transportation, communications, medical services, public health, disaster assistance, public works, and construction workers (Carafano, 2003). Given the potential for role conflict and ambiguity under these circumstances, understanding and managing interagency and team issues becomes an important component of stress risk management.

Simply bringing together representatives of agencies who have little contact with one another under normal circumstances will not guarantee a coordinated response. Rather, such ad hoc arrangements can and are more likely to increase interagency conflict, resulting in a blurring of roles and responsibilities, and fueling frustration and feelings of inadequacy and helplessness (McKinsey, 2002; Paton, 1994). A capability for more effective multiagency response, and a reduction in the likelihood of this facet of the operating environment making an independent contribution to stress risk, can be developed by integrating respective agency roles through interagency team development (Brake, 2001; Flin & Arbuthnott, 2002; Grant et al., 2003; Paton et al.,

1999) that focuses on building understanding of the respective contributions of different agencies, develops collaborative management systems, and ensures effective interagency communication.

At one level, this issue reflects the need for structural integration between agencies to be matched by corresponding procedural or operational capacity to act in concert during a crisis (Paton et al., 1999). However, it also encompasses participants' understanding of their respective contributions to the same plan and their shared understanding of each member's role in the response (Brake, 2001; FEMA, 2004; Paton & Flin, 1999). This contributes to their capacity to share a common understanding of evolving events, to work towards common goals over time, and, importantly, to anticipate the needs of those with whom they are collaborating (Burghardt, 2004; Department of Homeland Security, 2003; Paton & Flin, 1999; Pollock et al., 2003; van der Lee and van Vugt, 2004).

Stress risk during response can be managed by developing the interpretative team and information and decision-making competencies required to impose a sense of coherence on atypical experiences and to deal with them effectively. It is also important to ensure that these competencies are activated within an organizational culture that supports and protects officers' well-being and that establishes response protocols that do likewise. While facilitating the proactive mitigation of stress risk during response, it is, however, important to note that termination of involvement in a specific event does not eliminate risk.

Managing Risk after the Event

The unique nature of terrorist events requires new approaches to postevent stress risk management (Carafano, 2003). As the response phase winds down and draws to a close, officers will face the challenge of reintegration into routine work. During reintegration, stress risk management involves managing the emotional correlates of involvement in a terrorist event and providing a framework within which officers can render atypical, threatening experiences meaningful. In this section, discussion focuses on strategies that can be used to assist officers to render their experiences meaningful and to learn from a given event in ways that can contribute to building future resilience.

The period of transition from responding to an act of terrorism back into routine work and family life poses a unique set of demands. Stress risk is not restricted to event experiences. It can also arise as from readjusting to routine work, catching up with any backlog of work, dealing with reporting pressures, confronting any sociolegal issues associated with responding to a complex criminal act, and dealing with intense public and media scrutiny. Sociolegal processes and media coverage can extend the period of event experience, and thus stress risk, substantially. During this time, officers may have to contend with blame (e.g., media accounts regarding event preventability, response effectiveness) being directed towards them or coming to terms with self-blame as they reflect on their role in the response. There are several ways in which risk can be managed during the reintegration phase, with social support having a prominent role in this process.

Solomon and Smith (1994) warn that if the demands on a social network for support occur at a time when all members have support needs, support provision itself can become a source of stress. This is particularly likely in the aftermath of terrorist events that create substantial ripple effects from the pervasive climate of fear that can affect whole communities and influence how events are interpreted or reported (e.g., perceiving the environment as more threatening). This issue also needs to be considered in the context of the cohesive team context within which officers usually work.

While cohesive teams can constitute a protective resource (Park, 1998), team cohesiveness can, ironically, contribute to stress vulnerability if situational constraints result in a response being perceived as less effective than anticipated. Some level of failure, relative to expectations derived from routine experience, is likely given the complex nature of terrorist events. Officers may find it difficult to perceive the positive characteristics in the group necessary to maintain a positive social identity. Under these circumstances, support networks break down (Hartsough & Myers, 1985), a negative social identity develops (Paton & Stephens, 1996), and the risk of acute stress reactions increases. Countering this possibility requires team processes that facilitate the realistic interpretation of circumstances that confront, for example, the pervasive sense of fear that accompanies acts of terrorism and cultural predispositions to martyrdom that create a unique source of risk.

Lyons et al. (1998) discuss the use of "communal coping" as a means of achieving this. This is characterized by officers' collective acceptance of responsibility for event-related problems and the existence of mechanisms that facilitate the ability of officers to cooperate to define and resolve problems, and to use this process to build their future capabilities. Acknowledging and building on effective collaboration during the crisis, and working together after the crisis, to develop understanding and enhance future preparedness has an important role to play in mitigating stress and in developing future stress resilience. It should, however, be borne in mind that recovery and reintegration and support practices occur within an organizational context.

Stress risk is increased if reintegration is experienced within an organizational culture that discourages emotional disclosure, focuses on attributing blame to officers, or minimizes the significance of their reactions or feelings (Paton & Stephens, 1996; MacLeod & Paton, 1999). Recovery can be hastened if the organizational culture encourages managers to actively promote reintegration.

Managers can assist adaptation by helping officers appreciate that they performed to the best of their ability, and reducing performance guilt by realistically reviewing how situational factors constrained performance (MacLeod & Paton, 1999). Managers can also facilitate positive resolution by assisting staff to identify the strengths that helped them deal with the terrorist emergency and building on this to plan how future events can be dealt with more effectively. If these actions are not taken, risk management programs should review the climate of relationships between managers and staff (e.g., trust) and seek ways to build this capacity (Gist & Woodall, 2000; Paton et al., 2003). Such analyses can promote future response effectiveness and contribute to the development and maintenance of a resilient organizational climate. Pursuing this objective may require some organizational change. This issue is tackled in Chapter 8.

CONCLUSION

Terrorism adds a new, unique and challenging dimension to the hazards faced by police organizations and, consequently, contributes substantially to the risk of acute stress and posttraumatic stress faced by officers. Terrorism necessitates making changes to several interventions (e.g., training needs analysis, training simulations) required to facilitate officer's capacities to negotiate a new set of transitions and to optimize their journey through their career trajectory (see Chapter 1). Because it is essential that emergency organizations learn from experience and develop a culture that facilitates adaptive capacity, stress risk management should be viewed as an iterative process that encompasses personal and organizational learning (see Chapter 10). However, before proceeding to address the latter issue, it is important to understand how terrorism has changed the context in which police activities are based. This issue is the subject of the next chapter.

Chapter 8

ACCOMMODATING TERRORISM AS RISK FACTOR: THE ORGANIZATIONAL PERSPECTIVE

INTRODUCTION

A key facet of life-course theory is its adoption of the principle of contextualization (see Chapter 1). This principle highlights the fact that officers' progress through the career trajectory cannot be understood in isolation from the context in which these trajectories are embedded (see Chapter 2). Because the police organization has a ubiquitous influence on both the way trajectories unfold and the interventions provided to facilitate officers' ability to negotiate these trajectories, it plays a key role in the development of a life-course perspective on police careers. Normally, the characteristics of the organization appear stable, with change occurring incrementally over time. There can, however, occur events of such significance that they require organizational change to ensure that the organization can continue to support the life course of its members. One such change occurred on 11th September, 2001. The advent of terrorism is used in this chapter to illustrate why and how organizational change is required to ensure that the police organization remains relevant as a context in which the police career unfolds.

Since 9/11, the environment of policing has changed irrevocably, with terrorism being an ever-present hazard for police agencies. Discussion in this chapter builds on the fact that officers respond to incidents as members of law enforcement agencies (see Chapters 1 and 2). As such, the organizational culture influences officers thoughts and actions and represents the context in which challenging (e.g., critical incident) experiences (e.g., through interaction with colleagues, senior officers, and organizational procedures) are made sense of (Gist & Woodall, 2000; Mitroff & Aragnos, 2001; Paton et al., 1999; Paton et al., 2003; Weick, 1995). Agency culture, as a result of its prescribing, for example, officer induction and socialization, organizational structure, operating and reporting procedures, performance expectations, and training influences how officers think about their role, their work, and how they impose meaning on the incidents they attend and the outcomes experienced as a result of responding to critical incidents (Gist & Woodall, 2000; Paton, 1994; Weick, 1995). Because of its influence on the interventions that describe why and how career transitions take place, organizational culture exercises an important influence on the development of the schema or interpretive frameworks (that reflect assumptions/expectations derived from socialization, routine training, experience, and organizational practices) that officers use to plan and organize their response to any incident they are called upon to respond to.

An event becomes critical when incident characteristics fall outside expected operational or response parameters and officers' mental models are unable to make sense of such novel, challenging events (Janoff-Bulman, 1992; Paton, 1994; Tedeschi & Calhoun, 2003). Consequently, when significant change occurs in the environment of policing, organizational change is required to provide an appropriate context for the life trajectories of officers and to ensure that the interventions remain appropriate for managing risk. In this context, the focus should be on understanding how agencies and officers can learn from their experience of challenging events and develop more sophisticated interpretive schema that facilitates their capacity to respond to, cope with, and adapt to future challenges (Paton et al., 2003). This makes it important to consider how learning takes place and how the lessons learned are sustained in the form of enhanced resilience.

Given the role of the agency in the development and maintenance of schema, any sustained benefit will be strongly influenced by the degree to which new insights, perspectives, knowledge, and relationships that emerge from the formal review of operational experience become embedded in the culture of the organization in ways that enhance future adaptive capacity. Thus, it is argued here that developing a comprehensive critical incident, stress risk management program requires analysis at the level of both agency and officer, with the interaction between them playing a pivotal role in understanding and managing risk by increasing those factors that facilitate resilience and adaptation and reducing those that increase vulnerability (Paton et al., 2003).

The need for change can also be traced to recognition that terrorism has resulted in significant changes to the environment within which police agencies and their officers work. This environment has not only become more challenging, it has also become more dynamic than has been the case in the past. It is just this kind of circumstance that prompted Berkes, Colding, and Folke (2003) to argue for organizations to develop their capacity to adapt to an uncertain and riskier future. This chapter first discusses the nature of the environmental change that an age of terrorism has introduced and its implications for organizational change. The second part of the chapter considers how interaction between agency and officer influences stress risk and strategies for increasing resilience.

Acts of Terrorism and the Environment of Contemporary Policing

Despite a long history of effectively responding to emergency events, the nature of terrorist events presents police agencies with a unique set of problems (Carafano, 2003). As Carafano points out, events such mass traffic accidents, plane crashes, and even mass shootings present a relatively more coherent response environment. For example, the latter incidents have a clear starting point, tend to be localized, have a finite duration, present a relatively predictable set of demands, and allow established procedures to be employed to manage the response. However, greater unpredictability regarding the nature and complexity (e.g., terrorists devote time to developing and implementing new ways to deliberately create maximum harm and fear), location, timing, and duration of acts of terrorism has created new challenges for agencies and officers. With terrorist events, the agency context is also rendered more complex by the need to operate under different legislative requirements and in more complex multiorganizational and multijurisdictional contexts.

Agencies also have to plan to accommodate the implications of hazards that can be more complex and create more enduring consequences than those that typify the kinds of incidents to which officers normally respond. For example, a biohazard attack (e.g., pollution of water supplies, release of a biohazard such as smallpox) may have commenced prior to its existence being identified; present diffuse beginnings and ends; may be difficult to detect by those first on scene; spread in ways dictated by local conditions such as building density, topography, and prevailing weather (some of which can change over time); create relatively prolonged periods of impact; and result in a complex social environment characterized by confusion and uncertainty in the general population (Department of Homeland Security, 2003; Fisher, 2000; Lasker, 2004). Thus, when dealing with terrorist actions, the operating environment in which agencies plan their response and how they will deploy their officers is qualitatively different from that in which the prevailing organizational culture developed. A similar argument can be made regarding the experience of those who respond, with officers facing challenges that differ qualitatively from those they are likely to confront under normal circumstances.

Although police officers face danger on a daily basis (e.g., confrontation with armed offenders), terrorism can change the nature of the risk they face (see Chapter 7). For example, exposure to hazard agents (e.g., highly toxic chemical, biological or radiation hazards) that are difficult to detect, that can create significant acute and chronic health problems, and generate consequences that may persist for long periods of time create new sources of stress risk. Increased danger also emanates from the fact that, when responding to terror events, the scene could become an intentionally hostile environment for officers (Department of Homeland Security, 2003; FEMA, 2004; Maniscalco & Christen, 2002). Officers must attend events knowing that they themselves may be deliberately targeted and that the perpetrators are willing to die in the pursuit of their goal of inflicting the maximum level of loss and fear when targeting ordinary citizens. The latter point introduces a more insidious aspect of the environment of terrorism; the creation of a climate of fear (see Chapter 7).

What this means in practice is that the assumptions that had formerly enabled officers and community members alike to function effectively have become less reliable guides for behavior (Janoff-Bulman, 1992). Consequently, officers must explore a new way of being (Daw, 2001) and knowledge of terrorists, their culture, language, and psychology must be encapsulated in schema that can enhance their capacity to adapt to the new reality in which they have to respond. The police agency has a significant role to play in developing these new interpretive frameworks.

This brief discussion of the issues that agencies and officers may have to contend with illustrates how terrorist events create an environment that differs qualitatively from the operating environment in which agency and officer expectations have developed over years or decades. These historical expectations have driven the development and maintenance of the culture and thus the policies, procedures, and practices that govern present-day police work. The importance of acknowledging this issue stems from the fact that the foundation upon which agencies and officers respond to contemporary challenges (i.e., terrorism) derives from their historical assumptions (i.e., the organizational assumption that past experience is an appropriate predictor of future experience). Consequently, the issues facing agencies and officers have been underestimated because these assumptions and expectations are not accurate predictors of the conditions agencies could encounter in the new era of terrorism (Brake, 2001; Carafano, 2003; Kendra & Wachtendorf, 2003; Paton, 1992). This highlights the need for police agencies to consider both their ability to adapt to a changing, riskier, and more uncertain future and to identify the interventions and procedures required to facilitate the capacity of their officers to adapt to new demands. While it is undeniable that this new environment increases critical incident stress risk, it can also be conceptualized as creating a stimulus for the development of agency and officer capability.

ORGANIZATIONAL LEARNING, CHANGE, AND FUTURE CAPABILITY

Terrorism will not only increase over the coming years, it will also become more deadly (Cooper, 2001). Furthermore, difficulty defining who could perpetrate such acts, what they may do, and when and where they could do so add to this complexity and makes it imperative that agencies progressively develop the resilience of and adaptive capacity of their officers. Under these circumstances, it is important that police agencies learn from experience (theirs and others) and develop new ways of thinking and acting and commit to developing a capacity to manage the demands associated with acts of terrorism (Berkes et al., 2003; FEMA, 2004; Jackson et al., 2003; Kendra & Wachtendorf, 2003). What does this mean for organizational learning?

Police organizations must confront the assumptions derived from a long history of effective response to emergency events and accept that they now operate within an environment that is different and that may be more hostile and dynamic. Agencies thus have to develop in ways that facilitate their capacity to adapt rapidly to whatever occurs.

A capability to learn from experience should not be taken for granted (Berkes et al., 2003; Harrison & Shirom, 1999; Mitroff & Anagnos, 2001; Paton & Hill, 2006). These authors discuss how bureaucratic inertia, vested political interests, centralized power and authority, and operating expectations developed to manage historical conditions, conspire to block the perceived need to adapt to deal with changes in the environment. Change is also unlikely if organizations underestimate the potential consequences of new challenges by assuming that existing resources, procedures, and competencies will be adequate to deal with these new challenges (Berkes et al., 2003; Carapano, 2003). That is, if agencies fail to consider the possibility that the changes are significant enough to warrant new ways of thinking about and responding to environmental events.

Under these circumstances, agencies may underestimate or overlook threats or initiate inadequate actions, reducing their ability to match their capabilities to an environment that now includes highly unpredictable acts of terrorism whose occurrence will challenge their response capabilities and provide new sources of stress risk for their officers. Organizational cultures that embody these characteristics will attempt to render the consequences of acts of terrorism understandable by making them "fit in" with previous experience, making it difficult for agencies to consider, far less confront, the demands associated with unpredictable and dynamic terrorist events.

Assuming that pre-existing capabilities and procedures will suffice increases the likelihood that response to future events will occur in an ad hoc manner, with effective response occurring more by chance than by sound planning and good judgment. They thus fail to provide a context conducive to sustaining officers' career trajectories. Given the potential for terrorist acts to become more frequent and more unpredictable, it is essential agencies commit to developing ways of knowing and acting designed to enhance resilience and agency and officer capacity to adapt to future challenges.

Organizational Change

To enhance adaptive capacity to deal with complex terrorist events, organizations must learn from past failures and learn to think "outside the square" (Berkes et al., 2003; Kendra & Wachtendorf, 2003; Paton, 1994; Paton & Jackson, 2002). Not only must the organization learn to live with new forms of risk and greater uncertainty, it must develop a culture appropriate for a contemporary operating environment within which acts of terrorism are a fact of life. Recognition of the value of institutional learning thus becomes an important precursor of the culture change that should play an integral role in critical incident stress risk management for terrorist events. The question then becomes one of how this should be accomplished.

According to Berkes et al. (2003), this involves, first, ensuring that the memory of prior terrorism events and the lessons learned (in own and other agencies), whether positive or negative, are incorporated into institutional memory and accepted as an enduring fact of police agency life. Second, realistic estimates of new forms of risk can inform planning for the culture, procedures, and competencies required for effective response (Jackson et al., 2003). Knowledge of the personal characteristics and competencies and operational practices required will be determined through analysis of the demands officers are likely to encounter and the procedures required to respond effectively (see below—simulation). This process will inform future officer and organizational development. Finally, recognition of the risk posed by terrorist events and the importance of learning from them must be consolidated into a culture that espouses the policies, procedures, practices, and attitudes required to facilitate a capacity for adaptive response to an uncertain future (Berkes et al., 2003; Brake, 2001; FEMA, 2004; Jackson et al., 2003; Kendra & Wachtendorf, 2003; Paton & Jackson, 2002). That is, to commit to developing a culture that instils in officers, via, for example, induction, socialization, training, and performance management procedures, the development and maintenance of a capacity for agencies and officers to be able to adapt to future challenges. It is also important to recognize that change is required not only to better position police agencies to respond to terrorist events, but also to accommodate the fact that the agency culture and the procedures and expectations that flow from it have direct implications for officer well-being and response effectiveness.

Organizational Influences on Officer Thinking, Well-Being and Performance

Organizational factors have been identified as significant predictors of critical incident stress risk for officers responding to terrorist events (Carafano, 2003; Grant et al., 2003; Kendra & Wachtendorf, 2003). Officers' perception of organizational culture is not only a significant predictor of posttrauma risk (Huddleston et al., 2006; Paton, Smith, Violanti, & Eränen, 2000), it may even outweigh the influence of other factors. For example, compared with dispositional (hardiness), social support, and formal support (debriefing) factors, Paton et al. (2000) found that perception of organizational culture was three times more influential as a predictor of traumatic stress outcomes. In this section, factors contributing to the agency-officer relationship are discussed in terms of their implications for understanding resilience.

One way in which organizational culture influences officers' thinking and action is through its prescribing the way things are done in organizations; that is, through the relationship between organizational culture and organizational procedures. For officers working in this context, factors such as, for example, inadequate consultation, poor communication, a predisposition to protect the organization from criticism or blame, and excessive "red tape" can increase stress risk (Gist & Woodall, 2000; Huddleston et al., 2006; Burke & Paton, 2006). Furthermore, stress risk is greatest if response procedures (e.g., command structure, level of autocracy, degree of devolved authority) derived from routine work are assumed to be appropriate for terrorist response (Carafano, 2003; McKinsey, 2002; Kendra & Wachtendorf, 2003; Paton & Hannan, 2004). In contrast, a culture that supports autonomous response systems, a flexible, consultative leadership style, and practices that ensure that role and task assignments reflect incident demands can facilitate stress resilience (Gist & Woodall, 2000; McKinsey, 2002; Paton & Hill, 2006). The influence of response procedures on critical incident stress risk can be more specific. This can be illustrated with reference to the unique deployment, decision making, and interagency collaborating challenges that terrorist events pose for police agencies.

Agency Planning and Officer Deployment

Police agency involvement commences when an alarm is issued or a terrorist act occurs. During this initial phase, agencies are tasked with, for example, accessing intelligence about what has happened, differentiating fact from inference, making sense of confusing and often ambiguous information (Brake, 2001; HBWMD, 2001; Kendra & Wachtendorf, 2003), and negotiating operational arrangements with other agencies and jurisdictions (Brake, 2001; Department of Homeland Security, 2003; Grant et al., 2003). The uncertainty and complexity inherent in this phase define the context in which agencies must adapt plans to deal with emergent and evolving problems (Brake, 2001; Department of Homeland Security, 2003; Grant et al., 2003; McKinsey, 2002).

The degree to which agencies can manage the uncertainty inherent in this task has significant implications for the stress risk in officers deployed to respond (see Chapter 7). In order to enhance officers' capacity to adapt, it is important that agencies guard against mobilization plans being based on assumptions derived from routine emergencies or on unrealistic or untested plans (Carafano, 2003; Department of Homeland Security, 2003; Lasker, 2004). Response plans must be derived from accurate analyses of community (e.g., accommodate the need to reconcile different actions) and professional (e.g., concerns for self and family, having to adapt plans to accommodate emergent issues, multiagency/jurisdictional response, etc.) response needs and expectations, and be designed to accommodate the unique demands (e.g., a biohazard response) likely to be encountered. Because these community and professional issues fall outside the sphere of normal activities, organizational and training needs analyses must expand to identify the issues that will need to be accommodated in agency planning. The agency influence on critical incident stress risk does not stop here, but extends in several ways into the response itself, with decision-making and multiagency issues proving unique challenges for officers.

Decision-Making

The dynamic and complex nature of terrorist events generates a need for a level of creative decision making that exceeds that required for response to "routine" emergencies (Jackson et al., 2003; Kendra &

Wachtendorf, 2003). Creative decision making requires deviation from standard procedures and for decisions to be made in situ. To promote resilience in this domain, agencies need to train officers in creative and crisis decision making and develop procedures to devolve decision-making authority to those working in situ who need to produce contingent solutions to novel problems (Alper & Kupferman, 2003; Carafano, 2003; Endsley & Garland, 2000; FEMA, 2004; Grant et al., 2003; Jackson et al., 2003; McKinsey, 2002; Paton & Hannan, 2004; Paton et al., 1999). Furthermore, agencies must recognize that they may not be responding with the level of autonomy or authority that they would experience under normal circumstances.

The Multiagency and Multijurisdictional Context

The response environment for acts of terrorism is unique in its need for a multiagency and multijurisdictional response (Brake, 2001; Department of Homeland Security, 2003; FEMA, 2004; Grant et al., 2003; Jackson et al., 2003; Kendra & Wachtendorf, 2003). The complex nature of terrorist events brings together representatives of agencies (e.g., hazardous materials response teams, urban search and rescue teams, community emergency response teams, antiterrorism units, and so on—see Chapter 7) that rarely interact or collaborate with one another under routine circumstances, reducing opportunities to allow shared understanding of their respective roles to develop. Creating a context conducive for officer performance and resilience involves more than just bringing agency representatives together.

Several issues complicate the process of developing mechanisms capable of facilitating effective multiagency and multijurisdictional performance. For example, interagency rivalries, concerns about any budget implications of developing greater cooperation, and disagreements about who should be the lead agency and so on can result in the process of developing relationships one characterized by conflict rather that cooperation, result in a blurring of roles and responsibilities, and fuel frustration and feelings of inadequacy and helplessness in officers mobilized to respond under such circumstances (McKinsey, 2002; Paton, 1994).

However, effective multiagency collaboration can be developed by integrating respective agency roles through interagency team development activities and using training strategies designed to build understanding of the respective contributions of different agencies, develop collaborative management systems, and ensure effective interagency communication (Brake, 2001; Flin & Arbuthnott, 2002; Grant et al., 2003; Paton et al., 1999; Paton & Burke, 2007; Pollock et al., 2003). At one level, this issue reflects the need for structural integration between agencies to facilitate a capacity to collaborate during a crisis. However, the effectiveness of this collaboration is a function of the degree to which it is complemented by officers' understanding of their respective contributions to the same plan and their shared understanding of each member's role in the response (Brake, 2001; FEMA, 2004; Paton & Flin, 1999). The development of a more cohesive multiagency operating environment will make a significant contribution to officers' schema or interpretive frameworks by ensuring that they accommodate the characteristics of the multiagency response environment in which officers will find themselves working. This is, however, not the only aspect of schema development that must be developed to accommodate the unique demands of terrorist events. The interpretive frameworks used by officers provides the basis for rendering events coherent to the point where they can apply plans and competencies to manage the demands encountered (Janoff-Bulman, 1992; Paton, 1994).

Organizational Influence on Response Schema

The schema or mental models that guide response to terror events reflect officers' socialization into their profession and organization, their training, the experiences they accumulate over time, and the operating practices that prescribe how they respond to routine emergencies (Paton & Burke, 2007). These become implicit, or taken for granted, aspects of the mental models used by officers to make predictions about future events, organize experiences, and make sense of the consequences of events and their reactions to them. However, their importance as determinants of well-being and performance effectiveness tends to remain unrealized until officers encounter events that challenge these implicit assumptions (Paton, 1994). Terrorist events can result in officers having to contend with several factors that can challenge these assumptions.

In addition to the issues introduced earlier, several other aspects of a terrorist response may fall outside the parameters of schema developed from "routine" experience. For example, because the causes of acts of terrorism are always attributable to deliberate human action intended to cause harm, they threaten perceived control, a prominent stressor in officers whose training is designed to promote control (MacLeod & Paton, 1999; Myers, 2001). The magnitude of the death and injury encountered, coupled in many cases with uncertainty regarding cause of death or whether those people officers come into contact with are infectious, represents another conceptual departure from expectations developed from prior experiences (Jackson et al., 2003). Similar problems have been identified as predicting greater stress risk when performing body recovery and identification duties (North et al., 2002; Simpson & Stehr, 2003), as having insufficient, inadequate, or inappropriate resources to perform response tasks (Carafano, 2003; Paton, 1994) and dealing with the fact that, when responding to terror events, officers have to deal with the response environment being simultaneously a disaster area, a crime scene, and a mass grave. This adds to the complexity of the role relationships and tasking that officers have to deal with.

Consequently, developing the capability of officers to adapt to the challenges posed by terrorist hazards is of paramount importance for agencies, officers, and communities alike. New schema capable of facilitating a capacity to adapt to these new kinds of demands need to be developed. To do so, agencies and officers must confront prior assumptions and facilitate the development of interpretative competencies capable of accommodating the new reality of terrorism for contemporary policing.

The development of these interpretive mechanisms will be particularly important for police officers who may have to respond repeatedly to meet the challenges acts of terrorism pose to themselves and the communities they serve (Alper & Kupferson, 2003; Grant et al., 2003; Kendra & Wachtendorf, 2003; Paton & Hannan, 2004; Simpson & Stehr, 2003). In general, training that develops a capability of operational mental models (essential to response planning and organizing action) to impose coherence upon atypical and challenging experiences and to accommodate the demands encountered should be an essential component of stress risk management (Dunning, 2003; Paton, 1994; Paton & Jackson, 2002).

In the past, when dealing with "routine" events, training practices and information about officers' prior experiences served as fairly effective mechanisms for transmitting and sustaining operational schema. However, the qualitatively different nature of the terrorist environment renders these existing mechanisms less appropriate. Agencies cannot wait for officers to accumulate experience and need to develop new schema as quickly as possible. Consequently, agencies need a more sophisticated approach to confronting assumptions and reframing schema in ways that accommodate the reality of terrorist operating contexts. A capacity for reframing can be developed using simulations.

Simulations provide opportunities for officers to experience the kinds of demands they will have to contend with, develop realistic performance expectations, review and revise response plans and roles, facilitate adaptation to the demands associated with body recovery duties, understand their stress reactions, and rehearse strategies to deal with stressful circumstances and reactions (Crego & Spinks, 1997; Deahl et al., 1994; Paton & Jackson, 2002; Thompson, 1993). Training develops realistic outcome expectations, an ability to differentiate personal and situational constraints, and interpretive processes that review experiences as learning opportunities to enhance future competence and thus officers' capacity to adapt to challenging circumstances (Dunning, 2003; Paton, 1994).

Developing these more sophisticated psychological structures requires that simulations are constructed using information derived from two sources. One concerns the development of training needs analyses capable of accommodating atypical events that that can identify the competencies, relationships, and procedures required for effective response to terrorist events. The second involves designing simulations capable of reconciling event characteristics (e.g., exposure to biohazards, personal danger, dealing with human remains, and cross-cultural aspects of death and loss) with the competencies required to manage them (e.g., hazard identification and interpretation; adapting plans; team and multiagency operations; information and decision management) in ways that promote adaptive capacity (Paton & Hannan, 2004).

By including simulations within a training strategy, police agencies can proactively enhance officer resilience, develop their capacity to adapt to challenging circumstances and protect their well-being. Given the complexity and uncertainty inherent within the new environment, this strategy will not eliminate the risk of posttrauma reactions.

Consequently, postevent support resources will remain an important component of any critical incident, stress risk management strategy.

Organizational Influence on Managing Risk After the Event

It is important to remember that the support practices and procedures used to reintegrate officers back into routine work are developed and delivered within an organizational context. Stress risk is increased if support strategies are delivered in an organizational culture that discourages emotional disclosure, focuses on attributing blame for response problems to officers, or minimizes the significance of officers' reactions or feelings (Paton & Stephens, 1996; MacLeod & Paton, 1999). In contrast, an organizational culture that encourages supervisors to actively promote reintegration can complement other resilience strategies. Supervisors can assist adaptation by helping officers appreciate that they performed to the best of their ability, and reducing performance guilt by realistically reviewing how situational factors constrained performance (MacLeod & Paton, 1999). This kind of feedback, and the quality of supervisor-officer relationship to ensure it is effective, is essential for developing resilience (see Chapter 10).

Managers can also contribute to the development of stress resilience by working with officers to identify the strengths that helped them deal with the terrorist emergency and building on this to plan how future events can be dealt with more effectively. Similarly, when reviewing response problems, the focus should be on ensuring that it occurs in a positive climate in which discussion identifies ways in which issues can be constructively resolved or contained in the future. The feedback from this process can contribute to identifying future training and support needs and organizational practices. If these actions are not taken, risk management programs should review the climate of relationships between managers and staff (e.g., levels of trust) and seek ways to build this capacity (Gist & Woodall, 2000; Paton et al., 2003). Such analyses can promote future response effectiveness, facilitate the establishment and/or maintenance of a resilient organizational climate, and contribute to the next iteration of agency and officer change and development.

CONCLUSION

Terrorism adds a new, unique, and challenging dimension to the environment of contemporary policing, and one that differs qualitatively from that in which policing has historically occurred. It presents agencies and officers alike with a more complex, dynamic and threatening environment. As a result, agencies and officers must be able to learn from experience and incorporate in the agency culture and officer schemata ways of ensuring a capacity to adapt to future events. Given the importance of the agency-officer relationships in this process, organizational culture (e.g., attitudes to emotional disclosure, performance expectations, empowerment) and practices (e.g., devolving authority, incident management protocols, interagency collaboration) play an important role in creating and sustaining a context that supports officer well-being and effectiveness (Jackson et al,, 2003; Paton & Hill, 2006; Paton & Jackson, 2002). Cultural change can be transmitted to officers through, for example, induction and socialization procedures, training, simulation, and participative organizational development programs. Additional work is, however, required to identify those factors that influence how agency culture is enacted in ways that lead to resilience. Once identified, these predictors can be used by agency to plan and evaluate their resilience strategy. The dynamic nature of contemporary policing means that the development and maintenance of agency and officer resilience should be viewed as an iterative process that encompasses personal and organizational learning (see Chapter 10).

The degree to which police organizations are responsive to changes in the societal environment influences the long-term viability of the policed organization as a context conducive for guiding career trajectories that facilitate well-being and mitigate risk. Over time, however, the kinds of novel change introduced in this chapter become the norm and established facets of the organizational culture. At the same time, we should not lose sight of the fact that officers' life-course transitions unfold over time as a result of a progressive pattern of interactions between officer and agency (P-E Fit), making the career a highly dynamic entity that unfolds through a process of negotiation. While this process is, perforce, somewhat one-sided and dominated by the Environment (organizational) side of the P-E Fit equation, it nonetheless can be conceptualized as a process of negotiation (e.g., officers can decide to leave, reduce their input, etc.) that changes over time with the Person side of the P-E Fit equation becoming more influential as officers progress through their careers. What this negotiation process looks like for established officers is the subject of the next chapter.

Chapter 9

THE LIFE OF ESTABLISHED OFFICERS

INTRODUCTION

The core objective of this book is to examine the trajectory described by officers' transition through their career (see Chapter 1). The early stages of this trajectory were discussed in Chapter 3 (citizen to recruit) and Chapter 4 (recruit to operational officer). These chapters addressed very specific transition points in the career of police officers. Thereafter, however, until retirement, it becomes harder to identify such specific milestones in the career trajectory. This chapter discusses officer's perceptions of their role and experiences after some 32 months of involvement in the police organization. The goal is examine how several years of operational and organizational experience of police life come to define the officer how they dealt with the challenges and changes that emerged throughout the course of their policing career and what this means for their future capabilities. This raises the question of how to anticipate that future. Because it can capture the cumulative impact of positive and negative experiences and is a valid predictor of the likelihood of officers remaining in the profession over time, the job satisfaction construct represents a useful means for assessing this aspect of the career trajectory.

SATISFACTION AND ITS ANTECEDENTS

When assessing officers at this point in their career, Burke (2009) found that changes in patterns of stress and coping were consistent with their positive adjustment to the role of police officer. Evidence of successful socialization and acculturation were evident in the finding of growing homogeneity in how officers perceived and interpreted their work experience. However, Burke did find a gender difference, with female officers reporting higher levels of negative work experiences.

Burke argued that this pattern likely reflected a combination of exposure to the masculine nature of the police role and culture (see Chapter 4) and the major shift female officers had to make in relation to their traditional societal role. This appeared to have had a pervasive effect on many areas of occupational experiences for female officers. However, this gender difference did not manifest itself in differences in their reported levels of satisfaction. Nor did it influence female officers' capacity to perceive benefit from their experience of potentially traumatizing events. Taken together, these observations permit the tentative inference that socialization experiences relating to event response are introducing some level of homogeneity into how all officers are interpreting their organizational and operational experiences.

In order to put these observations on a more systematic footing, Burke (2009) then examined the relative influence of personal, operational, and organizational factors on job satisfaction in 106 officers who had been followed from the point they commenced work as police officers to their becoming serving officers. Following a multiple regression analysis, Burke (2009) found that organizational hassles, emotional social support, operational uplifts, denial, extraversion, and behavioral disengagement accounted for some 51 percent of the variance in job satisfaction (Figure 9.1).

Burke's (2009) finding that organizational hassles explained the most variance in job satisfaction confirms the findings of earlier work (Burke & Paton, 2006). These findings add weight to the argument that officers' experience of organizational systems and procedures plays an important role in defining their well-being. Operational uplifts also made a significant contribution to job satisfaction and it is likely that this reflects officers' reporting on operational experiences (e.g., involvement in operational incidents which entail dealing with victims of crime) that are consistent with their expectations of the core functions of policing, with consistency between expectations and reality validating their earlier assumptions about the job.

Burke's (2009) analyses also reiterated Hart et al.'s (1995) finding that positive (uplifts) and negative (hassles) work experiences coexist,

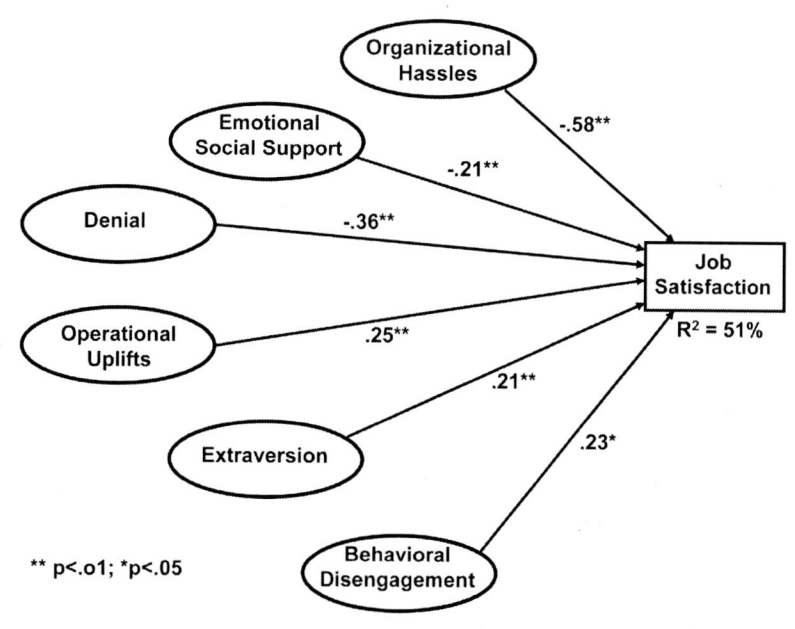

Figure 9.1. Summary of stepwise regression analysis examining individual and occupational predictors of job satisfaction (N=106) (adapted from Burke, 2009).

and that, at least to some extent, are interdependent. This has important implications for conceptualizing and managing critical incident stress risk. It means that while positive work experiences can increase well-being, they may do little to reduce psychological distress. In contrast, whereas minimizing negative experiences can reduce psychological distress, it may have little effect on enhancing well-being (Burke & Paton, 2006; Hart, 1999; Hart et al., 1995a). Consequently, positive and negative influences must be managed as separate strategies with a risk management program. At this point in their careers, officers are now more firmly entrenched as members of the culture of the police organization. This makes it pertinent to consider how this influenced their satisfaction.

Organizational Climate and Job Satisfaction

Burke (2009) found that organizational climate had positive relationships with organizational and operational uplifts, and negative relationships with hassles (both operational and organizational). This finding adds weight to the argument that the police organization can play a powerful role in the quality of the daily experiences of officers (e.g., Burke & Paton, 2006; Hart et al., 1995). Furthermore, her failure to find any gender differences in the perceptions of climate led Burke to suggest that similar work and organizational experiences underpin the development of more homogenous perceptions of the working environment in male and female officers alike, and one that stimulates the development of shared ways of imposing meaning and interpreting operational and organizational experiences.

Of particular interest was Burke's finding that while both operational and organizational hassles had moderate positive relationships with job satisfaction, neither facet of uplifts showed a similar association. This finding led Burke to suggest that, at least at this point in an officer's career, negative experiences exercise a stronger influence on satisfaction. It can be tentatively suggested that this reflects the experience of inconsistencies between officers' expectations of working in an environment focused on operational response and their coming to terms with the administrative demands imposed by agency life and the fact that bureaucratic imperatives are attributed with greater importance than operational performance (see below and Chapters 3 and 4). Notwithstanding, officers demonstrated levels of job satisfaction indicative of their being happy and content in their working life, with positive operational experiences making an additional contribution to the observed levels of satisfaction.

Occupational Experiences and Individual Characteristics

Burke (2009) found a positive relationship between negative work experiences and maladaptive coping strategies and with stress. She argued that this pattern of relationships reflected the continuing process of person-environment fit as well as capturing the consequences of the growing incidence of experience of operational incidents.

Socialization into a role is a difficult and challenging task. Fully understanding the relationships between negative work experiences, stress, and coping requires an examination of how these constructs change over the course of the officers' careers. Burke's analysis raised some interesting issues with regard to the relationships between coping strategies and satisfaction.

COPING

In Chapter 4, the point was made that behavioral disengagement was increasingly making its presence felt within officers' coping repertoires. This pattern appears to carry forward into later stages of officers' careers. Denial and emotional social support were also identified as coping strategies that impacted on satisfaction (Figure 9.1). What of the more positive strategies identified earlier (Chapter 4)?

On examining the negative association, she found between Operational Uplifts and the coping strategy of Planning, Burke (2009) found an intriguing negative relationship. Planning is typically seen as one of the more adaptive coping mechanisms and one which offers protection against distress and increases the likelihood of experiencing adaptive outcomes. It would, as a consequence, be expected to have a positive association with positive experiences. This raises a question. Why did this positive coping strategy not demonstrate any relationship with satisfaction? Burke answered this question by arguing that while Planning had one of the highest overall scores of the COPE subscales, the timing of its assessment coincided with officer's growing recognition that policing is an inherently unpredictable occupation. A combination of unpredictability, resource constraints, and complexity fuelled officers' realization that it was impossible to plan their actions and responses for all contingencies. This view is consistent with Carver's argument that adaptive problem-focused strategies are only effective if the individual has some ability to control the situation and thus deal with the problem directly. Faced with complex and uncontrollable experiences (in both operational and organizational contexts), it would be expected to see the emergence of strategies in response to this lack of control. The strategies that did emerge as significant predictors of job satisfaction were emotional social support, denial, and behavioral disengagement. Emotional social support and denial both had negative influences, while behavioral disengagement had a positive influence.

Emotional Social Support

While emotional social support is typically held to be a maladaptive strategy (and had a negative impact on satisfaction) (Figure 9.1), Carver et al. (1989) and Hart and Cooper (2001) argue that coping strategies can be both adaptive and maladaptive, with their specific function and their effectiveness being heavily dependent on the situation in which they are invoked. For example, a person who has been made to feel insecure by a stressful transaction can be reassured by seeking out emotional social support (e.g., officers coming to terms with new operational challenges, dealing with organizational demands, etc.), particularly when dealing with complex, uncontrollable events. Emotional social support mechanisms are used as outlets for ventilating feelings and emotions. However, this strategy can become maladaptive if the underlying problem is not addressed. Consequently, due to the necessarily high levels of teamwork and the emphasis placed on comradeship and solidarity within these occupations, particularly amongst police (Bartone, 2003; Pollock et al., 2003), the seeking of social support for emotional reasons, such as moral support, may well serve as an adaptive and protective function for officers and facilitate the use of other adaptive strategies.

Given the limited operational experience of these officers, it is likely that emotional social support is acting to assist them to adapt to the new experiences that unfold over the course of their careers. Furthermore, the high score obtained for these officers on the coworkers domain of organizational uplifts scale provided Burke with confirmation that officers continue to encounter many new challenges over time. As a result, they are seeking the moral support and advice of those who are going through similar experiences or from those who have previously dealt with the challenges that progressively unfold as officers negotiate their way through their career.

The negative influence of emotional social support on satisfaction (Figure 9.1) suggests that while officers are seeking the moral support of their colleagues and are recognizing the positive value associated with this, the fact that support was being sought to deal with the experience of negative events could have the observed negative relationship between emotional support and job satisfaction. Furthermore, emotional support in the form of having an outlet upon which to express emotion and vent feelings is not a positive strategy if these feelings are left unresolved. The negative relationship with satisfaction warrants further investigation of its longer-term implications.

It is possible to hypothesize that lack of training and inappropriate organization procedures may be fuelling officers' loss of perceived control. This creates a situation in which operational and organizational contexts can be rendered more coherent and which would provide a context more conducive for the development of adaptive coping, increasing satisfaction and well-being in the process. This can certainly be done for highly challenging events (Alexander & Wells, 1991; Paton, 1994). This explanation is consistent with low empowerment and the failure of the organization to provide an enabling environment (see Chapter 10).

Denial

The negative influence of denial on job satisfaction (Figure 9.1) makes sense intuitively. Denial reflects a maladaptive way of coping, particularly if the event, situation, or stressor is not going to abate simply by being ignored, as is likely the case with many of the adverse situations officers encounter over time. Furthermore, the fact that similar events are likely to be encountered in the future makes this a problematic issue. If events are appraised as threatening or aversive, and an officer decides to carry on regardless (i.e., denies that the stressor exists), he or she is more likely to experience a decline in satisfaction if the stressor does not abate. It is also possible that increased use of denial is a result of the positive influence of Behavioral Disengagement on Job Satisfaction (Figure 9.1).

Behavioral Disengagement

Behavioral Disengagement refers to the reduction in effort to deal with a stressor. In its most maladaptive form, it is characterized by giving up the attempt to cope with the event. However, the behavioral disengagement construct can also be construed in a manner akin to the notion of procrastination. It can also be implicated in the process of task prioritization. For example, if an officer has a number of tasks to be completed in a certain time frame, a process of prioritization often takes place. This involves focusing on the completion of one task while removing or leaving other tasks that are prioritized as less important until a later stage. Thus, the positive influence of behavioral disengagement may be reflective of the higher levels of hassles from administration reported by officers, and reflects the need they have felt to prioritize tasks. Certainly behavioral disengagement had a moderate positive correlation with Operational and Organizational hassles, suggesting that it is used more as hassles increase, but then has a positive influence on levels of job satisfaction (e.g., focus on positive tasks and disengage from administrative demands).

Extraversion

The influence of Extraversion on Job Satisfaction found by Burke is consistent with research that identified it being correlated with indices of individual well-being. Brief, Butcher, George, and Link (1993) argued that enduring personality characteristics influence the meaning given to an event. Thus, as job satisfaction is held to be cognitive in nature, it is probable that trait extraversion will play a role in determining judgments of satisfaction in a work context. This interpretation is supported by the finding that these officers were scoring higher on extraversion than the general population (see Chapter 3). Furthermore, Heady and Wearing (1989) argued that constructs such as life experiences, coping, and psychological well-being could be predicted on the basis of a person's personality characteristics. Thus the findings reported by Burke provide further evidence of their being a relationship between personality and well-being.

While the contents of the preceding section cannot be taken to be indicative of experiences over the entire career of a police office, there is a clear picture emerging of the events and situations which influence officers' perceptions of their work environment and their satisfaction with the job, with organizational aspects of the police role impacting on well-being. Insights into the nature of the officer-organization transactions that influence satisfaction and that define the context in which life trajectories influence critical incident stress risk can be gleaned from closer investigation of officers' interpretation of their experiences. This is the subject of the next section.

ESTABLISHED OFFICERS: PERCEPTIONS OF POLICE LIFE

In order to elucidate what being a police officer meant to the incumbents, Burke (2009) invited officers to discuss their best and worst experiences in the job since starting and how operational and organizational contexts influenced officers' satisfaction with their jobs. She also explored how officers' impressions of the public perception of police and inquired about the influence of the job on family and non-

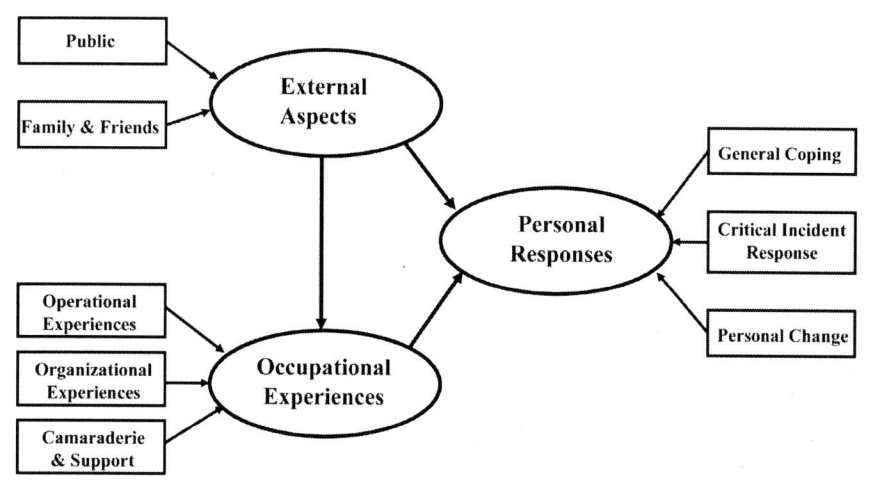

Figure 9.2. The themes and interactive effects described by established officers (adapted from Burke, 2009).

work life. Officers were also asked whether they regarded the job as stressful and what aspects they considered stressful, and/or frustrating, as well as positive and/or rewarding.

Burke identified three (*External Aspects, Occupational Experiences, and Personal Responses*) overarching categories that influenced officers' job satisfaction and intention to remain in policing (Figure 9.2). In so doing, she found that officers' comments reiterated several of the daily hassles and uplifts described earlier (see Chapter 2). However, others, particularly those relating to critical incidents, provided some novel insights into how officers experience such events.

External Aspects

With regard to the factors external to their job and job role that influenced their satisfaction and commitment, Burke (2009) identified two themes. These were, *Family and Friends* and *Public*.

Family and Friends

Officers indicated that over the course of their first few years on the job, their social circle had become almost exclusively police officers, with not wanting to expose people outside of policing to the profession being a prominent reason for this. Working a rotating shift roster and being tired of some people continually asking questions about the job were also cited as reasons for reducing their circle of friends outside the job. Officers also reported becoming somewhat distant from family.

While this loss of relationships outside policing was a source of regret for several officers, all believed it was necessary. It appears that the constriction of their social circle, and their distancing themselves from family, was a conscious decision intended to shield close family and friends from the down side of the profession (see below). This influence becomes important when the ways in which officers cope with the job are considered as they affect whom they feel comfortable turning to when difficult situations arise. Restrictions on one's social networks during employment can have significant implications for the course of an officer's retirement (see Chapter 11). In addition to reporting changes in their relationships with family and friends, changes in the quality of relationships with the public were also reported.

Public

Officers' relationships with the public had changed, with a mismatch between their actual powers and public expectations of police capabilities being identified as an important influence on the quality of this relationship. Officers were increasingly of the belief that the public saw them only as police and not as people, and believed that the ideals to which they were held were fuelled almost exclusively by stereotypes sustained by media reporting (see below). However, it should be noted that while some officers felt that the public needed to be educated about the powers of police officers, others liked the exclusivity they were afforded as police officers, and felt that education would make no difference anyway. The themes of "family," "friends," and "the public" were implicitly linked to job satisfaction.

The content of these themes has the potential to impact negatively on an officer's sense of well-being, in terms of regret from a smaller social circle, to the frustration experienced at the lack of public knowledge about policing. Despite these potential negative impacts, both appear to have become an accepted part of the job. For example, Carrie explained, "yeah my social circle is smaller, but in a way it has to be, you just can't put yourself out there as a cop, you're held to a higher ideal and you've really got to live up to it . . . you can't be seen to be vulnerable or weak or silly or too outgoing." Thus, potentially negative experiences are reconciled in a positive way. However, this can reduce access to opportunities to challenge assumptions regarding relationships with the public and the wider community and reduce opportunities to broaden the bases for imposing meaning on atypical critical incident experiences (Frederickson et al., 2003; Paton & Burke, 2007). In other words, increasing the likelihood of interaction occurring only with fellow officers will reinforce prevailing mental models and make it more difficult to challenge or change these mental models.

Occupational Experiences

This category described officers' experiences in their role over the first two to three years of their careers (Burke, 2009). It comprised the themes of "rewards," "frustrations," and "camaraderie and support." Officers' comments illustrated how operational and organizational aspects of policing interact and that they have an independent influence on well-being and on how officers interpret their experiences. This split between operational and organizational experiences is consistent with previous literature examining stress and well-being in the police profession (Hart et al., 1995; Kohan & Mazmanian, 2003), and with the conclusions presented earlier in this chapter.

REWARDS. The rewards theme describes officers' beliefs about what those facets of work experience they found intrinsically rewarding. In this sense, they are reminiscent of the content of the uplifts domain of the police daily uplifts scale (see Chapter 2). However, they tended to reflect officers' personal experiences rather than their interpretation of the impact of systems and procedures on themselves and their work. Many officers indicated that these experiences contributed to their wanting to continue to be police officers. Burke (2009) split rewards into operational (Table 9.1) and organizational (Table 9.2) components. The subthemes representing positive or rewarding operational experiences were heavily influenced by officers' expectations of their job and job role.

According to Burke (2009), officers' perceptions of positive outcomes from operational experiences reflect those that fit their expectations of what it is to be a police officer (helping people, solving crimes, and being able to use their initiative). For example, Brian stat-

TABLE 9.1
THE OPERATIONAL SUBTHEMES COMPRISING THE REWARDS THEME

Operational Theme	Indicative Quotes
Helping People Satisfaction from being able to help victims of crime and members of the community.	"the smile you get–even if they don't say it, sometimes you know just how thankful they are . . . that's what keeps you going, the one's who you know appreciate what you've done"
Crime Solving The investigation process and the satisfaction derived from solving a crime and charging an offender	"It's your job to sort out the chaos and then to fix the problem . . . there's no better feeling than working through it all and seeing the guy caught and made to pay for what he's done" (Amanda).
Autonomy & Intuition As their experience increased officers were given a greater level of autonomy and latitude to use their intuition which resulted in: - Feeling able to follow through the crime solving process and to trust using their intuition in an operational context. - Being trusted to use their initiative in operational situations	"Using your intuition can pay off and when you do you get so much more out of seeing the thing [the incident] through to the end." "There's no expectation anymore that you should be asking questions, you still can [ask questions], but there's a level of trust that you'll make the right decision, so you've got much more latitude for decision making than there was before [after only 2-4 months of operational duties]
Variety The variety of the job was an aspect they found rewarding	"No incident is exactly the same, so you're always going to something different and its so good not going to the same thing over and over again."

Adapted from Burke, 2009.

ed, "I love the job, being 'on the job'. I mean sometimes you don't know what's gonna happen when you get there, but you don't know what's gonna happen any day you come to work, and that's what's great about it [being a police officer]. There's no better feeling than when you look back and you know you've done everything you could and you've got the best outcome for everyone–the victim's happy, the crook's caught, and you [the officer] played a major role in that." Implicit in this was the notion that positive outcomes and benefits can be derived from exposure to negatively emotive events. All officers acknowledged that at times their job was extremely difficult, but that the benefits or rewards outweighed the disadvantages.

The ability to implicitly see the benefit in challenging events is a capacity officers' develop as they become more experienced. It follows that the more refined this "ability" becomes, the more likely officers were to report positive perceptions of their work environment, less likely to perceive organizational and role ambiguity, and more likely to indicate an intention to stay with the organization (Brunetto & Wharton, 2003; Giga, Noblet, Faragher, & Cooper, 2003). That these experiences tended to be consistent with officers' expectations of their job role (i.e., consistent with their mental model of the police role) also served to increase satisfaction. This has implications for the understanding the issues raised above regarding the use of (maladaptive) coping strategies to deal with uncontrollable experiences.

While additional work will be required before a conclusion can be drawn, the findings discussed above imply that, at this stage and with regard to the typical operational demands encountered, officers possess the competencies required to deal with operational demands and the capabilities to interpret them in ways that increase the likelihood of their experiencing beneficial outcomes. If the factors increasing the use of maladaptive coping strategies cannot be found in the operational domain, it becomes necessary to look elsewhere for an explanation (see below).

The rewards theme also contained references to the organizational context. In contrast to the intrinsic nature of those emanating from operational contexts (Table 9.1), officers' discussion of organizational rewards focused more on the more extrinsic and tangible aspects of their experience (Table 9.2). Prominent organizational rewards were the stability and financial security offered by police work. While the notion of financial and job security is linked to job satisfaction to a certain extent, it also plays a major role in organizational commitment. There was, however, one organizationally-derived reward which officers found intrinsically rewarding.

The ability to take on teaching, leadership, and mentoring roles was described as a positive and rewarding aspect of their work. The motivating aspects of these facets of work life derived from officers' beliefs that these activities had inherent value to their own knowledge and skills as police officers (i.e., it had intrinsic value). Furthermore, the fact that taking on teaching, mentoring, and leadership roles, as a result of it increasing officers' confidence in their own abilities, has important implications for job satisfaction and organizational commitment. This aspect of organizational experience takes on added significance in the context of the role that leadership plays in developing and sustaining resilience (see Chapter 10). While additional work is required to examine this issue in more detail, the opportunities afforded for rumination about and discussion of experiences and learning scenarios could positively influence the development of interpretive processes that facilitate resilience (see Chapter 10).

As introduced above, the content of the rewards theme is reminiscent of the uplifts domain (see Chapter 2). However, Burke (2009) also identified uplifts that had not been identified in previous research. For example, a sense of autonomy and intuition and feelings of being able

TABLE 9.2
THE ORGANIZATIONAL SUBTHEMES COMPRISING
THE MANIFEST THEM OF REWARDS.

Operational Theme	Indicative Quotes
Financial and Job Security Feelings that employment as a police officer provided a safety net for their future.	"There wouldn't be another job I could do that would give me the same benefits, so this is the plan for the next 10 to 12 years at least."
Flexible Hours The rotating shiftwork roster provided a degree of flexibility in hours worked because they weren't continually "stuck" on the same shift.	"Routine hours don't suit me, I like the varied shifts, I couldn't handle working 9 to 5, I think I'd feel like I was being unfairly restricted or something."
Leadership The opportunity to mentor and teach newer constables as a result of their "experience."	"I learnt stuff as well through mentoring . . . it gives you the opportunity to expand your own knowledge and skills . . . to find out answers to stuff you ought to know, but didn't."

Adapted from Burke, 2009.

to use these constructively was an item that was not included in the uplifts scale. This highlights the importance of how feeling empowered can contribute to satisfaction. The implications of this are discussed in more detail in Chapter 10.

Frustrations

This theme describes those facets of the job which officers found stressful, frustrating, or bothersome about their job. In some respects, its content mirrors the notion of the hassles experienced in the daily context of policing (see Chapter 2). As with rewards, frustrations could be split into two components: operational and organizational. Two operational subthemes (Table 9.3) and five organizational subthemes (Table 9.4) were identified by Burke (2009).

TABLE 9.3
THE OPERATIONAL SUBTHEMES COMPRISING
THE MANIFEST THEM OF FRUSTRATIONS.

Operational Theme	*Indicative Quotes*
Public Misconceptions Unrealistic public expectations of the power police possess, particularly in relation to neighborhood disputes, vehicle theft and burglary.	"They watch the tele and think that you can just dust for fingerprints and you can just swab and take DNA samples and match it up and catch the crook and everyone's happy. It just doesn't happen that way, and people don't want to hear that they might never get their car or their possessions back."
Workload Officer's belief that they were expected to accomplish much more than they were able to on a single shift. Workload was compounded by the amount of paperwork required to be completed for even simple offenses.	"At the end of a shift, I think about work and all the paperwork, and all the things I should've done that I'll now need to do tomorrow but that I probably won't get time to do . . . sometimes I worry about that stuff [admin and paperwork] quite a bit cos I know now that it's important and has to be done, there's just so much of it for every job, every offense, and it just gets to the point where it mounts up and you have to stay back and do overtime simply to get your paperwork done."

Adapted from Burke, 2009.

Burke's analyses of "frustrations" also revealed additional insights into how officers related to the organizational culture. In particular, greater acceptance of the hierarchical nature of the police organizational structure was evident, as the consequent belief that it was the people above them who had all the power. This aspect of work life was not necessarily liked, but it was accepted and indicates the emergence, or even embedding of a hierarchical cultural attitude. The sense of disempowerment that emerges as a result of officers' progressive immersion in the police culture has significant implications for understanding and managing critical incident stress risk (see Chapter 10).

The themes of *Processes and Procedures, Court and Justice System and Personnel and Staffing* all represent aspects of work life over which over which officers have little or no control, but which have highly significant implications for the quality of the outcomes they experience from exercising their operational role. This raises the possibility that it is these facets of work experience that underpin the development of the (maladaptive) coping strategies that influence satisfaction. Perceptions of incompatible guidelines and procedural limitations on officers' ability to exercise their discretion have particular significance from the perspective of increasing critical incident stress risk. This can arise as result of organizational cultural constraints on officers' flexibility to respond to rapidly changing and evolving incidents (Alexander & Wells, 1991; Paton & Flin, 1999). The issues raised under the *Processes and Procedures* theme provide additional insights into factors that will have a detrimental effect on empowerment (see Chapter 10).

Camaraderie and Support

The third theme identified in the occupational experiences category describes the relationships between officers and their colleagues and senior officers. This theme describes experiences accumulated in team and organizational contexts. It has a significant impact on officers' sense of well-being and on station morale, and provides several insights into the workings of the organizational culture, particularly with regard to its role in developing and sustaining a sense of cohesion through team activities and from support provided by the officers' immediate supervisor.

All the officers interviewed by Burke (2009) identified the people they worked with as one of the most positive aspects of policing. "The

TABLE 9.4
THE ORGANIZATIONAL SUBTHEMES COMPRISING
THE MANIFEST THEME OF FRUSTRATIONS.

Operational Theme	Indicative Quotes
Processes and Procedures Organizationally defined guidelines for action on certain situations are not always compatible with situations faced in front line policing. - The ability to use individual discretion is often limited by set polices and procedures	"Sometimes you just can't do what you think you need to do . . . domestics are a good example, I know there's a reason for the legislation, but a lot of the time having to drag some poor fella in just makes the whole situation worse." "You have to be careful, cos there's procedures for dealing with things and if you go outside of those and if it all goes wrong you'll find yourself in a whole heap of trouble, no one will back you in those circumstances."
Court & Justice System Lenient sentencing or cases thrown out of court.	"Officers that should have had the book thrown at them don't or they have the ability to make deals that get them lesser sentences . . . after all the work you've put in to making a case against them, they just walk away, it's extremely frustrating, and you wonder why on earth you bothered in the first place."
Personnel & Staffing Lack of staff "on the ground." This problem was particularly identified by, but certainly not limited to, smaller regional stations.	"There just isn't enough manpower. You go to jobs 1 or 2 [officers] up where there should be more."
Shiftwork Negative experiences and perceptions of shiftwork	"It's a lifestyle thing, when you're doing 24 hour rotational shiftwork, it mucks your whole life up." "I like it, but its really hard not being around for the kids, you miss the important things–assemblies, sports days, awards, it's hard."

Adapted from Burke, 2009.

people you work with, the camaraderie, the team atmosphere, that's what I like best [about the job]" (Aleisha). This was an inevitable consequence of the time spent around other cops and because there was a shared implicit understanding of the job. "It just works that way, cos you're forever surrounded by cops, and you've got people there that know the job and understand what you're doing. . ." (Walter). The notion of a sense of collegiality amongst the officers also highlights the idea that police see themselves as occupying a unique place in society, and that membership of this team affords them a level of exclusivity, by virtue of their job role, from the rest of society. ". . . everyone here knows what you're up against . . . unless you're in the job you really don't know what it's like, its so unique. . ." (Harry). These comments reinforce the validity of the issue raised earlier regarding how support networks comprised solely of fellow officers can lead to existing schema becoming increasingly entrenched, reducing access to experiences likely to challenge the assumptions inherent in these schema, making them more difficult to change (Paton & Wilson, 2001).

Officers' comments about camaraderie also furnish insights into how officers' early career experiences facilitate the adoption of shared norms and values through a socialization process that increasingly involves contact only with one's fellow officers. Officers' early experiences of organizational practices are assimilated as a result of their being interpreted as providing insights into how "cops are made." This socialization process is one mechanism for sustaining the organizational culture through the acculturation of new recruits and probationary officers. These team experiences appear to play an important role in the maintenance of job satisfaction and exercise a strong influence on officers' organizational commitment.

The notion of the team environment influencing officers' individual perceptions is important. While camaraderie manifests itself at the team level, the shared norms and values derived from collective experiences percolate into the schema of individual officers to exercise a consistent influence on their motivations and interpretive processes. In this way, team experiences influences both station morale and individual job satisfaction. The influence of these team experiences transcends the daily experiences of the officers to exercise a more pervasive influence on how officers actually perceive their day-to-day experiences. Officers believe that the sense of team cohesion they experience "makes the job." Consequently, it is probable that the presence of this component alone, if it is experienced in a positive way, can facilitate organizational commitment. It also has an important role to play in developing and maintaining resilience amongst members of a profession that can experience critical incidents repeatedly over the course of their career (see Chapter 10).

Personal Influences

This theme describes how officers perceived the relationship between their response to operational events and their overall sense of well-being. Three main aspects were identified, General Coping, Critical Incident Response and Individual Change.

General Coping

The coping strategies adopted by officers in response to the operational demands encountered were marked by considerable homogeneity. Officers were reluctant to define these responses as coping, as that would imply a level of vulnerability that most officers were not willing to admit to. In this respect, while the themes identified in this category were not explicitly identified by officers as coping mechanisms, they were directly identified as "things" the officers "did" in certain situations to ensure they maintained professionalism and "got the job done" despite the nature of the events they were facing. Burke (2009) extracted seven coping themes. These are outlined in Table 9.5.

Burke reported that officers were reluctant to talk about their feelings. This was linked to their perceived need to disengage themselves emotionally from specific incidents in order to effectively perform their role (e.g., "victims can't be seen as people if you're at the scene of a particularly gruesome event as it can cloud your judgment of what is necessary to resolve the situation"). Officers described how they place considerable reliance in such situations on automatic and "intuitive" responses. This observation provides an example of the role that situational awareness plays in promoting the effective response to critical incidents.

The importance of this competence can also be traced to its ability to enhance officers' resilience when responding to high-demand/low-time events (Paton & Hannan, 2004). Burke also found evidence of the development of team mental models; collective ways of thinking about and responding to events that arises from interaction with fellow

TABLE 9.5
COPING MECHANISMS IDENTIFIED BY OFFICERS
IN RESPONSE TO ON-THE-JOB EVENTS.

Coping Mechanism	Indicative Quotes
Disengagement/Automaticity Responses to jobs become automatic and officers appear to have learnt/taught themselves to disengage emotionally from operational incidents.	"It can take a lot of [mental] effort to sort out what's going one . . . you have to come back on your training and things become automatic."
Active Coping Tackling each situation based on its unique characteristics, dealing with one thing at a time and making decisions about priorities.	"You find you can make different evaluations based on the circumstances because you've done it before . . . if it's something new you do what seems right and you hope for the best."
Humor Used "after the fact"; as a mechanism for debriefing about situations that were difficult, novel or particularly gruesome.	". . . some of the things we go to, if you don't make a joke out it, it can get to you a bit. I guess it is a way of dealing with the job."
Social Support Turning to others as a means of dealing with difficult events on the job, both operational and organizational. Colleagues and close family and friends are used in different ways. - Colleagues are turned to discuss the dynamics of particular incidents and dissect the event itself rather than an individual's reaction to it. - Family and friends are used to discuss more organizationally based frustrations such as paperwork, workload and feelings of lack of support rather than specific incidents.	 "I'll talk to another cop before I'd talk to someone outside the job." "I've told my partner about being overloaded, you know paperwork and all that, but not about the op [operational] stuff. I don't think she'd get it, and I really don't think she needs to know anyway."
Positive Reinterpretation Seeing the positive in negative (challenging) events	"Even if you haven't managed to catch the offender, the fact that you've made a victim feel safe, or helped them take back some of the control they might have lost, that's a good thing, and you've got to give yourself credit for that." "There's not a lot of good stuff in policing, so you have to look for, and you have to consciously try and turn things around in your head so that you can see something positive in really bad, negative situations."

Adapted from Burke, 2009.

officers. This team competence makes an important contribution to resilience (Pollock et al., 2003). This, in turn, will be influenced by acculturation and the adoption of ways of thinking and knowing that are implicit within the organizational culture (see Chapters 1 and 2).

Burke singled out the fact that few officers talked in detail about re-engaging after events. This is a point that requires further investigation as officers move through their careers in order to ascertain if and how their use of disengagement changes. It is a particularly important construct as while disengagement at the time of the event is adaptive and helps protect the officer from the negative consequences of their involvement, a failure to re-engage can be detrimental in the long term.

Critical Incident Response

There appears to be a process of resolution to a critical incident response that extends from and draws upon some of those strategies identified in *General Coping*. Given the critical and exceptional nature of such incidents, it is not surprising that officers openly reported feeling vulnerable after these critical events, and described questioning themselves and their actions as a consequence. Several officers indicated some notion of "checking over their shoulder"; referring to a level of constant self-appraisal and self-monitoring that was either not present before, or became intensely heightened after the events. This is consistent with the notion of hyperarousal in PTSD symptomatology.

An interesting finding was Burke's observation that most officers were generally willing to disclose "coping" with these events, but were not so forthcoming with regard to their general day-to-day experiences (see above). This suggests several things. First, officers were willing to identify such events as "potentially" problematic, thereby conceding that these events did need to be "coped with." Second, it indicates that while this was the case, officers still expressed a level of reluctance at being seen as vulnerable during and/or after a critical incident. A third issue that emerged concerned officers being able to openly recognize these incidents as challenging (rather than threatening) events. The significance of this reframing was the role that it played in leading officers to realize that they could respond, rather than just react passively in ways that make them vulnerable, to the events defined in this way.

As a result, officers came to conceptualize these events as those over which they could exert a level of control. In other words, they could appraise these events in ways that increased their ability to perceive them as beneficial. However, this should not be taken to imply that this happens automatically.

When describing their critical incident experiences, officers reported feeling like it was necessary to quickly "shake off those feelings" or being seen as somehow inadequate as a police officer, "you run the risk of not being able to do your job if you dwell on things for too long" (Eric). Burke also found evidence that officers were ruminating over their involvement in critical incidents and asking themselves whether they could have done anything differently. Belinda said, "you get to a point where you realize that you do your job and you do it to the best of your ability . . . you've got to reach that point before you let yourself relax again." The level of rumination appears to be much deeper than for incidents dealt with utilizing general coping strategies. Rumination appears to lead officers to resolve their feelings of vulnerability (see Figure 9.2). The existence of this kind of natural review process has important implications for developing resilience (see Chapter 10).

In addition, consistent with its use as a general coping mechanism, officers reported a high use of humor in response to these events. However, while humor was generally evoked n situations in which officers felt vulnerable, it was unclear whether humor facilitated the resolution process or was an indirect mechanism of rumination which then led to resolution of vulnerable feelings. "Sure you have to find the funny side of things . . . but I wouldn't let them see that I was feeling weird about it [a critical event] either, I'd rather make a joke and then go away and deal with it myself . . . You don't want it to get out that you're weak" (Kathryn). This response also highlights the pervasively negative side of the police culture, in that seeking help to deal with emotions is looked upon as a weakness. This is consistent with the machismo often regarded as characteristic of professions such as policing (see Chapters 3, 4, and 6).

Officers also indicated that these events, and their response to them, influenced their future capabilities. This activity was not, however, restricted only to critical incidents, but was also used to assist officers to deal with the psychological consequences of their day-to-day activities. In Burke's work, this described a tendency for officers to hold

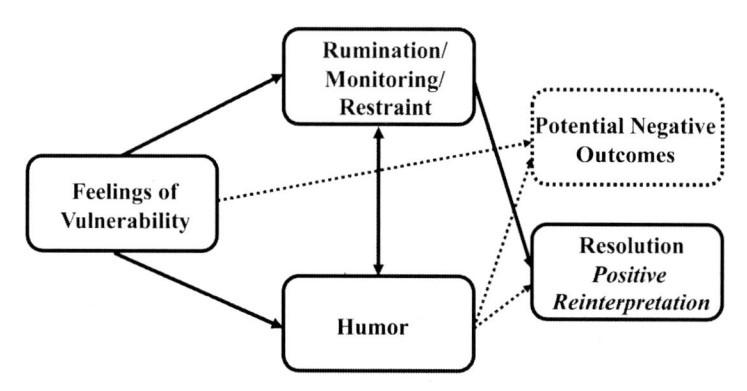

Figure 9.3. The process of resolution evident after critical incident experience. Note: Broken lines indicate possible relationships, and broken oblong indicates potential long-term consequences (adapted from Burke, 2009).

back, of trying to work out the appropriate course of action for dealing with their emotions rather than acting upon them and seeking some form of help or assistance. For example, Chad stated, "there's a lot of ways you can block it out [the memory of the event] eventually you're just not thinking about it anymore . . . but yeah, that threat is always there in the back of your mind, but you've just got to keep it there, you cant let it rule your life, you do that and you're no good as a cop anymore." The concept of restraint closely mirrors that of repression, and like disengagement, is not positive in the long term. This is another concept which requires further investigation in order to ascertain its role in the long-term coping profile across the careers of police officers. While Burke (2009) characterized activity of this nature as a restraint, this kind of feedback loop can, if developed as part of a risk management program, play a role on promoting resilience (see Chapter 10).

Personal Change

All officers identified some degree of change within themselves over the course of the previous three years as they made the transition from civilians to operational police officers. The most profound change involved their identifying themselves as police officers, with this forming an integral aspect of their own sense of identity (see Chapter 1). "The biggest change I see in myself is that I'm a cop now, so I'm always on duty, I'm always on guard and I'm always looking out for

TABLE 9.6
SUBTHEMES OF PERSONAL CHANGE IDENTIFIED BY OFFICERS
AS OCCURRING AS A RESULT OF THEIR BEING A POLICE OFFICER.

Change Aspect	Indicative Quotes
People Skills Ability to deal with people in many situations, knowing that people are unpredictable, having a store of skills to draw upon in tricky situations.	"I've learnt a lot about people . . . don't judge people, take things as they come and that each situation is different and people will react differently to different circumstances."
Cynicism Recognition that policing has resulted in a higher degree of cynicism towards people in general and towards certain sections of society.	". . . see the world in a more negative light. Before [becoming a Police Officer] you don't realize how many people there are living a different lifestyle, and they're the people we deal with all the time, you just don't realize how many of those people are around."
Confidence Heightened confidence in their role as police officers, but also as an individual.	"Eventually it all clicks and you suddenly realize you know what you're doing. That comes with experience, they can't teach it to you at the academy."
Factuality Approach to things tends to be more fact based. Things are often seen as black and white rather than varying degrees of right and wrong–either you break the law or you don't.	"I've changed in relation to how I deal with people, I'm less tolerant in some situations and I work through the facts and those, the the facts, what you can see, the evidence, sometimes that's all that matters."
Humor Move to a darker sense of humor which is not necessarily acknowledged as a way of coping, but in response to "horrible and gruesome" situations.	"My sense of humor is darker now, probably because I've got more ammunition! But you have to reign it in sometimes, you need to be conscious of your audience." "It [use of humor] lights the mood, takes the tension away."

Adapted from Burke, 2009.

things. . . . It can be problematic because it's not the sort of job you can walk away from and leave at work, and sometimes, you do just have to hold your tongue and let things go" (Frank). Alongside this identity shift, officers identified four major aspects of change since they had joined the profession (see Table 9.6).

Officers identified several changes, some of which can be regarded as positive, others appear to be more negative in nature, and some do not simply fit either a positive or negative profile, but could be regarded as either or both. For example, officers reported that their confidence as police officers had increased. On the surface, this appears to be positive and was certainly conceptualized as such by the officers. However, it is possible that this heightened confidence can come across as arrogance in a police role, and as harshness in, for example, a family context. Similarly, while most officers felt that their humor had become much darker, and that this was simply a way of dealing with events, and that was a necessary component of being a cop. Several officers also acknowledged that "other people" did not understand the function of this dark humor. Their recognition of the importance of context resulted in their acknowledging that they had to be careful when, and with whom, they used this kind of humor. For example, Chad said, "I certainly wouldn't go home and tell my wife some of the things we come up with at work, she just wouldn't get it, wouldn't understand."

Several issues emerged from examining officers' experiences of police life. Confirmation that individual (e.g., personality, coping) and organizational factors influence well-being support the need for their inclusion in strategies designed to manage critical incident stress risk. It also became evident that the team and social context in which police officers conduct their work and experience incidents exercises an additional influence on their stress risk. Taken together, this means that the comprehensive conceptualization of critical incident stress risk and its management will be incomplete unless it embraces the collective and interactive influence of person, team, and organizational factors. How this might be accomplished is the subject of the next chapter.

Chapter 10

MANAGING CRITICAL INCIDENT STRESS RISK: INTEGRATING PERSON, TEAM, AND ORGANIZATIONAL FACTORS

INTRODUCTION

As previous chapters have demonstrated, police officers face both predictable (e.g., transition from recruit to officer, transition to retirement) and unpredictable (e.g., 9/11) transition points over the course of their career. While some unpredictable transitions, such as 9/11, can be large-scale events that change the environments in which life-course trajectories occur for all concerned, such events are, fortunately, infrequent. However, officers will have to contend with the implications of several, smaller-scale transition points over the course of their career. Critical incidents represent just this kind of transition. Critical incidents challenge officers' mental models or interpretive schema (see Chapter 1). They thus create a sense of psychological and social (team) disequilibrium. As such, critical incidents can be conceptualized as transition points that represent catalysts for positive or negative changes to how officers come to view the world (see Chapter 1) and that define how they respond to future events (Paton, 2006). Critical incidents thus represent important transition points in the life-course trajectories of police officers. Furthermore, officers can expect to experience several such transitions over the course of a career that can span decades. The repetitive nature of critical incident experiences has important implications for risk management interventions developed within a life-course model.

It is important that any intervention can accommodate the iterative nature of critical incident exposure. It is also imperative that any intervention accommodates the natural review processes that officers adopt to assist their ability to learn from their experiences (see Chapter 9), but also be designed in ways that transcend the experience of any one officer in order to facilitate both the collective learning of all officers and the incorporation of lessons into the collective conscience of the police organization (see Chapter 8). To embrace the tenets of a life-course model that advocates accommodating the principle of contextualism (see Chapter 1), any intervention must encompass the interdependencies between officers, the teams in which they operate, and the overarching organizational context in which all activities are undertaken. How this might be accomplished is the subject of this chapter.

A LIFE COURSE CRITICAL INCIDENT INTERVENTION

The critical incidents that police officers have to contend with become "critical" when they create a sense of psychological disequilibrium. This disequilibrium represents that period when the existing interpretive frameworks or schemata that guide officers' expectations and actions have lost their capacity to organize experience in meaningful and manageable ways (Janoff-Bulman, 1992; Paton, 1994; Paton, 2006). In this chapter, the focus is on identifying the individual, team, and organizational resources that facilitate officers' ability to render discordant challenging events that create a sense of psychological disequilibrium coherent, manageable, and meaningful (Antonovsky, 1990). The challenge is to identify those factors that can be developed prior to exposure that predict officers capacity to develop schema that broaden the range of (unpredictable) experiences that officers can render coherent, meaningful, and manageable (Frederickson et al., 2003; Paton, 1994; 2006). That is, to increase resilience.

To accommodate the principle of contextualism, the process of rendering experiences coherent, manageable, and meaningful must be conceptualized in ways that accommodate complex patterns of interaction between officer, team, and organizational levels. This chapter outlines an approach to modeling how these factors interact to achieve this. By articulating these influences on meaning, and how they interact, police agencies will have at their disposal a comprehensive basis for developing critical incident stress risk management strategies.

Integrating Officer, Team, and Organizational Factors

While often considered primarily as a phenomenon that exists solely at the level of the individual officer, this chapter continues the theme developed in preceding chapters to argue that the comprehensive understanding of resilience must integrate person, team, and organizational levels of analysis. Because several person- and team-level (e.g., coping, social support) factors have been implicated as playing complementary roles in predicting resilience (Paton, 2006), they must be included in any comprehensive model. However, the understanding afforded by the incorporation of these factors will be incomplete until the context in which they are enacted is included in the model. The argument for the latter derives from the fact that the police organization defines the context within which its officers experience and interpret critical incidents and their sequelae and within which future capabilities are nurtured or restricted (Paton, 2006). That is, officers respond to incidents as members of law enforcement agencies whose organizational culture influences their thoughts and actions and within challenging experiences (using schema whose nature derives from patterns of interaction with colleagues, senior officers, and organizational procedures over time) are made sense of (Paton et al., 1999; Weick & Sutcliffe, 2007).

Modeling Resilience

In order to develop a risk management model consistent with the tenets of life-course theory, several conceptual challenges must be surmounted. One such challenge derives from the fact that resilience can only truly be assessed when officers are confronting a challenging event (Klein, Nicholls, & Thomalla, 2003). From the perspective of adopting a risk management strategy that proactively seeks to broaden the range of events officers will be able to adapt to means that research into resilience must be undertaken prior to such events. Consequently, the assessment of officers' resilience requires that the use of a proxy measure that can be assessed prior to any involvement in critical incident.

This would not be a problem if it were possible to predict exactly what officers will be called upon to confront. However, because critical incidents are characterized by considerable diversity (e.g., mass casualty incidents, school shootings, biohazard attack), police agencies cannot predict what their officers will encounter. The diversity of events that officers may be required to respond to and their often horrific nature means that there is currently no measure capable of capturing the diverse ways in which police officers can experience meaningfulness and manageability in work contexts. Until such measures are developed, what is needed is a measure that can capture the experience of coherent, meaningful and manageable outcomes irrespective of the specific outcomes officers' experience. It is argued here that the construct of job satisfaction can fulfill this role.

This argument is based on several lines of evidence. Thomas and Tymon (1994) found a relationship between perceptions of meaning found in work tasks (meaningfulness) and enhanced job satisfaction. Spreitzer, Kizilos, and Nason (1997) observed a positive relationship between competence (manageability) and job satisfaction. These findings have been echoed in the critical incident literature, with several studies finding meaning and benefit in emergency work being manifest in changes in levels of job satisfaction (Britt, Adler, & Bartone, 2001; Hart & Cooper, 2001; North et al., 2002). These findings suggest that the job satisfaction construct can be used to capture changes in the meaningfulness and manageability and so act as a proxy measure of resilience.

Having identified a suitable proxy measure of resilience, the next task is to identify the person-, team-, and organizational-level factors that influence how it develops over time following each successive critical incident experience. That is, to identify the resources and competencies that facilitate the proactive development of a general capacity to adapt (i.e., render any future experience meaningful and manageable) to unpredictable circumstances.

ORGANIZATIONAL CHARACTERISTICS, COPING, AND RESILIENCE

The starting point for this discussion concerns organizational climate. Perception of organizational climate has been implicated as significant predictor of posttrauma outcomes (Paton & Violanti, 2007).

Hart and Cooper (2001) proposed a conceptual model of organizational health that predicts that interaction between individual and organizational factors influences the experience of salutary outcomes. In their model, Hart and Cooper afforded organizational climate a significant role. Organizational climate describes officers' perceptions of how their organization functions, and these perceptions influence both their well-being and their performance in their organizational role (Hart & Cooper, 2001).

Burke and Paton (2006) tested the ability of the Hart and Cooper model to predict satisfaction in the context of emergency responders' experience of critical incidents. They found that organizational climate, officers' experience of organizational and operational practices prescribed by the organizational culture (measured using the police daily hassles and uplifts scale) (Hart et al., 1993), and officers' problem- and emotion-focused coping style accounted for 44 percent of the variance in job satisfaction. Organizational climate was the best single predictor of job satisfaction and, by inference, illustrates the important role that climate can play in how officers render their critical incident experiences meaningful and manageable.

This finding attests to the important role that organizational climate, and, by inference, the police agency that sustains this climate can play in facilitating staff adaptability and resilience. However, the fact that Burke and Paton's analysis left a substantial portion of the variance to be explained highlights the scope for developing a risk model. This chapter discusses how the model can be profitably developed by expanding understanding of the relationships between officers and teams and the organizational context within which they operate and work. To pursue this objective, it is first necessary to identify a construct that can unify these perspectives.

One construct that is capable of doing so is empowerment. Empowerment, or the lack of it, was earlier identified as playing a significant role in understanding the quality of officers' relationship with the police organization (see Chapter 3, 4, and 9). The remainder of this chapter builds on work by Burke and Paton (2006) and Johnston and Paton (2003) to construct a comprehensive, multilevel stress risk model. In this model, empowerment plays a central role as an integrating construct.

EMPOWERMENT

Before it is possible to proceed to develop a multilevel model, it is first necessary to demonstrate the existence of a relationship between empowerment and satisfaction (i.e., to demonstrate that empowerment is capable of influencing the proxy measure of resilience). Several studies have demonstrated that empowerment predicts satisfaction in individuals and teams (Kirkman & Rosen, 1999; Koberg, Boss, Senjem, & Goodman, 1999). The other issue concerns whether empowerment theories can encapsulate the individual, team, and organizational influences in ways that positively influence the meaningfulness and manageability of experiences (captured by job satisfaction). It is to a discussion of how empowerment satisfies this need that this chapter now turns. This discussion is based on the fact that empowerment *enables* people who operate in complex, unpredictable and challenging contexts to act. Discussion also addresses the capability of this enabling process to facilitate the learning required to build on experience and develop future adaptive capacity (see Chapter 9). The ability to facilitate future capacity is an essential feature of any risk management model that is to be applied to members of a profession whose members face repeated exposure to critical incidents over the course of their career. This will provide the foundation for a career-long, proactive approach to managing critical incident stress risk.

Empowerment as an Enabling Process

Empowerment is a construct that encompasses several organizational processes. Amongst those with which it is normally linked, processes such as participation and delegation enjoy a prominent position (Conger & Konungo, 1988). This aspect of empowerment helps introduces its relevance as a construct that can inform understanding critical incident stress and how it can be managed. For example, because delegation, as an attribute of organizational culture, can facilitate the effective response to complex events (e.g., delegating responsibility for crisis decision making), this facet of empowerment can contribute to increasing resilience (Paton & Flin, 1999). However, it is the finding that empowerment has demonstrated strong links to motivating action in conditions of uncertainty (Conger & Konungo, 1988; Spreitzer, 1997) that renders it capable of providing valuable insights into resilience and how it can be developed and sustained.

Motivational interpretations of empowerment derive from a theoretical perspective that argues that *having sufficient resources* (psychological, social, and physical) and the *capacity to use them* is a prerequisite for increasing officers' ability to effectively confront the challenges posed by events and the environment (Conger & Konungo, 1988; Spreitzer, 1997). The proactive management of critical incident stress risk calls for both resources and the capacity to use them. Of these two, making resources (e.g., physical resources, skill training) available is the relatively more straightforward option. Facilitating a capacity to use these resources effectively, particularly in the context of working in an autocratic, hierarchical organization (see Chapter 4) represents more of a challenge. It is in the context of the latter that the construct of empowerment comes into its own. Empowerment theories argue that the potential to use resources to accomplish tasks derives from the relationship between the organization and the officer. It thus provides a useful conceptual framework appropriate for exploring how to develop a multilevel (i.e., one that integrates person, team, and organizational factors) risk management framework.

Conger and Konungo (1988) conceptualize empowerment as an enabling process that facilitates the conditions necessary to effectively confront (i.e., develop meaning, competence, etc.) future challenges. Conger and Konungo argue that individual differences in meaning and competence reflect the degree to which the environment (i.e., the police organization) enables actions to occur. Empowerment thus describes a process that uses organizational strategies to remove conditions that foster powerlessness (e.g., organizational hassles) and encourages organizational practices (e.g., organizational and operational uplifts, self-efficacy information, competencies) that develop officers' learned resourcefulness (Johnston & Paton, 2003).

Thomas and Velthouse (1990) complement this position by adding that beliefs about future competence derive from the schema or interpretive frameworks (developed through the enabling process of empowerment) that provide meaning to officers' experiences and build their capacity to deal with future challenges. In addition to its ability to inform understanding of resilience directly, the notion of enabling through the development of (empowering) schema means that the empowerment construct can help explain how officers' experience of organizational culture (e.g., the hassles and uplifts that reflect

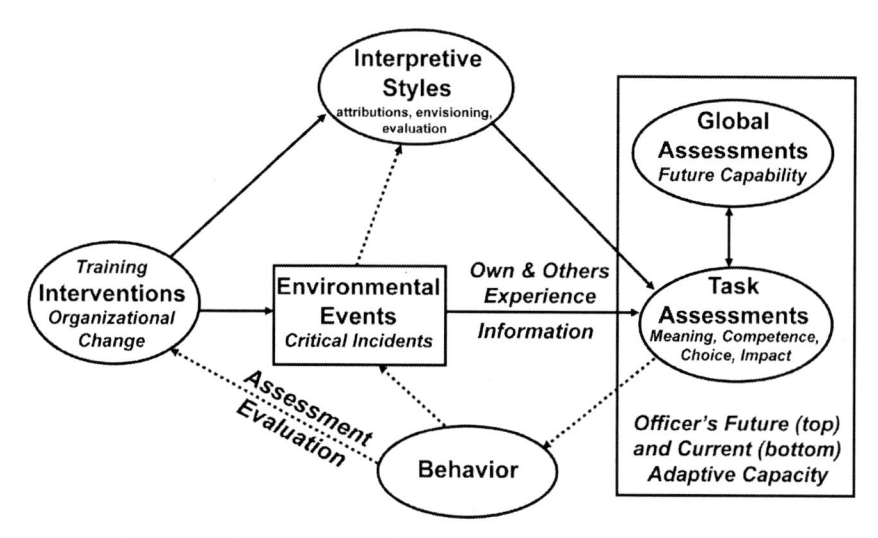

Figure 10.1. The cycle of environmental events, task assessments, and behavior. Broken lines indicate the input into organizational learning (adapted from Johnston and Paton, 2003).

how it is enacted) and critical incidents are translated into schema that facilitates their interpreting experience in meaningful and manageable ways (manifest as changes in levels of satisfaction). These relationships are illustrated in Figure 10.1.

By providing a mechanism that can offer explanation for the relationship between the organizational environment and the development and maintenance of schema (interpretive styles) that underpin future adaptive capacity, the empowerment construct has considerable potential to inform understanding how resilience is enacted in police agencies. This capability is further bolstered by the fact that empowerment is conceptualized as an iterative process in which a cycle of environmental events (critical incidents), task assessments (e.g., meaningfulness), and behavior interact via feedback mechanisms to facilitate the progressive development of adaptive capacity (Figure 10.1). This renders any model developed around this construct capable of (a) accommodating the repetitive nature of officers' critical incident experience and (b) ensuring that such experiences contribute to the learning process required to maintain adaptive capacity in the changing environment of contemporary policing.

Critical Incidents, Incident Assessment and Behavior

Environmental events (critical incidents) provide information to officers about both the consequences of their previous task behavior and the conditions they can expect to experience in future task behavior (Conger & Konungo, 1988). In addition to it emanating from their own experiences, task information (e.g., the assessment of critical incident experiences) can also be provided by peers, subordinates, and superiors at work, in the context of, for example, performance appraisals, training programs, and meetings. Given that the nature, content, and timing of these activities derive from decisions made by the organizational representatives, it is possible to understand the role the organization can play in sustaining resilience over time.

Through each progressive cycle of event (i.e., following a challenging critical incident), assessment (of specific critical incident experiences), and feedback, officers develop, maintain, and change the operational schema they use to plan for, interpret, and respond to critical incidents. This process is depicted in Figure 10.1. For it to inform the development of resilience, it is necessary to identify how empowerment cycles contribute to the development of future adaptive capacity. The environmental assessment process achieves this as a result of it translating into two outcomes: task assessment and global assessment.

According to Thomas and Velthouse (1990), officers' task assessments comprise several components (Figure 10.1). The first, meaningfulness (meaning), describes the degree of congruence between the tasks performed and one's values, attitudes, and behaviors. Empowered individuals feel a sense of personal significance, purpose, and commitment from their involvement in work activities (Spreitzer, 1997; Thomas & Velthouse, 1990). Meaningfulness is increased by experiencing uplifts (see Chapter 2) such as receiving recognition and being given responsibility, but constrained by organizational hassles (e.g., red tape) that shift emphasis from meaningful role performance to meeting administrative expectations. An example of the latter was offered in Chapter 4 (e.g., some officers reported feeling that they were being evaluated on administrative procedures rather than by their operational performance).

The second component, competence, is analogous to Bandura's (1977) notion of self-efficacy. Competence is fundamental to officers' beliefs in their ability to perform successfully in their operational role

(Spreitzer, 1997). This outcome is comparable to the manageability component of resilience. Importantly, Bandura (1977) points out that there is a direct relationship between levels of self-efficacy (i.e., competence) and the level of effort and persistence officers invest when facing challenging events. It thus makes an important contribution to officers' capacity to adapt to the unexpected. This issue reflects some of the comments discussed in Chapter 4 (e.g., officers' comments illustrated how inconsistencies between training and practice could adversely affect officers' perceptions of their level of competence). This, in turn, can adversely influence levels of self-efficacy. Furthermore, discrepancies of this nature make additional demands on officers by requiring them to fill in the gaps (especially within an organizational context in which there exist differing views regarding how certain tasks should be performed—see Chapter 4), thus increasing officers' stress risk.

The third component, choice, reflects the extent to which officers perceive that their behavior is self-determined (Spreitzer, 1997). A sense of choice is achieved when officers believe they are actively involved in defining how they perform their role (a prominent item when officers report uplifts), rather than just being passive recipients (as is often the case when officers describe hassles). A capacity for choice was evident with regard to officers discussing their having some choice about work assignments and having some autonomy and opportunities to use their discretion in some operational contexts (see Chapter 9).

A sense of choice is enhanced when the organization delegates responsibility for planning and task performance to officers (see the discussion of working in an hierarchical organization in Chapter 4). This facet of empowerment is comparable to the coherence component of resilience. A sense of choice is particularly important for dealing with emergent, contingent emergency demands and for creative and crisis decision making and the development and maintenance of situational awareness when responding to critical incidents (Paton & Flin, 1999). An ability to exercise choice also facilitates learning from training and operational experiences and, in an empowering climate, to facilitate others to do likewise and pass on learning.

The final component, impact, describes the degree to which officers perceive that they can influence important organizational outcomes (Spreitzer, 1997). Where choice concerns control over one's work behaviors, impact concerns the notion of personal control over organizational outcomes. Impact may, however, be inhibited in organizational contexts if officers encounter incompatible guidelines and procedural constraints on their ability to use their discretion or have their use of their intuition called into question on procedural grounds (see Chapter 9). Parallels can be drawn between the choice and impact elements of empowerment and perceived control, another factor that has been widely implicated in thinking on stress resilience and adaptability (see Chapter 3).

The ability to draw direct comparison between the components of task assessment and the concepts of meaningfulness, manageability, and coherence adds weight to the argument that empowerment represents a construct capable of informing how to understand and manage critical incident stress risk. It also illustrates how hassles and uplifts could affect core empowerment processes such as meaning and choice (see Figure 10.1). It thus affords an opportunity to see how empowerment research complements the earlier work (Burke & Paton, 2006; Johnston & Paton, 2003) and how their integration can contribute to the development of a comprehensive model of police resilience.

Before proceeding to advance this argument further, there remains one form of assessment that remains to be discussed. The final form of assessment, global assessment, further establishes empowerment as a construct that has an important role to play in informing understanding of officers' resilience and their capacity to adapt to future incidents.

While task assessments are localized within a singular task and time-period, global assessments describe an outcome of empowerment that embodies a capacity to generalize expectancies and learning across tasks and over time. Thomas and Velthouse (1990) observed that global assessments describe a capacity to fill in gaps when faced with new and/or unfamiliar situations. This facet of empowerment is essential for adaptive capacity in police officers who can't predict what they will be called upon to confront and who must be able to use current experiences as a basis for preparing to deal with future risk and uncertainty. The feedback loop described in Figure 10.1 provides the learning mechanism necessary to facilitate the iterative learning required to facilitate officers' ability to build on their experience and so develop their future capability. It does so through the progressive development of interpretive styles or schema.

Both global and task assessments, and thus capacity to adapt, are influenced by officer's interpretive styles (Figure 10.1), with these schema comprising separate but related components (Thomas & Velthouse, 1990). According to Thomas and Velthouse (1990), interpretive frameworks are influenced by the work context, with management practices (intervention–Figure 10.1) having an important influence on how schema are developed and sustained.

Empowerment Schema and Resilience

Because it is difficult to predict the specific nature or characteristics of the events police officers may be called upon to confront, it is important that the risk management strategy not only actively facilitate the development of the schematic or interpretive styles but also ensure that they can be generalized across events and over time (Frederickson et al., 2003; Paton, 1994, 2006). Empowerment identifies several schema or interpretive styles (Figure 10.1).

The first schema component concerns the attributions made by officers to account for success or failure. Empowerment is greater when officers attribute causes for failure to external (i.e., due to factors other than personal shortcomings), transient (i.e., factors likely to change over time), and specific (e.g., factors limited to a specific day or event) factors.

The role of this schema component is consistent with findings in the critical incident stress literature. For example, Paton and Stephens (1996) discuss how officers' frequent experience of successful outcomes under normal circumstances can lead to the development of the helper stereotype. The helper stereotype schema fuels officers' expectations that they are always resourceful, in control, and able to put things right. The suddenness, scale, and complexity of mass emergencies and disasters make it inevitable that officers will have to deal with failure or not being able to perform at the expected level (Paton, 1994). Under these circumstances, the helper stereotype results in officers internalizing failure (Raphael, 1986) rather than, more correctly, attributing problems to environmental complexity. Similarly, organizational hassles such as reporting practices that supersede concern for officers' well-being or that project blame on officers increase the likelihood that officers will perceive problems as emanating from internal sources (MacLeod & Paton, 1999). In contrast, feedback processes that differentiate personal and environmental influences on outcome contribute to officers' developing attributional schema that sustain adaptive capacity (MacLeod & Paton, 1999).

A second schema component, envisioning, refers to how officers anticipate future events and outcomes. It influences the quality of the attributional processes brought to bear on critical incident experiences. Officers who anticipate positive rather than negative outcomes experience stronger task and global assessments, and, thus, empowerment. With regard to response problems, the existence of a learning culture in police agencies that interprets problems as catalysts for future development and not as failure will increase positive expectations regarding performance and well-being (Paton, 2006; Paton & Stephens, 1996).

The final schema component, evaluation, refers to the standards by which one evaluates success or failure. Thomas and Velthouse (1990) argue that individuals who adopt less absolutist and more realistic standards experience greater empowerment. This observation is reinforced by findings in the critical incident literature. Officers who have realistic performance expectations, and acknowledge environmental limitations on their outcomes, are better able to adapt to highly threatening circumstances (Paton, 1994; Raphael, 1986).

In addition to being able to predict satisfaction and thus inform understanding of how meaning and manageability develop, by mediating the relationship between organizational characteristics and satisfaction, empowerment represents a mechanism that illustrates how officers' experience of organizational culture (e.g., hassles and uplifts) is translated (via the above schema components) into resilience and future adaptive capacity. Having identified the potential of empowerment theories to inform understanding of resilience, the next issue involves identifying its predictors.

Several antecedents to psychological empowerment have been identified. Prominent amongst these are social structural variables (access to resources and information, organizational trust, peer cohesion, and supervisory support) and personal characteristics (e.g., personality). This literature can contribute to identifying predictors of empowerment that can be included in the model used to guide the development of critical incident, stress risk management strategies. The model is illustrated in Figure 10.2.

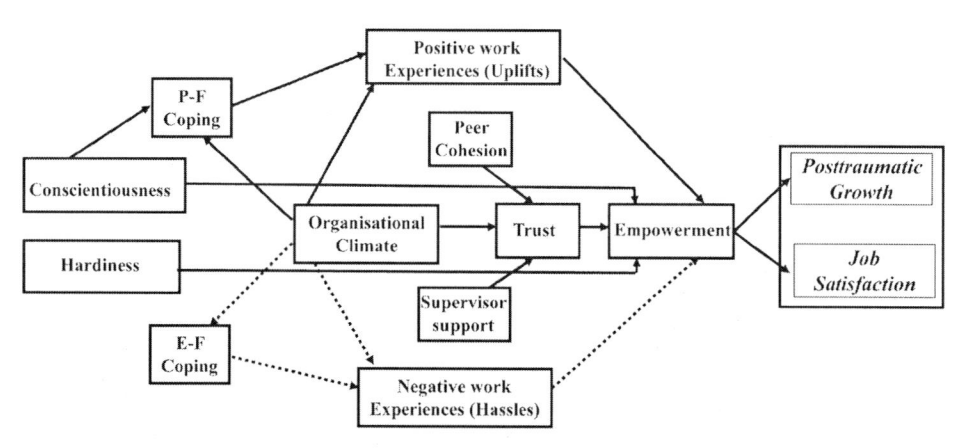

Figure 10.2. A critical incident, stress risk management model designed to accommodate repetitive critical incident experience. Solid lines indicate positive influences on empowerment. Dashed lines indicate pathways with a negative influence on empowerment. P-F = Problem-Focused Coping; E-F = Emotion-Focused Coping. For information on hassles and uplifts, see Chapter 2.

Access to Resources

Having insufficient, inadequate, or inappropriate resources to perform response tasks contributes to critical incident stress risk (Carafano, 2003; Paton, 1994). Having resources (physical, social, and informational) allows individuals to take initiative and enhance their sense of control (impact) and self-efficacy (competence) over environmental challenges (Gist & Mitchell, 1992; Lin, 1998; Paton, 1994). One resource that plays a pivotal role in predicting empowerment is information.

Crisis information management systems capable of providing pertinent information in conditions of uncertainty are essential to adaptive capacity in emergency responders (Paton & Flin, 1999), and play an important role in creating a sense of purpose and meaning (Conger & Konungo, 1988) amongst officers (Figure 10.2). However, information itself is not enough. The social context in which information is received is an equally important determinant of empowerment. In this context, one aspect of the agency-officer relationship becomes particularly important, and that concerns trust.

Trust

Trust is a prominent determinant of the effectiveness of interpersonal relationships, group processes, and organizational relationships (Barker & Camarata, 1998; Herriot, Hirch & Reilly, 1998), and plays a crucial role in empowering officers (Spreitzer & Mishra, 1999). People functioning in trusting, reciprocal relationships are left feeling empowered, and more likely to experience meaning in their work. Trust has been identified as a predictor of people's ability to deal with complex, high-risk events (Siegrist & Cvetkovich, 2000), particularly when relying on others to provide information or assistance.

Trust influences perception of other's motives, their competence, and the credibility of the information they provide (Earle, 2004). Individuals are more willing to commit to acting cooperatively in high-risk situations when they believe those with whom they must collaborate or work under are competent, dependable, likely to act with integrity (in the present and in the future), and to care for their interests (Dirks, 1999). Organizations functioning with cultures that value openness and trust create opportunities for officers to engage in learning and growth, contributing to the development of officers' adaptive capacity (competence) (Barker & Camarata, 1998; Siegrist & Cvetkovich, 2000). The quality of this aspect of the interpersonal environment is also influenced by officers' dispositional characteristics.

Dispositional Influences

Although less extensively researched than other variables, one dispositional factor that has attracted interest is the personality dimension of conscientiousness, particularly with regard to its attributes of achievement orientation and dependability (McNaus & Kelly, 1999). Conscientious individuals experience a stronger sense of meaning and competence in their work, particularly during times of change and disruption (e.g., responding to critical incidents in which officers need to adapt to unpredictable, emergent demands) (Thomas & Velthouse, 1990), demonstrate greater levels of perseverance in these efforts (Behling, 1998), and are more committed to contributing to collective efforts (Hough, 1998). This contributes positively to both the level of cooperation with and support for coworkers they demonstrate in work contexts and to sustaining a cohesive team response to complex events.

Modeling Empowerment and Resilience

Using these variables, Johnston and Paton (2003) described how empowerment mediated the relationship between the above predictors and resilience (job satisfaction) in hospital staff dealing with critical incidents. Johnston and Paton's analysis demonstrated that empowerment and its antecedents were good predictors of resilience, accounting for some 51 percent of the variance in job satisfaction. While providing good support for the core empowerment model, several other social structural and dispositional variables that have been implicated as predictors of empowerment have been identified and can be profitably included in the model. An important issue here concerns how procedures such as training needs analysis facilitates officers' capacity to deal with uncertainty. Importantly, decisions about the content and nature of training are made by senior officers.

Senior Officer Support and Empowerment

Training not only plays an important role in developing resilience resources such as hardiness and self-efficacy, and providing opportunities to capitalize on these personal characteristics (see Chapters 4 and 9), it also helps socialize officers into the fabric of the organizational culture that defines the context in which police agency responsibilities are exercised by bringing officers into contact with senior officers who play a significant role in transmitting and sustaining culture, including entrenched organizational beliefs about dealing with the consequences of critical incidents (e.g., attitudes to emotional disclosure, reporting requirements, etc.). This introduces a need to consider how sense making occurs in teams and in relationships with senior officers.

Senior officers play a central role in developing and sustaining empowering environments (Liden, Wayne, & Sparrow, 2000; Paton & Stephens, 1996). They have a major role to play in creating and sustaining a climate of trust and empowerment as a result of their being responsible for translating organizational culture into the day-to-day values and procedures that sustain the schema officers engage to plan for and respond to critical incidents (see Chapter 9).

Leadership practices such as positive reinforcement help create an empowering team environment (Bartone, 2004; Manz & Sims, 1996; Paton, 1994), particularly when they focus on constructive discussion (by officers, co-workers, and senior officers) of response problems and how they can be resolved in the future (Quinn & Spreitzer, 1997). The significance of this issue is heightened by the finding that one way in which the organizational culture in autocratic, hierarchical organizations is sustained is through negative reinforcement (see Chapter 4).

The importance of constructive discussion with senior officers, who are in a better position to provide the resources and training required to act on the outcomes of formal review sessions, derives from the fact that it draws one's emphasis away from personal weaknesses in a difficult or challenging situation and replaces it with an active approach to anticipating how to exercise control in future events (Paton & Stephens, 1996). In this way, senior officer behavior contributes to the development of the attributional, envisioning and evaluative schema components (see above) that are instrumental in translating officers' organizational experiences into resilient beliefs and competencies.

Quality supervisor-subordinate relationships, of which supportive supervisor behavior is a crucial factor (Liden, Sparrow & Wayne, 1997), create the conditions necessary for the personal growth of individuals (Cogliser & Schriesheim, 2000) enhancing general feelings of competence (global assessment) (see Figure 10.1). Furthermore, quality supervisor-subordinate relationships encourage the creation of similar value structures between officers (Cogliser & Schriesheim, 2000), building shared schema, enabling employees to find increased meaning in their task activities, and contributing to the development of a sense of cohesion between colleagues who operate in teams.

Peer Cohesion and Empowerment

The quality of relationships between coworkers predicts the meaning officers' perceive in their work (Major, Kozlowski, Chao, & Gardner, 1995; Liden et al., 2000; Mullen & Copper, 1994; Paton & Stephens, 1996; Perry, 1997), and increases levels of social support provided amongst coworkers (George & Bettenhausen, 1990). Members of cohesive work teams are more willing to share their knowledge and skills, an essential prerequisite for the development and maintenance of the learning culture that is fundamental to agency and officer resilience (see Chapter 9). Cohesive networks are also less dependent on senior officers for obtaining important resources. Peer relationships are an alternative source for such resources (Liden et al.,

1997) and high quality peer relationships contribute to a greater sense of self-determination (empowerment) in one's work (see Figures 10.1 and 10.2).

Taken together, the social structural variables of senior officer support and peer cohesion can make a valuable contribution to a model of resilience (see Figure 10.2). In the earlier discussion of the choice and impact components of empowerment (see above), a comparison between them and the construct of perceived control was made. Consequently, the final variable proposed for the model is a dispositional one that informs understanding of the relationship between perceived control and resilience: hardiness.

Hardiness and Empowerment

Hardiness has a long history as a predictor of resilience, and one which embraces the officer-agency relationship (Bartone, 2004). A growing body of literature shows that persons high in hardiness, marked by a strong sense of commitment, control, and challenge, tend to remain healthy under stress compared to those low in hardiness. (Bartone, 2003). Hardiness can be thought of as a personality style, reasonably stable over time and across situations—that somehow confers resiliency on those who possess it.

Furthermore, it may be an important adjunct to empowerment. Portraying empowerment as a multilevel process introduces another issue. While organizational decisions can provide the conditions necessary to enable officers, this cannot be taken to automatically imply that officers can fully utilize these opportunities. It is necessary to have an enabling (empowering) environment and officers with the dispositional characteristics to be empowered. The control, challenge, and commitment facets of hardiness represent a dispositional indicator of officers' potential to utilize environmental opportunities to learn from an empowering environment. For this reason, hardiness has the potential to play an important role in a comprehensive critical incident, stress risk management model. Importantly, theoretical considerations and recent research findings lend support to the notion that hardiness levels can be increased through team and organizational intervention (Bartone, 2004).

A key feature of hardiness training involves facilitating the adoption and application of new strategies for interpreting and making sense of experiences, especially highly stressful ones. A critical aspect of the hardiness resiliency mechanism probably involves the interpretations, or the meanings that people attach to events around them, as well as to their own place in the world of experiences. High hardy people will typically interpret experience as (1) overall interesting and worthwhile, (2) something they can exert control over, and (3) challenging, presenting opportunities to learn and grow. It is thus well placed to contribute to the development of the model (Figure 10.2).

CONCLUSION

From a life-course theory perspective, critical incidents represent significant transition points in the career trajectories of police officers. To develop a critical incident, stress risk management model compatible with the tenets of life-course theory, it was necessary to accommodate the iterative nature of critical incident exposure. It was also important to accommodate issues that officers themselves identified as influencing their performance, their well-being, and their satisfaction (see Chapters 3, 4, and 9). For this reason, constructs such as empowerment, supervisor relationships, and peer relationships were given prominent positions within the model.

The model is depicted in Figure 10.2. Paths contributing to the development of empowerment are shown in solid lines. Paths proposed to reduce empowerment are illustrated as hatched lines. Because it can capture changes in perceived coherence, meaningfulness, and manageability, satisfaction is retained as an outcome measure. However, because the occupational health and empowerment literatures have not examined posttrauma outcomes specifically, a measure capable of capturing this aspect of officers' experience must be included in any test of the model. For this reason, posttraumatic growth has been included as an outcome measure in the model (Figure 10.2).

If they are to exercise their duty of care to their officers, police agencies must develop critical incident, stress risk management strategies that decrease the probability of adverse (e.g., posttraumatic stress, PTSD) outcomes and increase the likelihood of officers experiencing adaptive and growth outcomes. Because the risk that police agencies have to manage includes the repetitive exposure to critical incidents, the effectiveness of their risk management strategy will be a function of the degree to which it facilitates the capacity of officers to learn and adapt and so increases their future capacity to deal with the unexpected. That is, risk management strategies must identify the resources and competencies that facilitate the proactive development of officers' general capacity to adapt (i.e., render any future experience meaningful and manageable) to unpredictable circumstances. The model discussed here satisfies these requirements. As such, it can be used to inform the development of practical risk management strategies.

All the model components (with the exception of conscientiousness whose influence can be accommodated in selection or assessment procedures) are amenable to change through organizational intervention and change strategies. Guidelines for changing hardiness, peer support, supervisor support, organizational hassles and uplifts, trust, and empowerment are available in the literature (Bartone, 2004; Cogliser & Schriesheim, 2000; Hart et al., 1993; Herriot et al., 1998; Perry, 1997; Quinn & Spreitzer, 1997). This confers upon the model both theoretical rigor and practical utility.

The focus of this chapter was on managing stress risk in serving officers. An important aspect of the model was its inclusion of a learning-feedback cycle to accommodate the repetitive and uncertain nature of critical incident exposure over a career that may span decades. At some point, the officer will decide to retire. While it is likely that the psychological consequences of many of the critical incident experiences they will have accumulated over time will have been satisfactorily resolved, some may not. This means that officers face the prospect of entering retirement with unresolved issues.

The review of factors influencing resilience, discussed above, identified several (e.g., peer and supervisor support) that will be less available to the retired officer. This raises questions about whether resilience can be sustained into retirement and, if so, what its predictors look like. Consequently, a comprehensive career perspective on critical incident stress risk will not stop at the point where the officer retires. Rather it must extend into the period of retirement. This is the topic of the next chapter.

Chapter 11

DISENGAGEMENT FROM POLICE SERVICE: THE IMPACT OF A CAREER END

INTRODUCTION

There are major transitions that characterize the police career. The first occurs when a person commences employment (see Chapter 3). The second is when they retire. By adopting a life-course perspective, the contents of previous chapters have identified how factors that characterize earlier stages of the career can have an impact on an event that may not occur for several decades. For example, as we shall see, the social and psychological distance that officers put between themselves and family and friends, that has its roots at an early stage in the police career (see Chapter 3) and that is reinforced by subsequent career experiences (see Chapter 9), can affect social and psychological adjustment to retirement. This is not the only career-long experience capable of affecting the transition to retirement.

When they make the transition to retirement, officers may bring with them a history of critical incident experiences that have accumulated over several decades. Police officers are just as susceptible to the effects of trauma at the end of their career as they are at the beginning. Just as some officers brought unresolved traumatic experiences with them when they commenced their police careers (see Chapters 3 and 4), some may take unresolved trauma with them into their retirement.

POLICE RETIREMENT

The course of trauma throughout a law enforcement career may have lasting impact. Considerable research has been done on the effects of adjusting to retirement. Unfortunately, much of this research has not included the police occupation. The research does, however, allow one to draw parallels between other occupations and police work. Adaptation to retirement may depend on one's experiences in early life. Mattilla, Joukamaa, and Salokangas (1988) studied a sample of 389 retired persons and found background factors that led to poor retirement adjustment. These were: (1) an unhappy childhood; (2) a tendency towards social withdrawal; (3) compulsive activity; (4) and preretirement stress. Creative integrity (the ability to be creative and original) and good social support facilitated adjustment to retirement.

Police officers approaching retirement have the same concerns as other workers. Fretz, Kluge, Ossana, and Jones, (1989) studied predictors of preretirement anxiety in individuals close to separation. Results indicated that the best predictors of preretirement anxiety were a low sense of self-efficacy, poor planning, financial insecurity, and bad health. Jakubowski (1985) assessed the impact of retirement on mental health, social adjustment, and factors which might help mediate potential stress. He found that health, irrational beliefs about aging, stressful life events, and prior occupational status all increased stress at retirement. The support of others appeared to help the retiree deal with impending mental stress. Jakubowski noted no significant decline in mental health after retirement, but did find a mild increase in psychological distress and depression.

Bosse, Aldwin, Levenson, and Eckerdt (1987) looked at mental health differences between retirees and workers. They examined psychological symptoms of 1513 men and found retirees reported more psychological symptoms than those still employed. The length of retirement did not matter, but timing did: both those who retired early and late in their careers had more symptoms. This finding is relevant to police officers, who often retire early. The misuse of alcohol among police officers has been noted by researchers (Kroes, 1976; Violanti, 1986). This problem may be exacerbated by the transition into retirement. Brody (1981), in an examination of demographic data, stated that alcohol abuse among retirees has increased. He noted four factors which make retirees susceptible to alcohol problems. These were (1) boredom, (2) concerns with death, (3) loneliness, and (4) poor health.

Brody cited evidence which suggests that a high proportion of retirees who seek medical attention actually have an alcohol problem. Eckerdt, DeLabry, Glynn, and Davis (1989) also examined changes in drinking behavior in retirees. Their findings indicated that as time in retirement increased, retirees reported more problems with drinking.

The retiring police officer faces a different perspective in retirement. The main difference is age. At a time when most workers are in the prime of their careers, the police officer may be retiring. In a sense, the officer is out of synchronization with societal perceptions of a retired person.

Druss (1965) viewed early retirement as a crisis point (transition) in the life of individuals. Such retirement may lead to intrapsychic conflicts in police officers. According to Druss, conflicts revolve around the fear of loss of (1) power and authority (see Chapter 3), (2) a familiar way of life, and (3) security (see Chapter 4).

The loss of a comfortable work position may thus severely disturb the psychological equilibrium of retired officers. McNeil and Griffin (1967) viewed the aspect of role confusion as adversely affecting early retirees. They stated that the period immediately following early retirement is a most difficult time for the person. He or she is suddenly thrust from the role of officer to that of civilian. This new role may produce conflict because officers do not understand, or society has not clearly defined, what their roles are as civilians. Furthermore, as discussed in Chapters 3 and 4, officers tend to isolate themselves from civilians very early in their career and maintain this separation throughout their period of service. On retirement this adds to the demands of adjusting to life as a civilian.

There is a marked contrast between the role of being a police officer and that of a civilian. As McNeil et al. (1983) (p. 107) point out, an individual's role in a military-like structure is predetermined through tradition and written regulation. Rank is strictly defined and individuals know their place in the organization. Deviation from expected roles is generally dealt with by disciplinary action. When officers retire, this structure of work is lost. They do not know what type of role to occupy, and may spend considerable time seeking out activity to restructure their lives. Personality characteristics may affect successful adjustment to retirement. Darnley (1975) found that persons who are flexible and develop long-range plans adjust well to retirement. Such people were found to adapt successfully to other major changes in their lives. Atchley (1976) suggests that successful adaptation to retirement depends not only on flexibility but also the degree of stress which accompanies retirement. This makes issues associated with the coping strategies that officers bring with them into their retirement an appropriate area for future work (see Chapter 9). Livson (1962) found that men with independent personalities adjusted better than those who depended on work for life satisfaction.

Kea (1988) conducted a study which compared well-being among retired and active Los Angeles police officers. His hypotheses were that (1) retired officers with low self-esteem will report less well-being, (2) retired officers who felt out of control of the situation will also report less well-being, (3) officers who retired voluntarily will have a higher level of life satisfaction, and (4) retired officers will have a higher life satisfaction in general than those still working.

Kea found that well-being for younger, older working, and retired officers increased with age. Well-being was highest for retired officers. Self-esteem appeared to be equivalent for younger and retired officers, but lower for older working officers. Feeling in control was lowest for retirees. Lastly, job satisfaction appeared to increase over time, with retirees being highest (in retrospect). The only exception to this finding was officers who were forced to retire. They had lower life satisfaction than those who voluntarily left police work.

The rank of a police officer may play a part in adaptation to retirement. Because of the difficulty in obtaining rank in police work, position is often viewed as a symbol of status among officers. Rank comes with privileges: respect, authority, and prestige. The officer who retires as a captain or inspector likely has much more to give up than the street patrol officer when they revert to the status of civilian. Initial levels of deprivation are apt to be more severe upon retirement for higher ranking officers, but, after initial adjustment, they may actually be at an advantage in retirement.

Dillard (1982) found that job rank influenced satisfaction more than retirement itself. Those in low status positions had less life satisfaction than those in higher status positions. Thus, higher-ranking officers not only enjoyed the benefit of additional skills for second careers, they also had greater life satisfaction than lower-ranking officers. Atchley (1976) suggested that the extent to which a job teaches people self-direction, intellectual flexibility, or sociability affects how well a person adjusts to retirement. Atchley added that skills learned in middle and higher echelon jobs are more useful in retirement. In addition, higher-ranked retirees have more opportunities for employment. They generally can, by virtue of their former position, find a job with similar status and higher pay than the patrol officer.

Police Retirement and Feelings of Loss

There are few officers who can retire from police work and not experience a sense of loss. Worden (1982, p. 10) points out that after one sustains loss, there are certain tasks that must be accomplished before psychological equilibrium can be restored. First, the retired officer must accept the reality of the loss. Officers may try to protect their feelings by denying that they are no longer in police work. Statements like "I'm glad to get out of the job" or "being a cop wasn't that important to me" are also attempts to deny the real meaning of the loss. Second, it is necessary to experience the pain of loss. If a retired officer continues denial, it may lead to psychological dysfunction. This makes it important to consider how police life influences the coping strategies that develop during active service and to investigate their implications for the retired officer. It is difficult for police officers who adapt the macho image to admit they feel pain. Third, the officer must learn to adjust to an environment without police work. The best way to deal with loss is to mentally redefine it in such a way that it benefits the new lifestyle. If officers dwell on the negative aspects of retirement, certain defeat will follow. Fourth, officers must withdraw emotional energy from police work and reinvest it into their new lives. If an officer retires and simply does nothing, he or she may soon experience depression. Most successful police retirees have in some way reinvested their energy into other activities. It does not necessarily have to be a job but some sort of activity. This does not mean that one should abandon one's feelings about police work; it means that one should realize other things are worthy of time and energy. This, of all tasks, appears to the most difficult for retired officers.

The retired police officer should realize that adjusting to the loss of work takes time. There will always be memories of police work. One should accept them and set goals in other directions. Worden comments that grief may be finished when a person can think of a loss without pain. There is no longer that "wrenching quality" associated with memories. In a larger sense, however, one never completely finishes mourning over a loss. How one adjusts is the important factor.

VESTIGES OF TRAUMA AFTER DISENGAGEMENT

We presently know little about the long-term course and stability of PTSD over a lifetime course. One major prospective study is of interest. Solomon and Mikulincer (2006) studied prospective data from a cohort of Israeli veterans with and without combat stress reactions followed up for 20 years. The study assessed posttraumatic symptoms in veterans one, two, three, and 20 years after their combat experience. The authors concluded that combat stress reaction was an important vulnerability marker. Veterans with combat stress reaction were 6.6 times more likely to endorse posttraumatic stress disorder (PTSD) at all four measurements, their PTSD was more severe, and they were at increased risk for exacerbation/reactivation. In both groups, the course fluctuated; PTSD rates dropped three years postwar and rose again 17 years later; 23 percent of veterans without combat stress reaction reported delayed PTSD. Solomon and Mikulincer's results suggest that the detrimental effects of combat are deep and enduring and follow a complex course, especially in combat stress reaction casualties.

Other studies have shown that exposure to combat or combat-like conditions such as the police experience can exacerbate symptoms of PTSD over long periods of time. Elder, Shanahan, and Clipp (1995), for example, found that World War II combat exposure affected long-term mental and physical health some 15 years after the war. Elder (1985) found that 56 percent of World War II veterans who experienced heavy combat were chronically ill or dead by age 65. Their findings also suggest that combat veterans are at risk of posttraumatic stress disorder (PTSD), and degree of combat exposure influences the severity of PTSD.

Residuals of Police Occupational Trauma

Violanti (1997) suggested that police officers continue to experience the "residual" of trauma even after separating from police service. The exposure of police officers to trauma, while generally not as intense as combat, may be for a period of 20 years or more. With such long-term exposure, officers who separate from policing are still likely to experience symptoms associated with posttraumatic stress disorder (PTSD) (Paton & Violanti, 1996). Police officers are in many ways similar to military combatants, experiencing events in their work that involve treachery, violence, and death. It is argued here that police officers with long-term exposure to trauma may, like the soldier, experience the after-effects of trauma long after separation from the war. For some, symptomatology may be full-blown; for others, a residual condition may exist.

With return to civilian life, police officers take with them emotional baggage remaining from traumatic work experiences. Solomon (1992) suggests that persons who leave traumatic situations tend to generalize avoidance to stimuli resembling the trauma in their new environment. As a result, they constrict their scope of activity, social ties, and civilian functioning (see Chapters 3 and 4). This is viewed as a detrimental pattern of residual trauma carried over into the new environment of the separated police officer. The officer's family and close friends may also contribute to this problem by adapting themselves to this widened avoidance.

Officers may experience full or residual PTSD at the time of their separation from service. The "residual stress hypothesis" proposes that prior trauma exposure leaves residual effects which are widespread, deep, and long lasting (Figley, 1978). Solomon (1989, 1990, 1993), in studies of Israeli Veterans, concluded that the trauma of combat leaves marked stress residues among combatants. On the whole, Solomon found that trauma-related symptomatology declined over time, but psychiatric symptomatology remained stable. Her conclusion was that war becomes internalized and continues to cast a shadow on the lives of veterans. Repeated trauma during the combat experience appears to be progressively more severe and limiting and leads to the deepening of symptoms. Scaturo and Hayman (1992) report clinical observations of separated combatants as displaying acute generalized anxiety, worry, and depression. Many of the patients seemed to experience a strong desire to resolve whatever ongoing psychological conflict they struggled with regarding the war. Yet it is possible that, unless diagnosed with full PTSD, those presenting with partial symptoms may not receive the attention they deserve, laying a foundation for future and more entrenched difficulties.

Weiss, Marmar, Schlenger, Fairbank et al. (1992) conclude that PTSD morbidity rates should include those individuals who experience partial as well as full PTSD symptoms. Evans (1987) stated that it is necessary to attend to subclinical phenomena because individuals who only partially meet the full set of diagnostic criteria for PTSD also contribute to the level of morbidity. Egendorf, Kadushin, Laufer, Rothbart, and Sloan (1981) noted that literature on problems of combat veterans seldom distinguishes between those with full or "partial" PTSD. The terminology of the person being in a "residual state" is used to describe the disorder. Weiss et al. (1992) commented that individuals who, on a life-time basis, never meet the full criteria for PTSD are indistinguishable from those who do.

Persons who experience long-term exposure to trauma and separate may have what Horowitz (1986) describes as "post-traumatic character disorder," or what Brown and Fromm (1986) call "complicated PTSD." These categories would better describe individuals who have exposure to repetitive, prolonged trauma (Kroll, Habennicht, & Mackenzie, 1989). Symptoms of persons chronically exposed to trauma appear to be amplified. Hilberman (1980) states that chronically traumatized people are hypervigilant, anxious, and irritated, and without any recognizable baseline of "calm." Studies of returning POWs exposed to repetitive trauma document increased mortality as a result of homicide, suicide, and suspicious accidents (Segal, Hunter, & Segal, 1976). The general conclusion that can be drawn from these studies is that, although not presenting with full PTSD following isolated traumatic episodes, repeat exposure can, over time, increase risk status. Consequently, it becomes necessary to consider the wider implications of such experiences, including the risk becoming addicted to traumatic incidents and carrying the effects of work experiences beyond the point of separation from police work.

Addiction to Prior Occupational Trauma

Police officers spend much of their careers preparing for the worst. Training generally emphasizes the "worst possible case scenario" and prepares officers to deal with that event only. As a result, many officers become occupationally and personally socialized into approaching situations with considerable suspicion. This defensive stance towards life activities can become an obsession and a liability for officers (Williams, 1987; Gilmartin, 1986). As one result of learned defensiveness, it is not uncommon to find a proportion of what Wilson (1980) refers to as "action junkies," officers who are addicted to risk behavior. Police work is mostly routine, but it is also interspersed with acts of violence, excitement, and trauma. Some officers become addicted to this excitement and cannot function effectively without it when they separate from service.

Addiction to highly stimulating and dangerous encounters has been explored by several authors. Solursh (1989) defined two factors which appear to exacerbate the addiction of those exposed to such encounters. The first is the "existence of a series of mutually reinforcing excitatory states beginning with multiple combat experiences and the recurring exciting recall of such experiences" (Solursh, 1988). Such "highs" are frequently followed by a depression or a "downer" mood which borders on numbing (Kolb, 1984). Solursh (1989, p. 251) describes such "highs" in his clinical experiences with Vietnam veterans:

> They (the experiences) appear to be highly reinforcing in the presence of a history of multiple combat exposures and seem to interact with other related excitatory experiences such as a compulsive need for presence of readied weapons, reenacting combat-like activities, seeking physical confrontation, and self-administered substance abuse patterns.

van der Kolk (1987) has discussed an "addiction to traumatic re-exposure" and theorizes that an endogenous opiod release could account for the calm upon re-exposure to stress that is reported by many traumatized persons. van der Kolk (1988) states that increased physiological arousal of traumatized persons decreases their ability to assess the nature of current challenges, and interferes with the resolution of the trauma. Such persons have difficulty in making calm and rational decisions and tend to rely on instant action rather than thought. Kolb (1993) hypothesizes that arousal of intense emotional response to traumatic events leads to hypersensitivity and impaired potential for habituation and relearning.

Grigsby (1991) states that "combat rush" is a conditioned emotional response to trauma. While war is frightening and traumatic, combat may be characterized by periods of intense pleasurable stimulation. These experiences may be reinforcing, leading persons to "seek out" similar trauma. Solursh (1989) views the "rush" experienced by traumatized persons as a response to dullness and boredom in life. They crave excitement as an alternative to a calm lifestyle.

An interesting hypothesis by Gilmartin (1986) purports that adrenaline addiction may result from learned behavior. The author suggests that police work creates a learned perceptual set which causes officers to alter the manner in which they interact with the environment. Statements by officers that "cop work gets into the blood" are provided as evidence describing a physiological change that becomes inseparable from the police role. The interpretation of the environment as always dangerous may subsequently reprogram the reticular activating system and set into motion physiological consequences. This will be interpreted by the officer as a feeling of energization, rapid thought patterns, and a general "speeding up" of physical and cognitive reactions (Gilmartin, 1986).

Gilmartin adds that police work often leads officers to perceive even mundane activities, not from a neutral physiological resting phase, but from a state of hypervigilance, scanning the environment for threats. Once a hypervigilant perception set becomes a daily occurrence, officers alter their physiology daily without being exposed to any types of threatening events. Thus, officers may continuously be on a physiological "high" without stimulation.

Prior Trauma and the Loss of Group Support

Many authors speak of the existence of a police subculture, a closed mini-society where officers maintain a sense of strong cohesion, a code of silence and secrecy, and dependence upon one another for survival (Skolnick, 1972; Neiderhoffer, 1967). The police subculture resembles military subgroups, where teamwork is necessary for survival against the enemy. One police officer commented that "the job is too tough without having to battle the public, the administration and the courts by yourself." It is not easy for police officers to leave this interpersonal web of protection. One of the major regrets of separated officers is that they no longer feel a part of the department. It is as if someone had removed an integral part of their personality (Violanti, 1992).

Separation and loss of support from the police group may serve to increase the already heightened physiological and psychological state associated with PTSD. Social interaction with such groups is important after a traumatic event to reduce psychological symptomatology (Green, Wilson, & Lindy, 1985; Green, 1993). Lindy, Grace, and Green (1981) first described this function as the "trauma membrane" effect, where a network of trusted, close persons served to protect traumatized persons from further distress.

Lin (1982, 1983) and Lin, Woelfel, and Light (1985) found that strong social ties, which resulted from association with others of similar characteristics, lifestyles, and attitudes, were successful in ameliorating distress. Kazak (1991) found that near-group "social context" is an important element in recovery from distress. Boman (1979) found that a cohesive social network helps to reduce the effects of trauma stress.

Tyler and Gifford (1991) found that cohesive military units facilitated trauma resolution in soldiers and their families. Studies of the absence of close ties have also demonstrated effects on psychological distress. Ottenberg (1987) suggested that members of dissimilar groups who experience trauma do not feel a sense of "connectedness" and therefore do not cope well with the traumatic event. Young and Erickson (1988) noted that victims who experience isolation from strong cultural ties had an increased vulnerability to traumatic stress disorders.

Matsakis (1987) found that military wives who experienced isolation from cohesive military social groups did not cope well with emotional distress. Ursano, Holloway, Jones, Rodriguez, and Belenky (1989) reported that military families who experience prolonged absences of spouses, isolation from the civilian community, and potential loss of a family member to war do not cope well with trauma.

The powerful role of social support, particularly in groups with a strong, cohesive identity, in ameliorating distress has been acknowledged. Upon separation from police service, officers exposed to trauma will lose ready access to the group and may no longer be able depend on other officers, the police agency, or police benevolent groups to reinforce a sense of understanding and recognition of their trauma (Williams, 1987; Reiser & Geiger, 1984).

The Police Family: Issues of Leftover Trauma

For police, as well as military families, traumatic duty experiences and emotions that follow are a genuine disruption of emotional attachment and bond (Scaturo & Hayman, 1992). Solomon, Mikulineer, Fried, and Wosner (1987) found that married soldiers had higher rates of PTSD than unmarried soldiers. Solomon attributed these results to many of the added pressures of marriage, including leadership, companionship, and taking care of one's family and other marital responsibilities. Married soldiers carried traumatic symptoms back to the family, which made many of these responsibilities seem more difficult.

Another factor that police officers must face upon separation is getting another job. Many officers who leave at mid-life are too young to actually retire. For the officer who has been exposed to trauma, job-related concerns may be affected in different ways. Blank (1983) has observed that persons involved with trauma in their lives often devote considerable amounts of psychic energy to deal with those traumas. This leaves the person void of energy to direct towards career and marriage.

Scaturo and Hayman (1992) note the lack of adequate and satisfying work for the trauma-exposed person has its emotional costs in the family. Often there is an "assault" upon the person's sense of accomplishment and place in the family. The authors add that therapy may help the traumatized person to reappraise previously unexamined aspects of their lives, including traumatic experiences.

Police family members may have never experienced or cannot fully understand the nature of trauma that officers faced in their daily work. What they see are the effects of such trauma. As Scaturo and Hayman (1992) state: "the therapist must assess the impact of two phenomenologically separate worlds which have collided in the family system." The integration of these two systems is necessarily the way to family well-being.

CONCLUSIONS

Retiring or leaving police work may not leave officers or their families free of the haunting vestiges of trauma. Recognition of this fact is needed among persons who work in this occupation. There are no easy answers to this dilemma, but effective intervention during the police career may help. Officers separated from the force may benefit from therapy which reorients the officers' perceptual set into other roles. As a civilian, the officer must learn to adjust to a role which does not involve constant scanning for threats. Therapy may require teaching the officer to learn new reactive patterns. In addition, the wider family consequences of trauma work must be recognized. More research into the implications of repetitive and addictive traumatic stress phenomena is required to augment support and therapeutic strategies.

Chapter 12

CONCLUSION

The careers of police officers are regularly punctuated by experiences of critical and traumatic events. Researching the psychological consequences of the these experiences is a topic that has attracted considerable attention over the years. Most of this work has emphasized the consequences of specific events located at a single point in time. Furthermore, the focus of these investigations has tended to be on how the relationship between the officer and the critical incident results in the development of, predominantly, pathological (e.g., acute stress disorder, posttraumatic stress disorder) consequences for the officer. While this work has provided valuable insights into this complex and important phenomenon, the emphasis on understanding how pathological outcomes arise following officers' experiences of specific incidents places limitations on the ability of this work to offer insights into a facet of police work that extends over several decades.

This book took the position that a more comprehensive understanding of critical and traumatic phenomena in police officers can be obtained by conceptualizing critical incident stress in policing as (a) an iterative, evolving processes that, (b) takes place within dynamic organizational and societal contexts, and which (c) can result in either positive (e.g., adaptation, growth) or negative (deficit or pathological) outcomes. The potential for critical incidents to be resolved in positive or negative ways was accommodated by adopting a risk management approach which seeks to understand the personal and organizational gains and losses that can arise from operating in an environment characterized by uncertainty, complexity, and danger. A corollary of adopting a risk management approach when working with police officers is a need for it to accommodate the career-long implications of responding repeatedly to the vicissitudes of life. This was accomplished by using life course theory to provide a theoretical foundation for exploring the interaction between career stage and critical incident stress risk.

The contents of this book were informed by two general principles derived from life-course theory. The first was the principle of *contextualism*. This principle argues that a comprehensive understanding of development can only ensue when it is investigated within the contexts (e.g., the police organization, the wider society) in which it occurs. The second is the *life stage principle*. This principle argues that the way personal experience and social events affect people is influenced by where they are in their career span when events occur.

Adopting these principles facilitated identifying the complex web of factors that are interwoven by officers' cumulative critical incident experience in the context of their progressive acculturation and socialization into the police organization to influence critical incident stress risk. This approach identified how people's experience of traumatic events prior to their becoming police officers; the personal and professional expectations of new recruits; the cultural beliefs, practices, and attitudes within the organization; officers' perceptions of their organizational and operational experiences; and their career progression all interacted to influence critical incident stress risk. Further complexity is added to the process of career progression by changes in officers' perception and experiences of the job over time and as a result of officers experiencing turning or transition points in their careers. Officer's careers never follow a smooth linear path. Rather their career paths are periodically punctuated by events that can change how officers define themselves, relate to their colleagues and their profession, and alter how they relate to society. Some of these transitions are expected and predicable; others are not.

Many of the transitions that officers encounter, such as those that mark entry into police work and disengagement from it on retirement, are predictable. Consequently, police organizations develop polices, procedures, and practices to facilitate officers' ability to negotiate these transitions. Some transitions, however, like the events of 9/11, are unpredictable, suddenly-occurring, crisis events that can have long-lasting implications for officers and agencies alike. Yet other transition events, such as the changing gender balance within police organizations, have unpredictable consequences, but take place at a slower, more incremental, pace over time.

If they are to manage critical incident stress risk effectively, police organizations must acknowledge the existence of these transitions in all their guises, understand their immediate, long-term, or more gradual influence, and accommodate the implications of these various types of transition in their risk management planning. This calls for a more proactive, future-oriented approach to risk management planning, and one that is responsive to how changes in the environment of policing can affect officers future risk.

The suddenness and scale of 9/11 made it relatively easy to research the consequences of this type of environmental transition. Not so those accompanying demographic shifts. Because the latter tend to occur at a slower pace, researching the implications of these more subtle changes (e.g., changes in gender composition) are less easy to investigate and can only be effectively investigated using a life-course approach. This means that police organizations must monitor changes in the societal environment in which they operate, assess the implications of these changes for their functioning, and instigate change as appropriate.

Police organizations can benefit from being receptive to these changes by planning how the organization, its culture, and its procedures can evolve in ways that will facilitate its ability to adapt to changes imposed on them by the external environment. The importance of this organizational adaptation can be traced to it being identified as an important precursor of organizational resilience. The development of sustained organizational resilience is a fundamental objective of any critical incident, stress risk management strategy. Organizational responsiveness to environmental change is also crucial to providing a context in which officer resilience is nurtured and sustained.

Irrespective of the pace of change, whether rapid onset as in the case of 9/11 or slow as in the case of demographic change, these emergent transition points have significant implications for how police officers relate to one another, the organization, and the wider society. The social networks that emerge and evolve over time as a result of officer's experience and interpretation of these transitions represent the context in which officers' mental models (schema, interpretive frameworks) of critical incident risk are developed and sustained, their uncertainties confirmed or resolved, and their competencies developed or constrained over time. It thus represents a context that can either nurture officers' future resilience or increase their future vulnerability. A police organization that responds to environmental change is more likely to evolve its culture, polices, and organizational and operational policies and practices in ways that provide a context that facilitates officers' ability to impose coherence and meaning on the challenges they encounter every day. In this way, organizational and officer resilience are intertwined.

By using life course theory to guide its contents, this book has demonstrated the benefits that can accrue to the understanding of critical incident stress risk and its management from placing it within a life-course framework. This perspective provides a more comprehensive conceptualization of traumatic stress processes as they apply to police officers and agencies than can be obtained by focusing on the analysis and interpretation of acute experiences alone. A life-course approach can guide research and intervention agenda in a manner that reflects the changes that characterize a police career that can in some instances span decades. This chapter reflects on the issues covered in the preceding chapters and summarizes the key findings and their implications for future research and intervention on critical incident stress risk and its management.

BENEFITS AND LIMITATIONS

It would, ideally, have been desirable to follow several cohorts of officers from the start of their career through into their retirement. However, issues such as the cost of conducting longitudinal research over several decades place some pragmatic constraints on this. Hopefully, by demonstrating the value of a career-length approach, the contents of this text will lay the foundation for future longitudinal investigations of critical incident stress risk.

An important issue that emerged was the demonstration that traumatic stress risk (i.e., the potential for traumatic events to be experienced in ways that result in their being resolved as either loss or adaptive/growth outcomes) is not restricted to periods of operational duty. It commences prior to the point where people decide to become a police officer and continues into the period of their retirement from active service. Furthermore, the adoption of a life-course perspective highlights the interdependencies between these phases of the police officer's career. Unless critical incident stress is investigated and understood within this life-course context, knowledge of risk will be incomplete and intervention developed to deal with isolated experiences will, at best, be only partially effective.

Recognition of the kinds of interdependencies introduced above highlights the importance of developing interpretive frameworks for the analysis of critical incident stress phenomena that encompass the entire career. A career-length or life-course perspective provides valuable insights into how the dynamic relationship between officer, organization, and society evolves over time. Acknowledging the important role that these dynamic relationships play in determining critical incident stress risk has significant implications for the nature of the interventions developed to manage critical incident stress risk. These must evolve in ways that complement the changes taking place in officers, organizations, and society. Consequently, interventions should be developed and delivered in a contingent rather than a prescriptive manner. Furthermore, the subtle influence of organizational culture and practices on risk that were highlighted throughout this text emphasize the need for risk management intervention to accommodate those dynamic aspects of critical incident experience that derive from officers' perceptions of both operational and organizational contexts and from how the experience of working in these contexts shapes the interpretive frameworks they use to make sense of operational and organizational life.

LESSONS AND IMPLICATIONS

Several lessons can be extracted from the contents of this text. Foremost amongst these is the need for a paradigm shift in the conceptualization and management of critical incident stress risk. In the past, this has tended to focus more on the relationship between officer and event at a single point in time. This is no longer adequate. Critical incident stress risk evolves over time as officers become progressively immersed in the organization and its culture.

Adopting a broader career-length perspective underpinned the realization that risk is something that is informed by the experiences that officers bring with them into the job, the experiences obtained during employment and it must encompass the residual effects of decades of challenging experiences that officers take with them into retirement.

Furthermore, the examination of officer's experiences over time introduced the fact that the consequences of cumulative experience of critical or traumatic events over the course of a career can be characterized by both common (e.g., shared perception of the organization as a result of uniform socialization practices) and idiosyncratic (e.g., individual differences in meeting expectations, incident experiences) factors. Consequently, not only must risk management intervention be embedded in the organization, its culture, and its procedures, it must also be capable of responding to diversity of experience and be capable of proactively preparing officers to deal with future events in ways that build their resilience and adaptive capacities.

This is difficult to achieve with interventions that focus on post event support and counseling. While such processes remain important, they should be complemented by activities designed to proactively enhance resilience. The approach being advocated for here is to adopt a proactive stance that recognizes the need for an iterative approach to risk management that accommodates the repetitive nature of critical incident experiences that take place in an organizational context. That is, intervention should be designed with the express goal of increasing officers' capabilities both before they encounter these challenging events and in ways that facilitate learning from those events officers do experience in ways that enhance future capacity and resilience. This laid down the challenge of producing a model capable of encapsulating these activities.

The risk management model proposed in Chapter 10 was developed to meet this challenge. Its emphasis on critical incident, stress risk management being a process that encompasses officers, the team environment in which they respond to events, and the organizational context in which experiences are embedded, is novel and requires a culture-shift in how police organizations think about risk management strategies in police work. Incorporating personality measures in the model allows it to be used at the start (e.g., accommodate the outcome of selection decisions) and throughout the police career. This was not the only aspect of personality with significant implications for managing stress risk.

Because it defines a relatively stable attributes of the person, personality assessment has featured prominently as a mechanism for selection. Its possible importance has also been boosted by claims for the existence of a unique rescue personality. By focusing on a police agency that does not use formal personality testing as part of its screening and selection process, it was possible to systematically examine whether people who self-select to enter police work can be described by their possessing a unique personality profile. It would appear that this is not the case.

Personality is not the only variable that can be used to distinguish between officers at the start of their careers. Officers can also be differentiated with regard to the nature and extent of their pre-employment traumatic experiences, the degree to which these have been resolved, and by the expectations they bring with them about policing and police work. The presence of these characteristics offers several novel ideas that could inform future selection and training strategies for police officers.

Several novel ideas for selection and training of police recruits can be extracted from the review of officers' selection and early career experiences in this book. At present, police selection processes do not consider either officers' pre-employment traumatic experiences or how they have been resolved as issues that could play a role in improving the level of Person-Environment Fit that can accrue from the selection process. The possibility that some officers may have disengaged from the police during the first year of their employment as a result of the residual consequences of traumatic events experienced prior to their entering police work suggests that the incorporation of this facet of police recruits' experience could play a valuable role in selecting officers.

Recruits who disengage early in their career create a substantial cost to police organizations. Not only will the return on the investment of resources in their training be lost, but early disengagement can also result in a shortfall of available human resources, increasing the demands on other officers as a consequence (e.g., from subsequent staff shortages). Other costs could be incurred if people with unresolved issues remain in employment.

Officers who continue with unresolved issues may not only be more vulnerable to mental health problems in the future, they may also increase the risk to colleagues and to members of the public. While this leads to the conclusion that using information on prior experience and levels of traumatic stress symptoms at time of application to "select out" would be an appropriate course of action, evidence was discussed that suggests that such a decision may be premature and not be the most effective way of using this knowledge. Prior traumatic experiences could have positive implications for nurturing resilient officers. However, achieving this outcome would only ensue following changes to how prior traumatic experiences are incorporated into training programs.

It was tentatively suggested, based on anecdotal accounts, that several officers who brought with them potentially pathological levels of posttrauma symptoms attributed the improvement in their mental health during their first year of police life to the fact that their training helped them impose a sense of coherence and meaning on their earlier traumatic event. While more work is needed to pursue this issue, this observation raises the possibility that incorporating officers' pre-employment traumatic experiences into the early-career training process could facilitate the development of more flexible and sophisticated mental models, enhance officers' capacity to make sense of their experiences, and to learn from their incident experiences in ways that contributes to their "challenge appraisal" and their capacity to cope with, and adapt to, future operational demands (Paton, 1994; Tugade & Frederickson, 2004). Clearly, more research into the relationship between pre-employment traumatic experiences and operational activities is called for.

Finally, knowledge of the fact that many officers enter police work with specific expectations about what the job will entail provides another avenue for the development of selection and training processes. Inconsistencies between officer's expectations about police work and the reality of the work was identified as contributing to stress risk at several points in officers' careers. Problems were attributed primarily to organizational aspects of work (e.g., reporting requirements). However, operational issues (e.g., downtime) were also cited. The importance of accommodating this issue during early career training can be traced to the knowledge that these kinds of organizational inconsistencies have been implicated as critical incident stress risk factors (Paton & Burke, 2007). This problem may be resolved, and officers' capacity for resilience developed, by including a greater focus on providing realistic orientation to operational and organizational realities during early career training.

While the above suggestions all have the potential to contribute to a risk management strategy by increasing officer resilience, it is acknowledged that implementation of the aforementioned suggestions may take some time. It is also recognized that the very precariousness of the role of the police officer in contemporary society makes it impossible to manage all sources of risk. Consequently, it is essential that the process of residual risk assessment (Violanti & Paton, 2006) is given a prominent role in the risk management strategies adopted by police organizations.

In conclusion, by conceptualizing critical incident stress risk as a process embedded in the life course, and in which dynamic organizational and social environments define the contexts in which police officers' life transitions (e.g., critical incidents) take place, the contents of this book can serve both to facilitate resilience research and inform the process of incorporating the findings into the fabric of police organizational life. When this happens, estimates of officers' capabilities to deal with hazardous and adverse work experiences will increase substantially as will confidence in the planning that precedes the deployment of police officers to deal with the emergencies and disasters that are all too frequent facets of the working lives of police professionals in contemporary society.

REFERENCES

Abdollahi, M. K. (2002). Understanding police stress research. *Journal of Forensic Psychology Practice, 2,* 1–24.

Abraham, R. (2000). Organizational cynicism: Bases and consequences. *Genetic, Social and General Psychology Monographs, 126,* 3, 126–141.

Affleck, G., & Tennen, H. (1996). Construing benefits from adversity: Adaptational significance and dispositional underpinnings. *Journal of Personality, 64,* 899–922.

Alexander, D. A., & Wells, A. (1991). Reactions of police officers to body handling after a major disaster: A before and after comparison. *British Journal of Psychiatry, 159,* 517–555.

Alkus, S., & Padesky, C. (1983). Special problems of police officers: Stress related issues and interventions. *Counselling Psychologist, 11,* 2, 55–64.

Allen, J. G. (1995). *Coping with trauma: A guide to self-understanding.* Washington, DC: American Psychiatric Press.

Allport, G. W. (1985). The historical background of social psychology. In G. Lindzey & E. Aronson (Eds.), *Handbook of social psychology* (3rd ed., Vol. 1, pp. 1–46). New York: Random House.

Alper, A., & Kupferman, S. L. (2003) *Enhancing New York City's emergency preparedness.* New York: New York Economic Development Corporation.

American Psychiatric Association. (2000). *Diagnostic and statistical manual of mental disorders* (4th ed., text revision). Washington, DC: Author.

Anderson, N. R., & West, M. A. (1998). Measuring climate for work group innovation: Development and validation of the team climate inventory. *Journal of Organizational Behavior, 19,* 235–258.

Andrews, B., Brewin, C. R., & Rose, S. (2003). Gender, social support, and PTSD in victims of violent crime. *Journal of Traumatic Stress, 16*(4), 421–427.

Anshel, M. H. (2000). A conceptual model and implications for coping with stressful events in police work. *Criminal Justice and Behavior, 27,* 3, 375–400.

Antonovsky, A. (1990). Personality and health: Testing the sense of coherence model. In H. S. Friedman (Ed.), *Personality and disease* (pp. 155–177). New York: John Wiley & Sons.

Atchley, R. C. (1976). *The sociology of retirement.* New York: Schenkman Publishing.

Bandura, A. (1977). Self-efficacy: Toward a unifying theory of behavioural change. *Psychological Review, 84,* 191–215.

Barker, R. T., & Camarata, M. R. (1998). The role of communication in creating and maintaining a learning organization: Preconditions, indicators, and disciplines. *The Journal of Business Communication, 35,* 443–467.

Barrick, M. R., & Mount, M. K. (1991). The big five personality dimensions and job performance: A meta-analysis. *Personnel Psychology, 44,* 1–25.

Bartol, C. R. (1996). Police psychology: Then, now and beyond. *Criminal Justice and Behavior, 23,* 70–89.

Bartone, P. T. (2003). Hardiness as a resiliency resource under high stress conditions. In D. Paton, J. M. Violanti & L. M. Smith (Eds.), *Promoting capabilities to manage posttraumatic stress: Perspectives on resilience* (pp. 59–72). Springfield, IL: Charles C Thomas.

Bartone, P. (2004). Increasing resiliency through shared sensemaking: Building hardiness in groups. In D. Paton, J. Violanti, C. Dunning & L. M. Smith (Eds.), *Managing traumatic stress risk: A proactive approach.* Springfield, IL: Charles C Thomas.

Baumann, U., Humer, K., Lettner, K., & Thiele, C. (1998). Die Vielschichtigkeit von sozialer Unterstützung [The complexity of social support]. In J. Margraf, J. Siegrist & S. Neumer (Hrsg.), *Gesundheits-oder Krankheitstheorie? Saluto-versus pathogenetische Ansätze im Gesundheitswesen* [Health or disease theory? Saluto-versus pathogenetic approaches in the health care system](S.101–113). Berlin: Springer.

Behling, O. (1998). Employee selection: Will intelligence and personality do the job? *Academy of Management Executive, 12,* 77–86.

Behr, R. (2002). Cop Culture–Der Alltag des Gewaltmonopols. Männlichkeit, Handlungsmuster und Kultur in der Polizei. *Betrifft JUSTIZ, 69,* 272–276. [Cop Culture–Daily job routine of the monopoly of force. Masculinity, patterns of acting and culture within the police.]

Benson, M. L. (2001). *Crime and the life course.* New York: Roxbury.

Berkes, F., Colding, J., & Folke, C. (2003). *Navigating social-ecological systems: Building resilience for complexity and change.* Cambridge: Cambridge University Press.

Beutler, L. E., Nussbaum, P. D., & Meredith, K. E. (1988). Changing personality patterns of police officers. *Professional Psychology: Research and Practice, 19,* 503–507.

Blank, A. (1983). *Clinical prospective of the chronically ill. Post-traumatic stress disorders.* Presentation: U.S. Veterans Administration: Northeast Regional Medical Education Center. New York.

Blau, G. (1981). An empirical investigation of job stress, social support, service length, and job strain. *Organizational Behaviour and Human Performance, 27,* 279–302.

Blau T. H. (1994). *Psychological Services for Law Enforcement.* New York: Wiley.

Blok, D., & Brown, J. (2005). *The gendered nature of policing among uniformed operational police officers in England and Wales.* Dept. of Psychology, School of Human Sciences, University of Surrey, November 2005, downloaded from the Internet.

Boman, B. (1979). Behavioral observations on the Grainville train disaster and the significance of stress for psychiatry. Social Sciences & Medicine, 13, 463–471.

Bonafacio, P. (1991). *The psychological effects of police work.* (pp. 169–174). New York: Plenum.

Bonger, B. M. (1991). *The suicidal patient: Clinical and legal standards of care.*

Washington, DC: American Psychological Association.

Bosse, R., Aldwin, C., Levenson, M., & Ekerdt, D. (1987). Mental health differences among retirees and workers: Findings from the normative aging study. *Psychology and Aging, 2,* 383–389.

Brake, J. D. (2001). *Terrorism and the Military's role in domestic crisis management: Background and issues for congress.* Washington, DC.: Congressional Research Service, The Library of Congress.

Braverman, M. (1995, September). *Beyond profiling: an integrated, multi disciplinary approach to preventing workplace violence.* Symposium conducted at the Work, Stress and Health '95 conference, Washington, DC.

Breslau, N., Chilcoat, H. D., Kessler, R. C., Peterson, E. L., & Lucia, V. C. (1999). Vulnerability to assaultive violence: further specification of the sex difference in post-traumatic stress disorder. *Psychological Medicine, 29,* 813–821.

Brewin, C. R., Andrews, B., & Valentine, J. D. (2000). Meta-analysis of risk factors for posttraumatic stress disorder in trauma-exposed adults. *Journal of Consulting and Clinical Psychology, 68,* 748–766.

Brief, A. P., Butcher, A. H., George, J. M., & Link, K. E. (1993). Integrating bottom-up and top-down theories of subjective well-being: the case of health. *Journal of Personality and Social Psychology, 64,* 646–653.

Britt, T. W., Adler, A. B., & Bartone, P. T. (2001). Deriving benefits from stressful events: The role of engagement in meaningful work and hardiness. *Journal of Occupational Health Psychology, 6,* 53–63.

Brody, J. (1981). Aging and alcohol abuse. Paper presented at the White House Conference on Aging, Washington, DC, November 30, 1981.

Brown, M. K. (1981). *Working the street: Police discretion and the dilemmas of reform.* New York: Russell Sage.

Brown, J. M., & Campbell, E. A. (1994). *Stress and policing: Sources and strategies.* Chichester: John Wiley.

Brown, J. M., & Fielding, J. (1993). Qualitative differences in men and women police officers' experience of occupational stress. *Work & Stress, 7,* 327–340.

Brown, D. P., & Fromm, E. (1986). *Hypnotherapy and hypnoanalysis.* Hillsdale, NJ: Erlbaum.

Brown, G. W., & Harris, T. O. (1989). *Life events and illness.* New York: Guilford.

Brown, J., Mulhern, G., & Joseph, S. (2002). Incident-Related Stressors, Locus of Control, Coping, and Psychological Distress Among Firefighters in Northern Ireland. *Journal of Traumatic Stress, 15,* 161–168.

Brunetto, Y., & Farr-Wharton, R. (2003). The impact of government practice on the ability of project managers to manage. *International Journal of Project Management, 21,* 2, 125–133.

Buchanan, G., Stephens, C. V., & Long, N. (2001). Traumatic experiences of new recruits and serving police officers. *Australasian Journal of Trauma and Disaster Studies.* 2001-2 (On-line serial) URL. Http://www.massey.ac.nz/%7Etrauma/-issues/2001-2/buchanan.htm

Burbeck, E., & Furham, A. (1985). Police officer selection: A critical review of the literature. *Journal of Police Science and Administration, 13,* 58–69.

Burghardt, P. (2004). *Combined systems.* Proceedings of ISCRAM 2004. Brussels: ISCRAM.

Burke, K. J. (2009). *Adjusting to life 'on the beat:' A longitudinal examination of adaptation to the police profession.* Unpublished Ph.D. Thesis. University of Tasmania.

Burke, K., & Paton, D. (2006a). Well-being in Protective Services Personnel: Organisational Influences. *Australasian Journal of Disaster and Trauma Studies,* 2006-2. http://trauma.massey.ac.nz/issues/2006-2/burke.htm

Burke, K. J., & Paton, D. (2006b). Predicting Police Officer Job Satisfaction: Traditional versus Contemporary Models of Trauma in Occupational Experience. *Traumatology, 12,* 189–197.

Burke, K. J., Shakespeare-Finch, J. E., Paton, D., & Ryan, M. (2006). Developing the Resilient Officer: Individual Characteristics at Point of Entry to Policing. *Traumatology, 12,* 178–188.

Burke, R. J., & Mikkelsen, A. (2005). Gender issues in policing: Do they matter? *Women in Management Review, 20,* 133–143.

Cantor, C. H., Tyman, R., & Slater, P. J. (1995). A historical survey of police in Queensland, Australia, 1843–1992. *Suicide and Life Threatening Behavior, 25,* 499–507.

Carafano, J. J. (2003). *Preparing responders to respond: The challenges to emergency preparedness in the 21st Century.* Heritage Lectures #812. Washington, DC: The Heritage Foundation.

Carlier, I. V. E., Lamberts, R. D., Gersons, B. P. R., & Berholdt (1997). Risk factors for posttraumatic stress in police officers: A prospective analysis. *Journal of Nervous and Mental Disease, 185,* 498–506.

Carlier, I. V. E., Lamberts, R. D., & Gersons, B. P. R. (2000). The dimensionality of trauma: A multidimensional scaling comparison of police officers with and without posttraumatic stress disorder. *Psychiatry Research, 97,* 29–39.

Carver, C. S.. Scheier, M. F., & Weintraub, J. K. (1989). Assessing coping strategies: A theoretically based approach. *Journal of Personality and Social Psychology, 56,* 267–283.

Chandler, E. V., & Jones, C. S. (1979). Cynicism - AN inevitability of police work. *Journal of Police Science and Administration, 7,* 1, 65–68.

Charbonneau, F. (2000). Suicide among the police in Quebec. *Population, 55,* 367–378.

Cogliser, C. C., & Schriesheim, C. A. (2000). Exploring work unit context and leader-member exchange: A multi-level perspective. *Journal of Organizational Behaviour, 21,* 487–511.

Cohan, C. L, Cole, S. W., & Steve, W. (2002). Life course transitions and natural disaster: marriage, birth, and divorce following Hurricane Hugo. *Journal of Family Psychology, 6,* 14–25.

Coleman, A. M., & Gorman, L. P. (1992). Conservatism, dogmatism and authoritarianism. *Sociology, 16,* 1–11.

Coman, G., & Evans, B. (1991). Stressors facing Australian police in the 1990s. *Police Studies International Review of Police Development, 14,* 4 153–165.

Conger, J. A., & Konungo, R. (1988). The empowerment process; Integrating theory and process. *Academy of Management Review, 13,* 471–482.

Cooper, H. H. A. (2001). Terrorism: The problems of definition revisited. *American Behavioral Scientist, 44,* 881–893.

Costa, P. T., Jr., & McCrae, R. R. (1989). *The NEO-PI/NEO-FFI manual supplement.* Lutz, FL: Psychological Assessment Resources.

Costa, P. T., & McCrae, R. R. (2003). *NEO-Five Factor Inventory.* Lutz, FL: Psychological Assessment Resources.

Costa, P. T., Somerfield, M. R., & McCrae, R. (1996). Personality and coping: A reconceptualization. In M. Zeidner & N. S. Endler (Eds.), *Handbook of coping: Theory, research, application* (pp. 44–61). New York: John Wiley.

Crank, J. P., Regoli, B., Hewitt, J. D., & Culbertson, R. G. (1993). An assessment of work stress among police executives. *Journal of Criminal Justice, 21,* 313–324.

Creamer, T. L., & Liddle, B. J. (2005). Secondary traumatic stress among disaster mental health workers responding to the September 11 attacks. *Journal of Traumatic Stress, 18,* 89–96.

Crego, J., & Spinks, T. (1997). Critical incident management simulation. In R. Flin, E. Salas, M. Strub & L. Martin (Eds.), *Decision making under stress.* Aldershot: Ashgate.

Cronin, T. J. (1982). *Police suicides: A comprehensive study of the Chicago Police Department 1970–1979.* Masters thesis, Lewis University, Illinois.

Dake, K. (1992). Myths of nature and the public. *Journal of Social Issues, 48,* 21–38.

Dannefer, D. (1984). Adult development and social theory: A paradigmatic reappraisal. *American Sociological Review, 49,* 100–106.

Darnley, F. (1975). Adjustment to retirement: Integrity or despair? *Family Coordinator, 24,* 214–221.

Darragh P. M. (1991). Epidemiology of suicide in Northern Ireland. *Irish Journal of Medical Science, 160,* 354–357.

Davison, E. H, Pless, A. P., Gugliucci, M. R., King, L. A., King, D. W., Salgado, D. M., Spiro, A., & Bachrach, P. S. (2006). Late-life emergence of early life trauma: The phenomenon of late-onset stress symptomatology among aging combat veterans. *Research on Aging, 28,* 84–114.

Davidson, M., & Veno, A. (1980). Stress and the policeman. In C. L. Cooper & J. Marshal (Eds.), *White collar and professional stress.* London: Wiley.

Davis, G. C., & Breslau, N. (1998). Are women at greater risk for PTSD than men? *Psychiatric Times,* July 1998, Issue 7, Vol. XV.

Daw, J. (2001). Responding to the nation's sadness, anger and fear. Monitor on *Psychology, 32.* Retrieved July 3, 2002 from www.apa.monitor/nov01/

Deahl, M. P., Gillham, A. B., Thomas, J., Searle, M. M., & Srinivasan, M. (1994). Psychological sequelae following the Gulf War: Factors associated with subsequent morbidity and the effectiveness of psychological debriefing. *British Journal of Psychiatry, 165,* 60–65.

Department of Homeland Security. (2003). *Top Officials (TOPOFF) Exercise Series: TOPOFF 2. After Action Summary Report.* Washington, DC: Department of Homeland Security.

Dillard, J. (1982). Life satisfaction of retired and nearly retired workers. *Journal of*

Employment Counseling, 19, 31–134.

Dirks, K. T. (1999). The effects of interpersonal trust on work group performance. *Journal of Applied Psychology, 84,* 445–455.

Disengagement Summit. (1998). *Attrition in the New Zealand Police.* Proceedings of the Disengagement Summit. Wellington: New Zealand Police.

Druss, R. G. (1965). Problems associated with retirement from the military. *Military Medicine, 130,* 382–385.

Dunning, C. (1999). Prevention strategies to reduce police trauma: A paradigm shift. In J. Violanti & D. Paton (Eds.), *Police trauma: The psychological aftermath of civilian combat.* (pp. 269–286). Springfield, IL: Charles C Thomas.

Dunning, C. (2003). Sense of coherence in managing trauma workers. In D. Paton, J. M. Violanti & L. M. Smith (Eds.), *Promoting capabilities to manage posttraumatic stress: Perspectives on resilience* (pp. 119–135). Springfield, IL: Charles C Thomas.

Earle, T. C. (2004). Thinking aloud about trust: A protocol analysis of trust in risk management. *Risk Analysis, 24,* 169–183.

Eckerdt, D., DeLabry, L., & Glynn, R. (1989). Change in drinking behaviors with retirement: Finding from the Normative Aging Study. *Journal of Studies on Alcohol, 50,* 347–353.

Egendorf, A., Kadushin, C., Laufer, R. S., Rothbart, C., & Sloan, L. (1981). *Legacies of Vietnam: Comparative adjustment of veterans and their peers.* Report to committee on veteran's affairs. Washington, DC: U.S. Government Printing Office.

Elder, G. H. (1985). Perspectives on the life course. In G. H. Elder (Ed.), *Life course dynamics* (pp. 23–49). Ithaca, NY: Cornell University Press.

Elder. G. H. (1992). The life course. In E. F. Borgatta & M. L. Borgatta (Eds.), *The encyclopedia of sociology,* vol. 3 (pp. 1120–1130). New York: McMillan.

Elder, G. H. (1995). The life course and human development. In: W. Damon & R. M. Lerner (Eds.), *Handbook of child psychology. Vol. 1: Theoretical models of human development.* (pp. 939–991). New York: John Wiley & Sons.

Elder, G. H., George, L. K., & Shanahan, M. J. (1996). *Psychosocial stress over the life course.* Orlando, FL: Academic Press. Retrieved February 27, 2007, from PILOTS Database.

Elder, G. H., Shanahan, M. J., & Clipp, E. (1994).When war comes to men's lives: Life-course patterns in family, work, and health. *Psychology and Aging, 9,* 5–16.

Elder, G. H., Shanahan, M. J., & Clipp, E. C. (1995). Linking combat and physical health: The legacy of World War II in men's lives. *American Journal of Psychiatry, 154,* 330–336.

Elder, G. H., Shanahan, M. J., & Clipp, E. C. (1994). When war comes to men's lives: Life-course patterns in family, work, and health. *Psychology and Aging, 9,* 5–16. Retrieved February 27, 2007, from PILOTS Database database.

Elder, G. H., George, L. K. Shanahan, M. J., & Kaplan, H. B. (1996). Psychosocial stress: Perspectives on structure, theory, life course, and methods (pp. 247–292). Orlando, FL: Academic Press.

Elder, G. H., Gimbel, C., & Ivie, R. (1991). Turning points in life: The case of military service and war. *Military Psychology, 3,* 215–231.

Endsley, M., & Garland, D. (2000). *Situation awareness. Analysis and measurement.*

Mahwah, NJ.: Lawrence Erlbaum.

Evans, A. S. (1987). Subclinical epidemiology. *American Journal of Epidemiology, 124,* 545–555.

FEMA. (2004). *Responding to incidents of national consequence.* Washington, DC: FEMA.

Fenster, C. A., & Locke, B. (1973). Neuroticism amongst policemen: An examination of police personality. *Journal of Applied Psychology, 57,* 3, 358–359.

Fisher, H. W. (2000). Mitigation and response planning in a bio-terrorist attack. *Disaster Prevention and Management, 9,* 360–367.

Figley, C. R. (1978). Psychological adjustment among Vietnam veterans: An overview of the research. In C. R. Figley (Ed.), *Stress disorders among Vietnam veterans–Theory, research, and treatment.* New York: Brunner/Mazel.

Figley, C. R. (1985). *Trauma and its wake.* New York: Brunner/Mazel.

Figley, C. R. (1999). Police compassion fatigue: Theory, research, assessment, treatment, and prevention. In J. Violanti & D. Paton (Eds.), *Police trauma: The psychological aftermath of civilian combat* (pp. 37–53). Springfield, IL: Charles C Thomas.

Fisher, H. W. (2000). Mitigation and response planning in a bio-terrorist attack. *Disaster Prevention and Management, 9,* 360–367.

Flin, R. (1996). *Sitting in the hot seat. Leaders and teams for critical incident management.* Chichester: Wiley.

Flin, R., & Arbuthnot, K. (Eds.). (2002). *Incident command: Tales from the hot seat.* Aldershot: Ashgate.

Forastiere, F., Perucci, C. A., DiPietro, A., Miceli, M., Rapiti, E., Bargagli, A., & Borgia, P. (1994). Mortality among urban policemen on Rome. *American Journal of Industrial Medicine, 26,* 785–798.

Fowlie, D. G., & Aveline, M. O. (1985). The emotional consequences of ejection, rescue, and rehabilittion in the Royal Air Force crew. *British Journal of Psychiatry, 146,* 609–613.

Foy, D. W., Sipprelle, R. C., Rueger, D. D., & Carroll, E. M. (1984). Etiology of posttraumatic stress disorder in Vietnam veterans: Analysis of pre-military, military, and combat exposure influences. *Journal of Consulting and Clinical Psychology, 52,* 88–96.

Fredrickson, B. L., Tugade, M. M., Waugh, C. E., & Larkin, G. (2003). What good are positive emotions in crises?: A prospective study of resilience and emotions following the terrorist attacks on the United States on September 11th, 2001. *Journal of Personality and Social Psychology* 84:365–376.

Freeman, T. W., Roca, V., & Moore, W. M. (2000). A comparison of combat related posttraumatic stress disorder patients with and without a history of suicide attempt. *Journal of Nervous and Mental Disease, 188,* 460–463.

Freedman, S. A., Gluck, N., Tuval-Mashiach, R., Brandes, D., Peri, T., & Shalev, A. Y. (2002). Gender differences in responses to traumatic events: A prospective study. *Journal of Traumatic Stress, 15*(5), 407–413.

Fremouw, W. J., de Perczel, M., & Ellis, T. E. (1990). *Suicide risk: Assessment and response guidelines.* Elmsford, NY: Pergamon Press.

Fretz, B., Kluge, N., Ossna, S., & Jones, S. (1989). Intervention targets for reducing pre-retirement anxiety and depression. *Journal of Counseling Psychology, 36,* 301–307.

Fridell, L. A., & Binder (1992). Police officer decision making in potentially violent confrontations. *Journal of Criminal Justice, 20,* 385–399.

Frye, J. & Stockton, R. A. (1982). Discriminant analysis of post traumatic stress among a group of Vietnam veterans. *American Journal of Psychiatry, 139,* 52–56.

Fullerton, C. S., Ursano, R. J., Epstein, R. S., Crowley, B., Vance, K., Kao, T. C., Dougall, A., & Baum, A. (2001). Gender differences in Posttraumatic Stress Disorder after motor vehicle accidents. *American Journal of Psychiatry, 158*(9), 1486–1491.

Galea, S., Ahern, J., Resnick, H., Kilpatrick, D., Bucuvalas, M., Gold, J., & Vlahov, D. (2002). Psychological sequelae of the September 11 terrorist attacks in New York City. *New England Journal of Medicine, 346,* 982–987.

Gecas, V., & Seff, M. A. (1990). Social class and self-esteem: Psychological centrality, compensation, and the relative effects of work and home. *Social Psychological Quarterly, 53,* 165–173.

Gerber, G. L. (2001). *Women and men police officers: Status, gender and personality.*

Genz, J. L., & Lester, D. (1976). Authoritarianism in policemen as a function of experience. *Journal of Police Science and Administration, 4,* 1, 9–13.

Gerson, E. M. (1976). On Quality of Life. *American Sociological Review, 41,* 793–806.

Gersons, B. (1989). Patterns of PTSD among police officers following a shooting incident: A two-dimensional model and treatment implications. *Journal of Traumatic Stress, 2,* 247–257.

Gershon, R. R., Lin, S., & Li, X. (2002). Work stress in aging police officers. *Journal of Occupational and Environmental Medicine, 44,* 160–167.

George, J. M., & Bettenhausen, K. (1990). Understanding prosocial behaviour, sales and turnover: A group level analysis in a service context. *Journal of Applied Psychology, 75,* 698–709.

Ghiselli, E. E., & Barthol, R. P. (1953). The validity of personality inventories in the selection of employees. *American Psychologist, 48,* 26–34.

Giga, S. I., Noblet, A. J., Faragher, B., & Cooper, C. L. (2003). The UK perspective: A review of research on organisational stress management interventions. *Australian Psychologist, 38,* 2, 158–164.

Gilmartin, K. M. (1986). Hypervigilance: A learned perceptual set and its consequences on police stress. In J. T. Reese & H. A. Goldstein (Eds.), *Psychological services for law enforcement* (pp. 443–446). Washington, DC: U.S. Government Printing Office.

Gilmartin, K. M. (1990). The brotherhood of biochemistry: Its implications for a police career. In H. E. Russel & A. Beigal (Eds.), *Understanding human behavior for effective police work* (pp. 397–418). New York: Basic Books.

Gist, M., & Mitchell, T. N. (1992). Self-Efficacy: A theoretical analysis of its determinants and malleability. *Academy of Management Review, 17,* 183–211.

Gist, R., & Woodall, S. J. (1998). Social sciences versus social movements: The origins and natural history of debriefing. *The Autralasian Journal of Disaster and Trauma Studies,* 1998-1.

Gist, R., & Woodall, J. (2000). There are no simple solutions to complex problems. In J. M. Violanti, D. Paton & C. Dunning (Eds.), *Posttraumatic stress intervention: Challenges, issues, and perspectives* (pp. 81–95). Springfield, IL: Charles C Thomas.

Goldfarb, D. A., & Aumiller, G. S. (2004). The heavy badge–10 reasons cops are different. Retrieved October 5, 2005, from http://www.heavybadge.com/10reason.htm

Grant, N. K. Hoover, D. A., Scarisbrick-Hauser, A., & Muffet, S. L. (2003). The Crash of United Flight 93 in Shanksville, Pennsylvania. In J. L. Monday (Ed.), *Beyond September 11: An account of post disaster research.* Special Publication #39. Boulder: Institute of Behavioral Science, Natural Hazards Research & Applications Information Centre, University of Colorado.

Green, B. L., Wilson, J. P., & Lindy, J. D. (1985). Conceptualizing PTSD: A psychosocial framework. In C. R. Figley (Ed.), *Trauma and its wake: The study and treatment of post-traumatic stress disorder* (pp. 53–69). New York: Brunner Mazel.

Green, B. L., Lindy, J. D., & Grace, M. C. (1989). Multiple diagnosis in posttraumatic stress disorder: The role of war survivors. *Journal of Nervous and Mental Disease, 177,* 329–335.

Green, B. L. (1993). Identifying survivors at risk. In J. P. Wilson & B. Rapheal (Eds.), *International handbook of traumatic stress syndromes* (pp. 53–69). New York: Plenum.

Grigsby, J. P. (1991). Combat rush: Phenomenology of central and autonomic arousal among war veterans with PTSD. *Psychotherapy, 28,* 354–363.

Gross, E. (1973). Work, organization, and stress. In S. Levine & N. A. Scotch (Eds.), *Social stress* (pp. 54–110). Chicago, IL: Aldine.

Haarr, R. N. (2005). Factors affecting the decision of police recruits to drop out of police work. *Police Quarterly, 8,* 4, 431–453.

Hackett, D. (2004). Suicide in the police. In D. Hackett & J. M. Violanti (Eds.), *Police suicide: Tactics for prevention.* Springfiled, IL: Charles C Thomas.

Halligan, S. L., & Yehuda, R. (2000). Risk factors for PTSD. *PTSD Research Quarterly, 11*(3), 1–8.

Harris, R. N. (1973). *The police academy: An inside view.* New York: Wiley Publishing, pp. 45–78.

Harrison, M. I., & Shirom, A. (1999). *Organizational diagnosis and assessment.* Thousand Oaks, CA: Sage.

Hart, P. M. (1999). Predicting employee life satisfaction: A coherent model of personality, work and non-work experiences, and domain satisfaction. *Journal of Applied Psychology, 84,* 564–584.

Hart, P. M., & Cooper, C. L. (2001). Occupational Stress: Toward a more integrated framework. In N. Anderson, D. S. Ones, H. K. Sinangil & C. Viswesvaren (Eds.), *International handbook of work and organizational psychology, vol. 2: Organizational psychology.* London: Sage.

Hart, P. M., Wearing, A. J., & Heady, B. (1993). Assessing police work experiences: Development of the police daily hassles and uplifts scales. *Journal of Criminal Justice, 21,* 558–572.

Hart, P. M., Wearing, A. J., & Heady, B. (1995). Police stress and wellbeing: Integrating personality, coping and daily work experiences. *Journal of Occupational* and *Organizational Psychology, 68,* 133–156.

Hartley, T. A., Violanti, J. M., Fekedulegn, D., Andrew, M. E., & Burchfiel, C. M. (2006). Associations between major life events, traumatic incidents and depression among Buffalo police officers. *International Journal of Emergency Mental Health, 9,* 25–35.

Hartsough, D. M., & Myers, D. G. (1985). *Disaster work and mental health: Prevention and control of stress among workers.* Rockville, MD. U.S. Department of Health and Human Services, No. (ADM) 85–1422.

Hartwig, D., & Violanti, J. M. (1999). Suicide by police officials in North Rhine-Westphalia. An evaluation of 58 suicide between 1992–1998. *Archives of Kriminologie, 204,* 129–142.

Helmkamp J. C. (1996). Occupation and suicide among males in the US Armed Forces. *Annals of Epidemiology, 6,* 83–88.

Herriot, P., Hirsh, W., & Reilly, P. (1998). *Trust and transition: Managing today's employment relationship.* Chichester: John Wiley & Sons.

Hewitt, P. L., & Flett, G. L. (1991). Perfectionism in the self and social contexts: Conceptualization, assessment and association with psychopathology. *Personality and Social Psychology, 60,* 456–470.

Hilberman, E. (1980). The 'wife-beater's' wife reconsidered. *American Journal of Psychiatry, 137,* 1336–1347.

Hitz, D. (1973). Drunken sailors and others: drinking problems in specific occupations. *Quarterly Journal on Studies in Alcohol, 34,* 496–505.

Hodgins, G. A., Creamer, M., & Bell, R. (2001). Risk factors for posttrauma reactions in police officers: A longitudinal study [Electronic version]. *Journal of Nervous and Mental Disease, 189,* 541–547.

Hough, L. M. (1998). Personality at work: Issues and evidence. In M. D. Hakel (Ed.), *Beyond multiple choice: Evaluating alternatives to traditional testing for selection* (pp. 131–166). Mahwah, NJ: Lawrence Erlbaum.

Hovanitz, C. A. (1986). Life event stress and coping style as contributions to psychopathology. *Journal of Clinical Psychology, 42,* 34–41.

Huddleston, L. M., Paton, D., & Stephens, C. (2006). Conceptualizing traumatic stress in police officers: Pre-employment, critical incident and organizational influences. *Traumatology, 12,* 170–177.

Huff, M. B. (1999). *Does the timing of life course events really matter: The perceptions of Vietnam veterans.* Dissertation (249 pp.) University of Kentucky.

Human Behavior and WMD Crisis/Risk Communication Workshop (HBWMD, 2001). *Final Report.* Washington, DC.: Defense Threat Reduction Agency, Federal Bureau of Investigation, & US Joint Forces Command.

Hyer, L. E., & Summer, M. N. (1994). *Trauma victim: theoretical issues and practical suggestions.* Muncie, IN: Accelerated Development. (pp. 633–679).

Jackson, B. A., Baker, J. C., Ridgely, M. S., Bartis, J. T., & Linn, H. I. (2003). *Protecting emergency responders, Volume 3: Safety management in disasters and terrorism response.* Cincinatti, OH: National Institute for Occupational Safety and Health.

Janoff-Bulman, R. (1992). *Shattered assumptions.* New York: Free Press.

Janoff-Bulman, R., & Freize, I. H. (1983). A theoretical perspective for understanding reactions to victimization. *Journal of Social Issues, 39,* 1–17.

Jensen, A. R. (1957). Authoritarian attitudes and personality maladjustment. *Journal of Abnormal and Social Psychology, 54,* 303–311.

Johnston, P., & Paton, D. (2003). Environmental resilience: Psychological empowerment in high-risk professions. In D. Paton, J. M. Violanti & L. M. Smith (Eds.), *Promoting capabilities to manage posttraumatic stress: Perspectives on resilience* (pp. 197–219). Springfield, IL: Charles C Thomas.

Joiner, T. E., & Rudd, D. M. (1995). Negative attributional style for interpersonal events and the occurrence of severe interpersonal disruptions as predictors of self-reported suicide ideation. *Suicide and Life Threatening Behavior, 25,* 297–304.

Kaczmarek, A., & Packer, J. (1997). *Determination of a job related test battery for the psychological screening of police applicants.* Payneham, South Australia: National Police Research Unit.

Kahneman, D., & Tversky, A. (1973). On the psychology of prediction. *Psychological Review, 80,* 237–251.

Kampanakis, J. (2000). Police organizational culture and policemen's integrity. In M. Pagon (Ed.), *Policing in Central and Eastern Europe: Ethics, integrity and human rights.* Ljubljana, Slovenia: College of Police and Security Studies (pp. 497–506).

Kates, A. (1999). *Cop shock.* Tucson, AZ: Holbrook Street Press.

Kazak, A. E. (1991). The social context of coping with childhood chronic illness: Family systems and social support. In A. LaGreca, L. J. Siegel, J. L. Wallander & C. E. Walker (Eds.), *Stress and coping in child health* (pp. 262–278). New York: Guilford Press.

Kea, W. (1987). *Loss of locus of control, self-esteem and job satisfaction on subjective wellbeing in retired and active duty police officers in a metropolitan police department.* Doctoral Dissertation, University Microfilms International, Ann Arbor, Michigan, 1987.

Kelling, G. E., & Pate, M. (1975). The person-role fit in policing: The current knowledge and future research. In W. Kroes & J. J. Hurrell Jr. (Eds.), *Job stress and the police officer: Identifying stress reduction techniques* (pp. 117–129). Health, Education and Welfare Publication no. 76-187(NIOSH), Washington, DC: U.S. Government Printing Office.

Kendler, K. S., Karkowski, L. M., & Prescott, C. A. (1998). Stressful life events and major depression: Risk period, long-term contextual threat, and diagnostic specificity. *Journal of Nervous and Mental Disease, 186,* 661–669.

Kendler, K. S., Kessler, R. C., Neale, M. C., Heath, A. C., & Eaves, L. J. (1993). The major depression: Risk period, long-term contextual threat, and diagnostic specificity. *Journal of Nervous and Mental Disease, 186,* 661–669.

Kendra, J., & Wachtendorf, T. (2003). Creativity in emergency response to the World Trade Center disaster. In J. L. Monday (Ed.), *Beyond September 11: An account of post disaster research.* Special Publication #39. Boulder: Institute of Behavioral Science, Natural Hazards Research and Applications Information Centre, University of Colorado.

Kenny, D. (2000). Occupational stress: Reflections on theory and practice. In D. T. Kenny (Ed.), *Stress and health: Research and clinical applications.* Amsterdam:

Harwood.

Kirkman, B. L., & Rosen, B. (1999). Beyond self-management: Antecedents and consequences of team empowerment. *Academy of Management Journal, 42,* 58–74.

Kirmeyer, S., & Diamond, A. (1985). Coping by police officers: A study of role stress and type A and type B behaviour patterns. *Journal of Occupational Behavior, 6,* 3, 183–195.

Kirschman, E. (1983). *Wounded heroes: A case study and systems analysis of job-related stress and emotional dysfunction in three police officers.* Doctoral Dissertation, University Microfilms International, Ann Arbor, Michigan.

Klein, R., Nicholls, R., & Thomalla, F. (2003). Resilience to natural hazards: How useful is this concept? *Environmental Hazards, 5,* 35–45.

Kobasa, S. C. (1979). Stressful life events, personality, and health: An inquiry into hardiness. *Journal of Personality and Social Psychology, 37,* 1–11.

Koberg, C. S., Boss, R. W., Senjem, J. S., & Goodman, E. A. (1999). Antecedents and outcomes of empowerment. *Group & Organization Management, 24,* 71–91.

Kohan, A., & Mazmanian, D. (2003). Police work, burnout and pro-organisational behaviour: A consideration of daily work experiences. *Criminal Justice and Behavior, 30,* 559–583.

Kohler, S., & Kamp, J. (1992). *American workers under pressure.* (Technical Report). St Paul, MN: St Paul Fire and Marine Insurance Company.

Kolb, L. C. (1984). The post-traumatic disorders of combat: A subgroup with conditioned emotional response. *Military Medicine, 149,* 237–243.

Kolb, L. C. (1993). The psychobiology of PTSD: Perspectives and reflections of the past, present, and future. *Journal of Traumatic Stress, 6,* 293–304.

Kop, N., Euwema, M., & Schaufeli, W. (1999). Burnout, job stress and violent behaviour among dutch police officers. *Work & Stress, 13,* 326–340.

Krause, N., Shaw, B. A., & Cairney, J. (2004). A descriptive epidemiology of lifetime trauma and the physical health status of older adults. *Psychology and Aging, 19,* 637–648.

Kroes, W. H. (1974). Job stress in policemen: An empirical study. *Police Stress, 1,* 9–10.

Kroes, W. H. (1976). *Society's victim: The policeman.* Springfield, IL: Charles C Thomas.

Kroes, W. H. (1986). *Society's victim: The police.* Springfield, IL: Charles C Thomas.

Kroes, W. H., Margolis, B. L., & Hurrel, J. J. (1974). Job stress in policemen. *Journal of Police Science and Administration, 2,* 2, 145–155.

Krohne, H. W. (1996). Individual differences in coping. In M. Zeidner & N. S. Endler (Eds.), *Handbook of coping* (pp. 381–409). New York: John Wiley.

Kroll, J., Habenicht, M., & Mackenzie, T., et al. (1989). Depression and post-traumatic stress disorder in southeast Asian refugees. *American Journal of Psychiatry, 146,* 1592–1597.

Kumpfer, K. L. (1999). Factors and processes contributing to resilience. In M. D. Glantz & J. L. Johnson (Eds.), *Resilience and development: Positive life adaptations.* New York: Kluwer Academic/Plenum.

Lasker R. D. (2004). R*edefining readiness: Terrorism planning through the eyes of the public.* New York: The New York Academy of Medicine.

Laub, J. H., Nagin, D. S., & Sampson, R. J. (1998). Trajectories of change in criminal offending: Good marriages and the desistance process. *American Sociological Review, 63,* 225–238.

Lazarus, R. S. (1981). The stress and coping paradigm. In C. Eisdorfer, D. Cohen, Kleinman & P. Maxim (Eds.), *Models for clinical psychopathology* (pp. 177–214). New York: Spectrum.

Lazarus, R. S., & Folkman S. (1984). *Stress, appraisal, and coping.* New York: Springer.

Lee, T. W. (1999). Using qualitative methods in organizational research. CA: Sage.

Lefcourt, H. M. (1992). Perceived control, personal effectiveness and emotional states. In B. M. Carpenter (Ed.), *Personal coping: Theory, research and application* (pp. 111–131). Westport, CT: Praeger.

Lennings, C. J. (1994). *Suicide ideation and risk factors in police officers and justice students.* Paper presentation at the Public Health Association Conference, Canberra, Australia.

Leong, C., Furnham, A., & Cooper, C. (1996). The moderating effect of organisational commitment on the occupational stress outcome relationship. *Human Realtions, 49,* 1345–1363.

Lester, D. (1995). The association between alcohol consumption and suicide and homicide rates: A study of 13 nations. *Alcohol, 30,* 465–468.

Liden, R. C., Sparrow, R. T., & Wayne, S. J. (1997). Leader-member exchange theory: The past and potential for the future. Research in Personnel and Human Resources Management, 15, 47–119.

Liden, R. C., Wayne, S. J., & Sparrow, R. T. (2000). An examination of the mediating role of psychological empowerment on the relations between the job, interpersonal relationships, and work outcomes. *Journal of Applied Psychology, 85,* 407–416.

Lin, N. (1982). Social resources and instrumental action. In P. Marsden & N. Lin (Eds.), *Social structure and network analysis.* CA: Sage.

Lin, N. (1983). Social resources and social actions: A progress report. *Connections 6,* 10–16.

Lin, N., Woelfel, M. W., & Light, S. C. (1985). The buffering effect of social support subsequent to an important life event. *Journal of Health & Social Behavior, 26,* 247–263.

Lin, C. Y. (1998). The essence of empowerment: A conceptual model and a case illustration. *Journal of Applied Management Studies, 7,* 223–238.

Lindy, J. D., Grace, M. C., & Green, B. L. (1981). Survivors: Outreach to a reluctant population. *American Journal of Orthopsychiatry, 51,* 468–479.

Linley, P. A., & Joseph, S. (2004). Positive change following trauma and adversity: A review. *Journal of Traumatic Stress, 17,* 11–21.

Linville, P. W. (1987). Self-complexity as a cognitive buffer against stress-related illness and depression. *Journal of Personality and Social Psychology, 52,* 663–676.

Liston, M. C. (2003). *Social work practice with World War II veterans: impact of the war experience on the life course and adjustment in late life* (dissertation) (131 pp.). University of Denver.

Loo, R. (1995, September). *Police suicide: Issues, prevention and postvention.* Poster session conducted at the Work, Stress and Health '95 conference, Washington, DC.

Lotz, R., & Regoli, R. M. (1977). Police cynicism and professionalism. *Human Realtions, 30,* 2, 175–186.

Lyons, R. F., Mickelson, K. D., Sullivan, M. J. L., & Coyne, J. C. (1998). Coping as a communal process. *Journal of Social and Personal Relationships, 15,* 579–605.

MacLeod, M.D., & Paton, D. (1999). Police officers and violent crime: Social psychological perspectives on impact and recovery. In J. M. Violanti & D. Paton (Eds.), *Police trauma: Psychological aftermath of civilian combat.* Springfield, IL: Charles C Thomas.

Madamba, H. J. (1986). The relationship between stress and marital relationships in police officers. In J. T. Reese & H. A. Goldstein (Eds.), *Psychological services for law enforcement* (pp. 463–466). Washington, DC: U.S. Government Printing Office.

Maercker, A., & Muller, J. (2004). Social acknowledgment as a victim or survivor: A Scale to measure a recovery factor of PTSD. *Journal of Traumatic Stress, 17,* 345–351.

Magnusson, D., & Bergman, L. (1990). A pattern approach to the study of pathways from childhhod to adulthood. In L. Robins & M. Rutter (Eds.), *Straight and devious pathways from childhood to adulthood* (pp. 101–115). Cambridge, MA: Cambridge University Press.

Major, D. A., Kozlowski, S. W., Chao, G. T., & Gardner, P. D. (1995). A longitudinal investigation of newcomer expectations, early socialization outcomes, and the moderating effects of the role development factors. *Journal of Applied Psychology, 80,* 418–431.

Maniscalco, P. M., & Christen, H. T. (2002). *Understanding terrorism and managing the consequences.* Upper Saddle River, NJ: Prentice Hall.

Manz, C. C., & Sims, H. (1996). *Super-leadership: Teaching others to lead themselves.* New York: Prentice-Hall.

Marks, S. R. (1977). Multiple roles and role strain: Some notes on human energy, time, and commitment. *American Sociological Review, 42,* 921–936.

Marshall, R. D., Olfson, M., Hellman, F., Blanco, C., & Struening, E. L. (2001). Comorbidity, impairment, and suicidality in subthreshold PTSD. *American Journal of Psychiatry, 158,* 1467–1473.

Maslow, A. (1968). *Toward a psychology of being.* Princeton, NJ: Van Nostrand.

Mattila, V., Joukamaa, M., & Salokangas, R. (1988). Retirement, aging and adaptation: The Turva Project II. Design of the projects and some preliminary findings. *European Journal of Psychiatry, 2,* 46–58.

Matsakis, A. (1987). But military wives never. In A. Matsakis (Ed.), *Vietnam wives: Women and children surviving life with veterans suffering from post traumatic stress disorder* (pp. 147–161). Baltimore: Woodbine House.

McCafferty, F. L., McCafferty, E., & McCafferty, M. A. (1992). Stress and suicide in police officers: Paradigm of occupational stress. *Southern Medical Journal, 85,* 233–243.

McCrae, R. R., & Terracciano, A. (2005). Personality profiles of cultures, I: Aggregate personality traits. *Journal of Personality and Social Psychology, 89,* 407–425.

McKinsey. (2002). *Improving NYPD emergency preparedness and response.* New York: McKinsey.

McNeil, J., Lecca, P., & Wright, R., Jr. (1983). *Military retirement: Social, economic, and mental health dilemmas.* New Jersey: Rowman and Allanheld.

McNaus, M. A., & Kelly, M. L. (1999). Personality measures and biodata: Evidence predicting their incremental predictive value in the life insurance industry. *Personnel Psychology, 52,* 137–148.

Mitchell, J. T. (1983). When disaster strikes... The critical incident stress debriefing process. *Journal of Emergency Medical Services, 8,* 1, 36–39.

Mitchell, J., & Bray, G. (1990). *Emergency services stress: Guidelines for preserving the health and careers of emergency services personnel.* Englewood Cliffs, NJ: Prentice-Hall.

Mitchell, J. T., & Everly, G. S. (2001). *Critical incident stress debriefing: An operations manual for CISD, defusing and other group crisis intervention services.* Ellicott City, MD: Chevron.

Mitchell, M. (1991). The police after Lockerbie: What were the effects? *Police, 23,* 30–31.

Mitroff, I. I., & Anagnos, G. (2001). *Managing crises before they happen.* New York: AMACOM.

Moran, C., & Colless, E. (1995). Positive reactions following emergency and disaster responses. *Disaster Prevention and Management, 4,* 55–61.

Mullen, B., & Copper, C. (1994). The relation between group cohesiveness and performance: An integration. *Psychological Bulletin, 115,* 210–227.

Myers, D. G. (2001). Do we fear the right things? *APS Observer.* Retrieved July 3, 2002 from www.psychologicalscience.org/1201/

Neiderhoffer, A. (1967). *Behind the shield: The police in urban society.* New York: Doubleday.

Nelson, D. (1987). Organisational socialisation: A stress perspective. *Journal of Occupational Behaviour, 8,* 311–324.

Newman, D. W., & Rucker, R. M. (2004). Police stress, state-trait anxiety and stressors among US Marshals. *Journal of Criminal Justice, 32,* 631–641.

Niland, C. (1996, July). The impact of police culture on women and their performance in policing. Paper presented at the Australian Institute of Criminology Conference, First Australasian Women Police Conference, Sydney.

Norris, F. H. (1992). Epidemiology of trauma: Frequency and impact of different potentially traumatic events on different demographic groups. *Journal of Consulting and Clinical Psychology, 60,* 409–418.

North, C. S., Tivis, L., McMillen, J. C., Pfefferbaum, B., Cox, J., Spitznagel, E. L., Bunch, K., Schorr, J., & Smith, E. M. (2002). Coping, functioning, and adjustment of rescue workers after the Oklahoma City bombing. *Journal of Traumatic Stress, 15,* 171–175.

O'Toole, B. I., Marshall, R. P., Schureck, R. J., & Dobson, M. (1998). Risk factors for posttraumatic stress disorder in Australian Vietnam veterans. *Australian and New Zealand Journal of Psychiatry, 32,* 21–31.

Ottenberg, D. J. (1987). Initiation of social support systems: A grass roots perspective. In E. Gottheil, K. A. Druley, S. Pashko & S. P. Weinstein (Eds.), *Stress and addiction* (pp. 209–224). New York: Brunner Mazel.

Park, C. L. (1998). Stress-related growth and thriving through coping: The roles of personality and cognitive processes. *Journal of Social Issues, 54,* 267–277.

Paton, D. (1992). Disaster research: The Scottish dimension. *The Psychologist, 5,* 535–538.

Paton, D. (1994). Disaster Relief Work: An assessment of training effectiveness. *Journal of Traumatic Stress, 7,* 275–288.

Paton, D. (1999). Disaster business continuity: Promoting staff capability. *Disaster Prevention and Management, 8,* 127–133.

Paton, D. (2003). Stress in Disaster Response: A risk management approach. *Disaster Prevention and Management, 12,* 203–209.

Paton, D. (2005). Posttraumatic growth in protective services professionals: Individual, cognitive and organizational influences. *Traumatology, 11,* 4, 335–346.

Paton, D. (2006). Posttraumatic growth in emergency professionals. In L. Calhoun & R. Tedeschi (Eds.), *Handbook of posttraumatic growth: Research and practice.* Mahwah, NJ: Lawrence Erlbaum.

Paton, D., & Burke, K. J. (2007). Personal and organizational predictors of posttraumatic adaptation and growth in police officers. *Australasian Journal of Disaster and Trauma Studies,* 2007–1. http://www.massey.ac.nz/%7Etrauma/issues/2007-1/paton-burke.htm

Paton, D., & Flin, R. (1999). Disaster Stress: An emergency management perspective. *Disaster Prevention and Management, 8,* 261–267.

Paton, D., & Hannan, G. (2004). Risk factors in emergency responders. In D. Paton, J. Violanti, C. Dunning & L. Smith (Eds.), *Managing traumatic stress risk: A proactive approach.* Springfield, IL, Charles C Thomas.

Paton, D., & Hill, R. (2006). Managing company risk and resilience through business continuity management. In D. Paton & D. Johnston (Eds.), *Disaster resilience: An integrated approach.* Springfield, IL, Charles C Thomas.

Paton, D., & Jackson, D. (2002). Developing disaster management capability: An assessment centre approach. *Disaster Prevention and Management, 11,* 115–122.

Paton, D., & Smith, L. M. (1999). Assessment, conceptual, and methodological issues in researching traumatic stress in police officers. In J. M. Violanti & D. Paton (Eds.), *Police trauma: Psychological aftermath of civilian combat* (pp. 13–21). Springfield, IL: Charles C Thomas.

Paton, D., Smith, L. M., Ramsay, R., & Akande, D. (1999). Assessing the impact of trauma in work-related populations: Occupational and cultural determinants of reactivity. In R. Gist & B. Lubin (Eds.), *Response to disaster: Psychosocial, community, and ecological approaches* (pp. 83–99). Philadelphia: Brunner/Mazel.

Paton, D., Smith, L. M., Violanti, J. M., & Eränen, L. (2000). Work related trauma stress: Risk, vulnerability and resilience. In J. M. Violanti, D. Paton & C. Dunning (Eds.), *Posttraumatic stress intervention: Challenges, issues and perspectives* (pp. 187–202). Springfield, IL: Charles C Thomas.

Paton, D., & Stephens, C. (1996). Training and support for emergency responders. In D. Paton & J. Violanti (Eds.), *Traumatic stress in critical occupations: Recognition, consequences and treatment.* Springfield, IL: Charles C Thomas.

Paton, D., & Violanti, J. M. (1996). *Traumatic stress in critical occupations: Recognition, consequences, and treatment.* Springfield, IL: Charles C Thomas.

Paton, D., & Violanti, J. M. (2007). Terrorism stress risk assessment and management. In B. Bonger, L. Beutler & P. Zimbardo (Eds.), *Psychology of terrorism.* San Francisco: Oxford University Press.

Paton, D., Violanti, J., Dunning, C., & Smith, L. M. (2004). *Managing traumatic stress risk: A proactive approach.* Springfield, IL: Charles C Thomas.

Paton, D., Violanti, J. M., & Smith, L. M. (2003). *Promoting capabilities to manage posttraumatic stress: Perspectives on resilience.* Springfield, IL: Charles C Thomas.

Patterson, G. T. (1999). Coping effectiveness and occupational stress in police officers. In J. M. Violanti & D. Paton (Eds.), *Police trauma: Psychological aftermath of civilian combat* (S. 214–226). Springfield, IL: Charles C Thomas.

Patterson, G. T. (2001). The relationship between demographic variables and exposure to traumatic incidents among police officers. *The Australian Journal of Disaster and Trauma Studies, 2.* http://trauma.massey.ac.nz/.

Patton, G. C., Coffey, C., Posterino, M., Carlin, J. B., & Bowes, G. (2003). Life events and early onset depression: Cause or consequence? *Psychological Medicine, 33,* 1203–1210.

Pearlin, L., & Schooler, C. (1978). The structure of coping. *Journal of Health and Social Behavior, 19,* 2–21.

Peck, D. L. (1984). Post-traumatic stress and life destructive behavior. *Journal of Sociology and Social Welfare, 10,* 15–21.

Pennebaker, J. W. (2000). The effects of traumatic disclosure on physical and mental health: The values of writing and talking about upsetting events. In J. M. Violanti, D. Paton & C. Dunning (Eds.), *Posttraumatic stress intervention: Challenges, issues and perspectives* (pp. 97–114). Springfield, IL: Charles C Thomas.

Perry, I. (1997). Creating and empowering effective work teams. *Management Services, 41,* 8–11.

Pieper, G., & Maercker, A. (1999). Männlichkeit und Verleugnung von Hilfsbedürftigkeit nach berufsbedingten Traumata (Polizei, Feuerwehr, Rettungspersonal). *Verhaltenstherapie, 9,* 222–229. [Masculinity and denial of need for help after occupational trauma. (Police, fire fighters, emergency medical services)].

Pogrebin, M. R., & Poole, E. D. (1991). Police and tragic events: The management of emotion. *Journal of Criminal Justice, 19,* 395–403.

Pollock, C., Paton, D., Smith, L. M., & Violanti, J. M. (2003a). Team resilience. In D. Paton, J. M. Violanti & L. M. Smith (Eds). *Promoting capabilities to manage posttraumatic stress: Perspectives on resilience* (pp. 74–88). Springfield, IL: Charles C Thomas.

Pollock, C., Paton, D., Smith, L. M., & Violanti, J. M. (2003b). Training for resilience. In D. Paton, J. M. Violanti & L. M. Smith (Eds.), *Promoting capabilities to manage posttraumatic stress: Perspectives on resilience* (pp. 89–102). Springfield, IL: Charles C Thomas.

Presidents Commission of Law Enforcement and the Administration of Justice. (1967). *Task force report: The police.* Washington DC: Government Printing Office.

Quinn, R. E., & Spreitzer, G. M. (1997). The road to empowerment: Seven questions every leader should consider. *Organisational Dynamics,* Autumn, 37–49.

Raphael, B. (1986). *When disaster strikes.* London: Hutchinson.

Regoli, R., & Poole, E. (1979). Measurement of police cynicism: A factor scaling approach. *Journal of Criminal Justice, 7,* 35–51.

Regoli, R. M., Poole, E. C., & Hewitt, J. (1979). Exploring the empirical relationship between police cynicism and work alienation. *Journal of Police Science and Administration, 7,* 2, 37–51.

Reiner, R. (1992). Policing and the media. In T. Newburn, *Handbook of policing* (pp. 259–281). London: Willan.

Reiser, M. (1974). Some organizational stressed on policemen. *Journal of Police Science and Administration, 2,* 156–159.

Reiser, M., & Gieger, S. P. (1984). Police officer as victim. *Professional Psychology: Research & Practice, 15,* 315–323.

Repetti, R. L., Mathews, K. A., & Waldron, I. (1989). Effects of paid employment on women's mental and physical health. *American Psychologist, 44,* 1394–1401.

Richmond, R. L., Kehoe, L., Hailstone, S., Wodak, A., & Uebel-Yan, M. (1999). Quantitative and qualitative evaluations of brief interventions to change excessive drinking, smoking and stress in the police force. *Addiction, 94,* 1509–1521.

Riley, M. W. (1986). Overview and highlights of a sociological perspective. In A. B. Sorenson, F. Weinert & L. R. Sherman (Eds.), *Human development and the life course.* Hillsdale, NJ: Erlbaum.

Romanov, K., Hatakka, M., Keskinen, E. Laksonen, H., Kaprio, J., Rose, R., & Koskenvuo, M. (1994). Self-reported hostility and suicidal acts, accidents, and accidental deaths: A prospective study of 21,443 adults aged 25 to 29. *Psychosomatic Medicine, 56,* 328–336.

Rosenberg, M., & Pearlin, L. I. (1978). Social class and self-esteem among children and adults. *American Journal of Sociology, 84,* 53–77.

Roszell, D. K., McFall, M. E., & Malas, K. L. (1991). Frequency of symptoms and concurrent psychiatric disorder in Vietnam veterans with chronic PTSD. *Hospital and Community Psychiatry, 42,* 293–296.

Rudd. D. M., Dahm, F., & Rajab, M. H. (193). Diagnostic comorbidity in persons with suicidal ideation and behavior. *American Journal of Psychiatry, 150,* 928–934.

Scaturo, D. J., & Hayman, P. M. (1992). The impact of combat trauma across the family life cycle: Clinical observations. *Journal of Traumatic Stress, 5,* 273–288.

Sced, M. (2004). *Screening for corruption using standard psychological tests of personality.* SA: Australasian Centre for Policing Research.

Scheier, M. F., Weintraub, J. K., & Carver, C. S. (1986). Coping with stress: Divergent strategies of optimists and pessimists. *Journal of personality and Social Psychology, 51,* 1257–1264.

Schneidman, E. S. (1986). *Definition of suicide* (pp. 121–147). New York: Wiley.

Schein, H. (1990). Organizational culture. *American Psychologist, 45*(2), 109–119.

Scotti, J. R., Beach, B. K., Northrop, L. M. E., Rode, C. A., & Forsyth, J. P. (1995). The psychologcial impact of accidental injury. In J. R. Freedy & S. E. Hobfall (Eds.), *Traumatic stress: From theory to practice.* New York: Plenum.

Segal, J., Hunter, E. J., & Segal, Z. (1976). Universal consequences of captivity: Stress reactions among divergent populations of prisoners of war and their families. *International Journal of Social Science, 28,* 593–609.

Sewell, J. D. (1993). Traumatic stress of multiple murder investigations. *Journal of Traumatic Stress, 6,* 103–118.

Shakespeare-Finch, J. (2006). Individual differences in vulnerability to posttrauma deprivation. In J. Violanti & D. Paton (Eds.), *Who gets PTSD? Issues of posttraumatic stress vulnerability* (pp. 33–49). Springfield, IL: Charles C Thomas.

Shakespeare-Finch, J., Paton, D., & Violanti, J. M. (2003). The family: Resilience resource and resilience needs. In D. Paton, J. M. Violanti & L. M. Smith (Eds.), *Promoting capabilities to manage posttraumatic stress: Perspectives on resilience* (pp. 243–265). Springfield, IL: Charles C Thomas.

Short, P. Victims and helpers. In: R. L. Heathcote and B. G. Tong (Eds.), *Natural hazards in Australia.* Canberra: Australian Academy of Science, 1979.

Shuster, M. A., Stein, B. D., Jaycox, L. H., Collins, R. L., Marshall, G. N., Elliott, M. N., Zhou, A. J., & Kanouse, D. E. (2001). A national survey of stress reaction after the September 11, 2001, terrorist attacks. *New England Journal of Medicine, 345,* 1507–1512.

Siegrist, M., & Cvetkovich, G. (2000). Perception of hazards: The role of social trust and knowledge. *Risk Analysis, 20,* 713–719.

Simpson, D. M., & Stehr, S. (2003). Victim management and identification after the World Trade Center collapse. In J. L. Monday (Ed.), *Beyond September 11: An account of post disaster research.* Special Publication #39. Boulder, CO: Institute of Behavioral Science, Natural Hazards Research and Applications Information Center, University of Colorado

Skolnick, J. (1972). a sketch of the policeman's working personality. In G. F. Cole (Ed.), *Criminal justice: Law and politics* (pp. 20–42). Belmont, CA: Wadsworth.

Skolnick, J. (2005). A sketch of the policeman's 'working personality.' In T. Newburn (Ed.), *Policing: Key readings* (pp. 264–278). London: Willan.

Soldz, S., & Vaillant, G. E. (1999). The big 5 personality traits and the life course: A 45 year longitudinal study. *Journal of Research in Personality, 33,* 2, 208–232.

Solomon, Z. (1989). A 3-year prospective study of post-traumatic stress disorder in Israeli combat veterans. *Journal of Traumatic Stress, 2,* 59–73.

Solomon, Z. (1990). Does the war end when the shooting stops? The psychological toll of war. *Journal of Applied Social Psychology, 20,* 1733–1745.

Solomon, Z. (1993). Immediate and long-term effects of traumatic combat stress among Israeli veterans of the Lebanon war. In J. P. Wilson & B. Raphael (Eds.), *International handbook of traumatic stress syndromes* (pp. 321–332). New York: Plenum.

Solomon, Z., & Mikulincer, M. (2006). Trajectories of PTSD: A 20-year longitudinal study. *American Journal of Psychiatry, 163,* 659–666.

Solomon, Z., Mikulineer, M., Fried, B., & Wosner, Y. (1987). Family characteristics and post-traumatic stress disorder: A followup of Israeli combat stress reaction casualties. *Family Process, 26,* 383–394.

Solomon, S. D., & Smith, E. S. (1994). Social support and perceived control as moderators of responses to dioxin and flood exposure. In R. J. Ursano, B. G.

McCaughey & C. S. Fullerton (Eds.), *Individual and community responses to trauma and disaster.* Cambridge, MA: Cambridge University Press.

Solursh, L. P. (1988). Combat addiction- PTSD re-explored. *Psychological Journal of the University of Ottawa, 13,* 17–20.

Solursh, L. P. (1989). Combat addiction: Overview of implications in symptom maintenance and treatment planning. *Journal of Traumatic Stress, 2,* 451–462.

Spector, P. E. (1982). Behavior in organizations as a function of employee locus of control. *Psychological Bulletin, 91,* 482–497.

Spielberger, C., Westberry, L., Grier, K., & Greefield, G. (1981). *The police stress survey: Sources of stress in law enforcement.* Tampa, FL: Human Resources Institute.

Spreitzer, G. M. (1997). Toward a common ground in defining empowerment. *Research in Organizational Change and Development, 10,* 31–62.

Spreitzer, G. M., Kizilos, M. A., & Nason, S. W. (1997). A dimensional analysis of the relationship between psychological empowerment and effectiveness, satisfaction and strain. *Journal of Management, 23,* 679–704.

Spreitzer, G. M., & Mishra, A. K. (1999). Giving up control without losing control: Trust and its substitutes' effect on managers involving employees in decision making. *Group & Organization Management, 24,* 155–187.

Stephens, C. V., & Long, N. (2000). Communication with police supervisors and peers as a buffer of work-related traumatic stress. *Journal of Organizational Behavior, 21,* 407–424.

Stephens, C. V., Long, N., & Flett, R. (1999). Vulnerability to psychological disorder: Previous trauma in police recruits. In J. M. Violanti & D. Paton (Eds.), *Police trauma: Psychological aftermath of civilian combat* (pp. 65–74). Springfield, IL: Charles C Thomas.

Storch, J. E., & Panzarella, R. (1996). Police stress: State-trait anxiety in relation to occupational and personal stressors. *Journal of Criminal Justice, 24,* 2, 99–107.

Stratton, J. (1978). Police stress: An overview. *Police Chief,* April, 58–62.

Stryker, S., & Serpe, R. T. (1982). Commitment, identity salience, and role behavior. In W. Ickes & E. S. Knowles (Eds.), *Personality, roles, and social behavior* (pp. 199–218). New York: Springer-Verlag.

Syme, S. L. (1991). Control and health: A personal perspective. In A. Stepoe & A. Appels (Eds.), *Stress, personal control and health* (p. 3–8). Chichester: John Wiley & Sons.

Tedeschi, R. G., & Calhoun, L. G. (2003). Routes to posttraumatic growth through cognitive processing. In D. Paton, J. M. Violanti & L. M. Smith (Eds.), *Promoting capabilities to manage posttraumatic stress: Perspectives on resilience* (pp. 12–25). Springfield, IL: Charles C Thomas.

Tett, R. P., Jackson, D. N., & Rothstein, M. (1991). Personality measures as predictors of job performance: A meta-analytic review. *Personnel Psychology, 44,* 703–742.

Thoits, P. A. (1983). Multiple identities and psychological well-being: A reformulation and test of the social isolation hypothesis. *American Sociological Review, 48,* 174–187.

Thoits, P. A. (1986). Multiple identities: Examining gender and marital differences in distress. *American Sociological Review, 51,* 259–272.

Thomas, K. W., & Tymon, W. (1994). Does empowerment always work: Understanding the role of intrinsic motivation and interpretation. *Journal of Management Systems, 6,* 84–99.

Thomas, K. W., & Velthouse, B. A. (1990). Cognitive elements of empowerment: An "interpretive" model of intrinsic motivation. *Academy of Management Review, 15,* 666–681.

Thompson, J. (1993). Psychological impact of body recovery duties. *Journal of the Royal Society of Medicine, 86,* 628–629.

Thompson, J., & Solomon, M. (1991). Body recovery teams at disasters: Trauma or challenge? *Anxiety Research, 4,* 235–240.

Toch, H., & Grant, J. D. (1991). *Police as problem solvers.* New York: Plenum.

Tugade, M. M., & Frederickson, B. L. (2004). Resilient individuals use positive emotions to bounce back from negative emotional experiences. *Journal of Personality and Social Psychology, 86,* 320–333.

Turkewitz, G., & Darlynne, A. S. (1993). *Developmental time and timing.* Hillsdale, NJ: Erlbaum.

Turner, R. J., & Roszell, P. (1994). Psychosocial resources and the stress process. in W. R. Avison & I. H. Gotlib (Eds.), *Stress and mental health* (pp. 179–210). New York: Plenum.

Turvey, B. (1996). Police officers: Control, hopelessness, and suicide. http://www.connix.com

Tyler, M. P., & Gifford R. K. (1991). Field training accidents: The military unit as a recovery context. *Journal of Traumatic. Stress, 4,* 233–249.

Unkovic, C., & Brown, W. (1978). The drunken cop. *Police Chief, 6,* 22–27.

Ursano, R. J., Holloway, R. C., Jones, D. R., Rodriguez A. R., & Belenky G. L. (1989). Psychiatric care in the military community: Family and military stressors. *Hospital & Community. Psychiatry, 40,* 1284–1289.

van der Kolk, B. A. (1987). *Psychological trauma.* Washington, DC: American Psychiatric Press.

van der Kolk, B. A. (1988). The trauma spectrum: The interaction of biological and social events in the genesis of the trauma response. *Journal of Traumatic Stress, 1,* 273–290.

van der Lee, M., & van Vugt, M. (2004). *IMI–An information system for effective multidisciplinary incident management.* Proceedings of ISCRAM 2004. Brussels: ISCRAM.

Van Raalte, R. C. (1979). Alcohol as a problem among police officers. *Police Chief, 44,* 38–40.

Vena, J. E., Violanti, J. M., Marshall, J. R., & Feidler, F. (1986). Mortality experience. *Stress Medicine, 2,* 233–240.

Verna, J. E., Violanti, J. M., Marshall, J. R., & Feidler, R. (1986). Mortality of a municipal worker cohort III: Police officers. *American Journal of Industrial Medicine, 10,* 383–397.

Verbugge, L. M. (1983). Multiple roles and physical health of women and men. *Journal of Health and Social Behavior, 24,* 16–30.

Violanti, J. M. (1981). Police stress and coping: An organizational analysis.

Unpublished dissertation, State University of New York at Buffalo, NY.

Violanti, J. M. (1983). Stress patterns in police work: A longitudinal study. *Journal of Police Science and Administration, 11,* 211–216.

Violanti, J. M. (1990). Post-trauma vulnerability: A proposed model. In J. T. Reese, J. M. Horn & C. Dunning (Eds.), *Critical incidents in policing* (pp. 503–510). Washington, DC: US Government Printing Office.

Violanti, J. M. (1992). *Police retirement: The impact of change.* Springfield, IL: Charles C Thomas.

Violanti, J. M. (1993a). Coping in a high stress police environment. *Journal of Social Psychology,* 717–730.

Violanti, J. M. (1993b). High stress police training: What does it teach police recruits? *Journal of Criminal Justice, 21,* 411–417.

Violanti J. M. (1997). Suicide and the police role: A psychosocial model. *Policing: An International Journal of Police Strategy and Management, 20,* 698–715.

Violanti, J. M. (1997). Residuals of police trauma. *Autralasian Journal of Disaster and Trauma Studies, 3,* http://trauma.massey.ac.nz/

Violanti, J. M. (1999). Alcohol in policing: Early prevention. *FBI Law Enforcement Bulletin.*

Violanti, J. M. (2001). Coping strategies among police recruits in a high stress training environment. *The Journal of Social Psychology, 132,* 6, 717–729.

Violanti, J. M. (2001). Post traumatic stress disorder intervention in law enforcement: Differing perspectives. *Autralasian Journal of Disaster and Truama Studies,* 2001–2.

Violanti, J. M. (2003). Suicide and the police culture. In D. Hackett & J. M. Violanti (Eds.), *Police suicide: Tactics for prevention.* Springfield, IL: Charles C Thomas.

Violanti, J. M. (2004). Predictors of police suicide ideation. *Suicide and Life-Threatening Behavior, 4,* 277–283.

Violanti, J. M., & Aron, F. (1993). Sources of police stressors, job attitudes and psychological distress. *Psychological Reports, 72,* 3, 899–904.

Violanti, J. M. & Aron, F. (1994). Ranking police stressors. *Psychological Reports, 75,* 824.

Violanti, J. M., Marshall, J. R., & Howe, B. (1985). Stress, coping and alcohol use: The police connection. *Journal of Police Science and Administration, 31,* 2, 106–110.

Violanti, J. M., Marshall, J. R., & Howe, B. (1986). Occupational demands, psychological distress, and the coping function of alcohol. *Journal of Occupational Medicine, 25,* 455–458.

Violanti, J. M., Vena, J. E., & Marshall, J. R. (1986). Disease risk and morality among police officers: New evidence and contributing factors. *Journal of Police Science and Administration, 14,* 1, 17–23.

Violanti, J. M., Vena, J. E., & Marshall, J. R. (1996). Suicides, homicides, and accidental deaths: A comparative risk assessment of police officers and municipal workers. *American Journal of Industrial Medicine, 30,* 99–104.

Violanti, J. M., & Paton, D. (Eds.). (1999). *Police trauma: Psychological aftermath of civilian combat.* Springfield, IL: Charles C Thomas.

Violanti, J. M., & Paton, D. (2006). *Who gets PTSD?* Springfield, IL: Charles C Thomas.

Violanti, J. M., Paton, D., & Dunning, C. (2000). *Posttraumatic stress intervention: challenges, issues and perspectives.* Springfield, IL: Charles C Thomas.

Volpicelli, J., Balaraman, G., Hahn, J., Wallace, M. A., & Bux, D. (1999). The role of uncontrollable trauma in the development of PTSD and alcohol addiction. *Alcohol Research and Health, 23,* 256–262.

Vrij, A., van der Steen, J., & Koppelaar, L. (1994). Aggression of police officers as a function of temperature: An experiment with the fire arms training system. *Journal of Community and Applied Psychology, 4,* 365–370.

Wagner, S. L. (2005). The rescue personality: Fact or fiction? *The Australasian Journal of Disaster and Trauma Studies,* 2005-2.

Weik, K. E. (1995). *Sensemaking in organizations.* Thousand Oaks, CA: Sage.

Weick, K. E., & Sutcliffe, K. M. (2007). *Managing the unexpected: Resilient performance in an age of uncertainty* (2nd ed.). San Francisco: CA: Jossey-Bass.

Weiss, D. S., Marmar, C. R., Schlenger, W. E., Fairbank, J. A., Jordan, K., Hough, R. L., & Kulka, R. A. (1992). The prevalence of lifetime and partial post-traumatic stress disorder in Vietnam theater veterans. *Journal of Traumatic Stress, 5,* 365–376.

Wells, C., Getman, R., & Blau, T. (1988). Critical incident procedures: The crisis management of traumatic incidents. *The Police Chief, 55,* 1, 70–74.

Williams, C. (1987). Peacetime combat: Treating and preventing delayed stress reactions in police officers. In T. Williams (Ed.), *Post-traumatic stress disorders: A handbook for clinicians* (pp. 267–292). Cincinnati, OH: Disabled Association of Veterans.

Wilson, J. P. (1980). Conflict, stress and growth: The effects of the Vietnam war on psychological development of Vietnam veterans. In C. R. Figley & S. Leventman (Eds.), *Strangers at home: Vietnam veterans since the war.* New York: Praeger.

Wilson, J. Q. (1968). *Varieties of police behaviour: The management of law and order in eight communities.* Cambridge, MA: Harvard.

Williams, T. (1993). Trauma in the workplace. In J. P. Wilson & B. Raphael (Eds.), *International handbook of traumatic stress syndromes* (pp. 925–933). New York: Plenum Press.

Wilt, G. M., & Bannon, J. (1976). Cynicism or realism: A criticism of Neiderhoffer's research into police attitudes. *Journal of Police Science and Administration, 7,* 340–345.

Woody, R. H. (2005). The police culture: Research implications for psychological services. *Professional Psychology: Research and Practice, 36*(5), 525–529.

Worden, W. (1982). *Grief counseling and grief therapy.* New York: Springer.

Wright, J. P., Carter, D. E., & Cullen, F. T. (2005). A life-course analysis of military service in Vietnam. *Journal of Research in Crime and Delinquency, 42,* 1, 55–83.

Young, M. B., & Erickson, C. A. (1988). Cultural impediments to recovery: PTSD in contemporary America. *Journal of Traumatic Stress, 1,* 291–298.

Zimbardo, P. (2001). *The psychology of terrorism: Mind games and healing.* Retrieved July 3, 2002 from American Psychological Association website: www.apa.org/science/.

INDEX

A

Adaptive capacity, 15, 85, 146, 153
Alcohol abuse, 103, 106, 114
    absenteeism, 104
    intervention, 111
    PTSD, 104
Anxiety, 105
Assessment centers, 56
Assimilation, into police organizations, 16, 17, 18
Authoritarianism, 54

B

Behavioral disengagement, 99, 100, 158, 161, 163
Big 5 personality measure, 52, 53
Blame, 139, 148
Bureaucracy, 18, 34, 35, 38, 43, 50, 90, 146

C

Change, organizational, 145, 147
Cohesion, 18, 42, 46
    organizational, 46, 58
Contextualism, 6, 141, 183, 216
Coping, 14, 16, 50, 66, 68, 98, 101, 161, 175, 178
    acceptance, 14, 98, 99
    alcohol abuse, 99, 101, 103, 105
        intervention, 111
    behavioral disengagement, 99, 100, 158, 161, 163
        hassles, operational, 163
        hassles, organizational, 163
    communal, 138
    coping efficacy, 101
    denial, 99, 158, 161, 163
    disengagement, from duties, 176
    emotion-focused, 101
    escape-avoidance, 101
    humor, 176, 179, 180, 181
    maladaptive, 15, 101
    planning, 14, 98, 161
    police role, 20
        constrictive inflexibility, 20
        diminished use of social roles, 20
    positive reinterpretation, 14, 98, 99, 176, 179
    problem-focused, 101
    and risk management, 108
    social support, 98, 161, 176
Counseling, 113, 220
Critical incident risk, 4, 41, 67
Critical incident stress debriefing, 57
Culture, 18, 134
    assimilation, 39
    blame, 139, 148
    change, 155
    communication, 148
    consultation, 148
        leadership, 148
    emotional disclosure, 139
    empowerment, 186
        learning, 194
    gender, 117
    organizational, 33, 37
        autocratic practices, 34
        bureaucracy, 34, 35, 38, 50, 146
            "red tape," 148
        politics, 34, 35, 43, 146

threat, underestimate, 146
police, 18
    loyalty, 19
posttrauma outcomes, 39
resilience, 155, 184
socialization, 19
    recruitment, 19
    selection, 19
teams, 172
Cynicism, 55, 180

D

Decision making, 103, 149
    contingent, 150
    creative, 149
    crisis, 150
Delegation, 187, 191
Denial, 99, 158, 161, 163
Depersonalization, 101
Depression, 105
Disequilibrium, psychological, 25, 26, 182, 183
Drug abuse, 104

E

Empowerment, 94, 187, 186, 187, 193
    autonomy, 94
    conscientiousness, 196
    delegation, 187, 191
    hardiness, 199, 201
    hassles, organizational, 188, 190, 193, 201
    leadership, 197
    learning, 187, 189, 192, 194
    motivation, 187, 188
    participation, 187
    peer cohesion, 198, 201
        social support, 198
    and resilience, 193, 197
    resource needs, 195
        information, 195
    satisfaction, 189, 194, 197
    schema, 188, 193, 194
    self-efficacy, 188, 191

supervisor support, 197, 201
teams, 196, 197
training, 190
trust, 196, 201
uplifts, organizational, 188, 201

F

Family, 6, 63, 64, 65, 97, 109, 122, 164, 165, 181, 213
    disruption, 109
    retirement, 213
Female officers, 117
    critical incident stress risk, 120

G

Gender, 4, 99, 115, 117, 216
    acculturation, 115
    critical incident type, 116, 120
    family, 122
    police culture, 118
        constructions of masculinity, 119
    and PTSD, 115
    and risk, 115, 116, 120
    social networks, 122
    social support, 121, 122
    socialization, 118

H

Hardiness, 50, 54, 148, 199, 201
Helper stereotype, 66, 67, 119, 193
Humor, 176, 179, 180, 181

I

Invulnerability, 107
    perceptions of, 107

J

Judicial system, 35

L

Late-onset stress symptomatology, 28
Leadership, 135, 148, 170, 197
Life course model, 4, 183, 184, 216
Life course theory, 4, 5, 46, 200, 202, 216, 218
   concepts, 8
   contextualism, 6, 141, 183, 216
   cumulative continuity, 8
   development, 5
   historical conditions, 5
   life-stage principle, 7
   social environment, 5, 8
   and terrorism, 8
   and trauma, 7, 9
   trajectories, 5, 8
      risk, 9
   transitions, 5, 6, 8, 11, 49, 73, 89, 182, 203, 216
      citizen to recruit, 48
      recruit to trainee, 73
      training to operational duties, 89
      officer to retiree, 203

M

Media, 35, 96, 138
Mental health, 81
Mentoring, 94, 170

O

Organization, 33, 41
   bureaucracy, 18, 34, 35, 38, 43, 50, 90, 146
   change, 145, 147
      estimating new forms of risk, 147
      learning lessons, 147
   climate, 39, 159, 185
      satisfaction, 186
      practices, organizational, 186
   coherence, 42
   culture, 33, 39, 135, 148, 155
      blame, 38, 139
      coherence, 37
   environment, 36, 217
      adaptation to, 217
   hassles, 40, 42, 44, 66, 80, 82, 158
   history, 146
   influence on well-being, 148
   learning, 145, 155
   politics, 146
   risk, 33, 37, 42, 74, 87
   resilience, 46, 154, 217
   role standards, 18
   socialization, 37, 38
      performance appraisal, 38
      selection, 37
      training, 37, 38
   terrorism, impact of, 143, 144
   uplifts, 42, 43, 80, 82, 158
Operational issues
   experiences, 15, 35
   hassles, 42,
   risk, 35, 42
   uplifts, 44
Optimism, 54

P

Pathogenic paradigm, 35
Peer support programs, 113
Personality, 14, 53, 49, 58, 220
   five factor model, 52
      Big 5, 52, 53
         agreeableness, 52, 53, 59
         conscientiousness, 52, 53, 59, 196
         extraversion, 14, 15, 50, 52, 53, 54, 59, 60, 62, 158, 164
            satisfaction, 164
            well-being, 164
         introversion, 54, 56
         neuroticism, 15, 52, 56, 59, 62
            emotional stability, 53
         openness to experience, 52, 53, 59, 62
   police, 56
   police performance, 53
   police recruits, 58
   recruits versus general public, 59
   risk, 51
   selecting in, 51, 54

selecting out, 51, 54
Person-environment fit, 49, 50, 66, 73, 84, 85, 155, 160, 221
Pessimism, 54
Physical health, 81
Police career, 3, 11, 66, 97, 164
   and trauma, 11
   stages, 12
      reality stage, 12
      disenchantment stage, 12
      personalization stage, 13
      introspection stage, 13
   transitions, 11, 73, 203, 216
      citizen to recruit, 48
      recruit to trainee, 73
      training to operational duties, 89
      officer to retiree, 203
Police personality, 56
Police role, 16, 68
   ambiguity, 169
   cohesion, 18
   control, 162
      organizational procedures, 162
      training, 162
   as coping, 16, 20
   dependence, 17, 103
   disengagement, 76
   family, 164
   image, 18
   individual assimilation, 16, 17
   loss of support, 211
      and relationships, 21
      retirement, 204
   social assimilation, 16, 17, 18
Police supervisor, 112
   empowerment, 197
   post event support, 154
      recognizing strengths, 154
      reintegration, promotion of, 154
   suicide prevention, 112
Politics, organizational, 34, 35, 43, 146
Positive reinterpretation, 14, 98, 99, 176, 179
Pre-employment traumatic experience, 15, 70, 74
   and resilience, 77
   and vulnerability, 76
   and posttraumatic growth, 82
Prejudice, 52
   gender, 120
   racial, 52
   ethnic, 52
Psychological contract, 42
PTSD, 10, 11, 14, 27, 31, 108
Public expectations and reactions, 35, 94, 95, 166
   satisfaction, 166

R

Recruit, 14, 48
   family history, 48, 63, 64
   life experience, 63, 66
   motivations, 48
   personality, 48, 59
   prior trauma experience, 15, 48, 69, 70, 71, 74, 75
      vulnerability, 69
      resilience, 69, 70
Rescue personality, 56, 57, 58, 62, 221
Resilience, 15, 27, 37, 42, 85, 143, 146, 184
   adaptive capacity, 15, 85, 146, 153
   organizational, 46
   pre-employment traumatic experience, 77
   person factors, 184
   organizational factors, 184
   team factors, 184
Retirement, 24, 27, 203
   addiction to stress, 209, 210
      "action junkies," 210
      adrenaline addiction, 211
      "combat rush," 210
      learned defensiveness, 210
   aging, beliefs about, 203
   coping, 205
   family issues, 212
   financial insecurity, 203
   health, 203
   loss, feelings of, 206
      adjustment, 206
      coping, 206
   loss of group support, 211, 212
      "trauma membrane" effect, 212
   planning, 203
   psychological disequilibrium, 204

satisfaction, 205
self-efficacy, 203
trauma, residuals of, 207
Risk, 9, 14, 24, 217, 223
   terrorism, 129, 141
   organizational influence, 30
      socialization, 30
      training, 30
   operational influence, 31
   residual, 26, 154, 223
      post-event management, 154

S

Satisfaction, 32, 50, 58, 157, 160, 185
   coping strategies, 160, 161
   gender differences, 160
   in police officers, 157
      occupational experience, 160
   organizational climate, 159
   retirement, 205
   social support, 162
Schema, 133, 134, 142, 144, 151, 152, 183, 217
   socialization, 151
   training, 152
Selection, 6, 48, 50, 77, 221, 222
   Assessment center, 56
   personality, 51
      selecting in, 51, 54
      selecting out, 51, 54
   screening, 50
Self-confidence, 55
Self-efficacy, 50, 188, 191, 203
Self-esteem, 55
Simulation, 92, 134, 139, 153
   competency analysis, 153
      decision making, 153
      multi-agency operations, 153
      planning, 153
   event characteristics, 153
   training needs analysis, 153
Situational awareness, 135
Socialization, 6, 11, 83, 84, 85, 86, 94, 133, 142, 151, 158, 160, 174
   academy training, 86
   acculturation, 33, 83, 84, 158

organizational practices, 174
Social identity, 21, 30, 138, 212
   identity role complexity, 21
   identity, loss of, 212
Social support, 15, 76, 94, 129, 148, 154, 158, 161, 162, 198, 217, 220
   empowerment, 198
   support, loss of, 211, 212
      retirement, 211
   "trauma membrane" effect, 212
Suicide, 105, 106
   assessment, 114
   prevention, 111
      police supervisor role, 112, 113
         training, 112
      peer support, 113
   and trauma, 105, 107

T

Teams, 137, 138, 150, 172, 174, 181, 196
   cohesion, 138
   communication, 151
   empowerment, 196
   multi-agency, 150
      training, 151
   organizational culture, 172
   satisfaction, 174
Terrorism, 4, 125
   deployment of officers, 128, 149
   mobilization, 127
   multi-agency issues, 134, 136, 150
   organizational issues, 135, 143
      decision making, 149
      influence on officers, 148
      organization, impact on, 143, 144
      organizational change, 147
      organizational learning, 145
   planning, 149
   response, 126, 148
      intelligence, accessing, 149
   risk management, 126
   stress risk, 125, 126, 129
   uncertainty, 149
Terrorist acts, 131
   characteristics, 131
   and the environment of police work, 143

post-event support, 137
safety and security, sense of, 130
training for, 133
Training, 6, 15, 30, 36, 76, 142, 152, 221, 222
   decision making, 103, 149
   emotional, 103
   empowerment, 190
   needs analysis, 153
   problem-solving, 103
   simulation, 92, 134, 139, 153
   terrorism, training for, 133
Traumatic experience, 82
   addiction, 17, 209
   early career, 78
      number of events, 78
      off-duty events, 79
      on-duty events, 79, 80
   loss of group support, 211
   police organization, 22

posttraumatic growth, 25
pre-employment, 69, 74, 76
psychological disequilibrium, 25, 26, 182, 183
   retirement, 204
residual, 4, 207
   residual stress hypothesis, 208
   retirement, 207
suicide, implications for, 107
vicarious, 78, 83
Trust, 113, 130, 139, 154, 196
Type A personality, 54

V

Vulnerability, 16, 25, 37, 42, 100, 108, 129, 143, 177, 179
   organizational influence, 46
Vulnerability coefficient, 129

ABOUT THE AUTHORS

Douglas Paton, Ph.D., C. Psychol. is a Professor in the School of Psychology, University of Tasmania, a Research Fellow at the Institute of Geological and Nuclear Sciences, New Zealand, and Research Associate with Aragon Consulting 7 Law, Perth, WA. His research and consulting work focuses on (a) developing and testing models of community preparedness for and resilience to natural hazards; (b) developing and testing emergency response systems (with a particular focus on information management, decision making and integrated/team emergency management) in emergency management and law enforcement agencies; and managing well-being in high risk professions.

Douglas has recently consulted to the General Accounting Office (Washington, D.C.) to develop national standards for HR aspects of disaster business continuity planning and with the U.S. National Centre for Disaster Psychology and Terrorism (Stanford University) to develop multiagency and interdisciplinary aspects of disaster response management policy for terrorist events. He is also a member of a NATO working group concerned with developing community and emergency agency resilience to the consequences of acts of terrorism. Douglas is also developing material for the Auckland District Health Board and Emergency Management Australia training programs on information and decision-making and crisis team development for managing natural hazards and health-related (e.g., pandemic) crises, and is the Australian delegate to the UNESCO Education for Natural Disaster Preparedness in the Asia-Pacific program. Douglas has worked with several protective services (fire, police) and health care organizations in Australia and New Zealand on developing traumatic stress management policy, training and organizational development to support crisis management, and stress management. He is Editor of the Australasian Journal of Disaster and Trauma Studies and serves on the *Editorial Advisory Board of Disaster Prevention and Management.* He has published ten books on traumatic and disaster stress, and has published some 160 papers and chapters in this area.

John M. Violanti Ph.D. is a research professor in the Department of Social and Preventive Medicine (SPM), School of Public Health and Health Professions at the State University of New York at Buffalo. John is a member of the SUNY Medical School graduate faculty. He is a police veteran, serving with the New York State Police for 23 years as a trooper, the Bureau of Criminal Investigation (BCI), and later as a coordinator of the Psychological Assistance Program (EAP) for the State Police. He has been involved in the design, implementation, and analysis of numerous police-related stress and health studies over the past 20 years. Major projects included a 40-year retrospective police mortality study and studies on police stress and health. His most recent work involves stress, fatigue, and subclinical cardiovascular and metabolic consequences in police officers. Dr. Violanti has authored over 45 peer-reviewed articles on police stress and PTSD, police mortality and suicide. He has also written and edited eight books on topics of police stress, psychological trauma, and suicide. He has been an invited lecturer on topics of police stress and suicide to the FBI Academy at Quantico, Virginia several times. He has lectured nationally and internationally at academic institutions and police agencies on stress and trauma at work.

Karena Burke is a recent Ph.D. graduate at the University of Tasmania, Australia. Her research focuses on understanding the role of organizational influences on stress and traumatic stress processes. Karena's current work is building her research on organizational determinants of satisfaction in police, fire, and ambulance personnel.

Anne Gehrke is currently working at the BG Institute of Work and Health in Dresden, Germany in the field of emergency psychology. She received her graduate degree in psychology at the University of Technology, Dresden, Germany with specialization in occupational health psychology. Her major interests are in police, trauma, and PTSD with the focus on secondary prevention.

Cover design and photo by Lt. Michael Kaska, Buffalo, New York Police Department.

Charles C Thomas
PUBLISHER • LTD.
P.O. Box 19265
Springfield, IL 62794-9265

ORDER ONLINE AT CCTHOMAS.COM

- Coleman, John L.—**POLICE ASSESSMENT TESTING: An Assessment Center Handbook for Law Enforcement Personnel. (4th Ed.)** '10, 300 pp. (7 x 10), 15 il, $54.95, hard, $36.95, paper.

- Covey, Herbert C.—**STREET GANGS THROUGHOUT THE WORLD. (2nd Ed.)** '10, 328 pp. (7 x 10), 1 table, $63.95, hard, $43.95, paper.

- Harmening, William M.—**THE CRIMINAL TRIAD: Psychosocial Development of the Criminal Personality Type.** '10, 304 pp. (7 x 10), 40 il, $62.95, hard, $42.95, paper.

- Mendell, Ronald L.—**PROBING INTO COLD CASES: A Guide for Investigators.** '10, 324 pp. (7 x 10), 5 il., 34 tables, $63.95, hard, $43.95, paper.

- Rivers, R. W.—**TECHNICAL TRAFFIC CRASH INVESTIGATORS' HANDBOOK (LEVEL 3): A Technical Reference, Training, Investigation and Reconstruction Manual. (3rd Ed.)** '10, 494 pp. (7 x 10), 252 il., 8 tables, $113.95, hard, $77.95, paper.

- Schafer, John R.—**PSYCHOLOGICAL NARRATIVE ANALYSIS: A Professional Method to Detect Deception in Written and Oral Communications.** '10, 220 pp. (7 x 10), 10 il., $49.95, hard, $29.95, paper.

- Smith, Cary Stacy & Li-Ching Hung—**THE PATRIOT ACT: Issues and Controversies.** '10, 284 pp. (7 x 10), 2 tables, $58.95, hard, $38.95, paper.

- Slatkin, Arthur A.—**COMMUNICATION IN CRISIS AND HOSTAGE NEGOTITIONS: Practical Communication Techniques, Stratagems, and Strategies for Law Enforcement, Corrections, and Emergency Service Personnel in Managing Critical Incidents. (2nd Ed.)** '10, 230 pp. (7 x 10) $39.95, spiral (paper).

- Vardalis, James J.—**ISSUES AND CASES IN LAW ENFORCEMENT: Decisions, Ethics and Judgment.** '10, 210 pp. (7 x 10), $53.95, hard, $33.95, paper.

- Weinzetl, Mitchell P.—**ACTING OUT: Outlining Specific Behaviors and Actions for Effective Leadership.** '10, 270 pp. (7 x 10), 15 il., $55.95, hard, $35.95, paper.

- Weiss, Peter A.—**PERSONALITY ASSESSMENT IN POLICE PSYCHOLOGY: A 21ST Century Perspective.** '10, 402 pp., (7 x 10), 70 il., 26 tables, $79.95, hard, $55.95, paper.

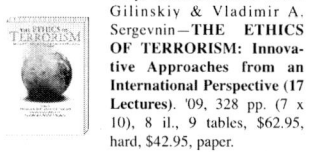

- Gilly, Thomas Albert, Yakov Gilinskiy & Vladimir A. Sergevnin—**THE ETHICS OF TERRORISM: Innovative Approaches from an International Perspective (17 Lectures)**. '09, 328 pp. (7 x 10), 8 il., 9 tables, $62.95, hard, $42.95, paper.

- Slatkin, Arthur A.—**TRAINING STRATEGIES FOR CRISIS AND HOSTAGE NEGOTIATIONS: Scenario Writing and Creative Variations for Role Play.** '09, 232 pp. (7 x 10), 11 il., $36.95, spiral paper.

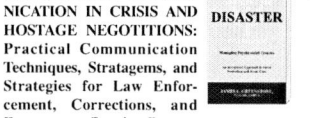

- Greenstone, James L.—**THE ELEMENTS OF DISASTER PSYCHOLOGY: Managing Psychosocial Trauma - An Integrated Approach to Force Protection.** '08, 288 pp. (7 x 10), 16 il., 1 table, $62.95, hard, $42.95, paper.

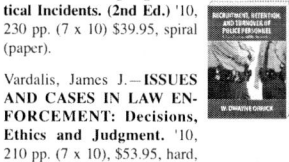

- Orrick, W. Dwayne—**RECRUITMENT, RETENTION, AND TURNOVER OF POLICE PERSONNEL: Reliable, Practical, and Effective Solutions.** '08, 250 pp. (7 x 10), $54.95, hard, $34.95, paper.

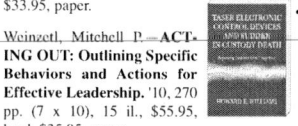

- Williams, Howard E.—**TASER ELECTRONIC CONTROL DEVICES AND SUDDEN IN-CUSTODY DEATH: Separating Evidence from Conjecture.** '08, 226 pp. (8 x 10), 15 tables, $59.95, hard, $39.95, paper.

- Campbell, Andrea and Ralph C. Ohm—**LEGAL EASE: A Guide to Criminal Law, Evidence, and Procedure. (2nd Ed.)** '07, 376 pp. (7 x 10), 31 il., $79.95, hard, $59.95, paper.

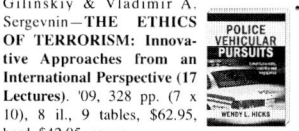

- Hicks, Wendy, L. **POLICE VEHICULAR PURSUITS: Constitutionality, Liability and Negligence.** '07, 128 pp. (7 x 10), 8 tables, $39.95, hard, $24.95, paper.

- Jurkanin, Thomas J., Larry T. Hoover, & Vladimir A. Sergevnin—**IMPROVING POLICE RESPONSE TO PERSONS WITH MENTAL ILLNESS: A Progressive Approach.** '07, 206 pp. (7 x 10), 21 il., 17 tables, $37.95, paper.

5 easy ways to order:

PHONE: 1-800-258-8980 or (217) 789-8980
FAX: (217) 789-9130
EMAIL: books@ccthomas.com
Web: www.ccthomas.com
MAIL: Charles C Thomas • Publisher, Ltd. P.O. Box 19265 Springfield, IL 62794-9265

Complete catalog available at www.ccthomas.com or email books@ccthomas.com

Books sent on approval • Shipping charges: $7.75 min. U.S. / Outside U.S., actual shipping fees will be charged • Prices subject to change without notice